VICTORIAN
TRADE CARDS

Historical Reference
& Value
Guide

MAMA! WHY CAN'T SIS AND I HAVE

MUNDELL'S

THE BEST SOLE LEATHER TIP MADE

SOLAR TIP

TRADE MARK
PHILA.
JOHN MUNDELL & CO.

PAT? FEBRUARY 19, 1878.

SOLAR TIP SHOES FOR CHILDREN

LIKE THE REST OF THE BOYS AND GIRLS.

DONALDSON BROTHERS, N.Y.

Dave Cheadle

with prices & introduction by Russ Mascieri

COLLECTOR BOOKS
A Division of Schroeder Publishing Co., Inc.

**To Audrey, Erica, and Evan Cheadle
and Donna, Amanda, and Andrew Mascieri**

*(and all the other family members
who have ever had to share a bathtub
with a soaking Victorian scrap book).*

The Authors:

Dave Cheadle has published over 100 articles on trade cards and Victorian history. He is a regular trade card columnist for *Paper Collectors' Marketplace* and *Bottles & Extras*, and has published trade card articles in magazines ranging from *Sports Collectors Digest* to *The Collector*. He is co-founder of the Trade Card Collector's Association, and co-editor of *The Advertising Trade Card Quarterly*. He is also the author of the trade-card-illustrated book, *Arctic Obsession: The Victorian Race for the North Pole*. Dave has been collecting trade cards for over 20 years, with a collection currently numbering over 15,000 cards.

Russ Mascieri, who wrote the introduction and provided the 1996 price information, is the owner of Victorian Images, the acknowledged leading firm in trade cards and one of the top ephemera auction houses in the county. He is a nationally recognized expert and speaker on the commercial aspects of trade cards and ephemera, and is the co-founder of the Trade Card Collector's Association and co-editor of *The Advertising Trade Card Quarterly*. Russ has been a lifetime collector and the author of numerous articles on trade cards, collecting, and the preservation of ephemera.

The current values in this book should be used only as a guide. They are not intended to set prices, which vary from one section of the country to another. Auction prices as well as dealer prices vary greatly and are affected by condition as well as demand. Neither the Author nor the Publisher assumes responsibility for any losses that might be incurred as a result of consulting this guide.

Searching For A Publisher?

We are always looking for knowledgeable people considered to be experts within their fields. If you feel that there is a real need for a book on your collectible subject and have a large comprehensive collection, contact Collector Books.

Cover Design: Beth Summers
Book Design: Benjamin R. Faust

Printed in the U.S.A. by Image Graphics

Contents

*NOTE: Over 700 of the illustrations in this book are shown at 75% of actual size.
The remaining cards are shown at actual size.

Preface
How to Best Use this Resource

Two Books in One

As my vision for this project evolved, I came to realize that a resource was needed for collectors, dealers, and historians that would convey the spirit and historical significance of advertising trade cards while at the same time addressing the practical concerns of those needing price information. My experience with historical reference works is that they frequently bog down, typically opting for another thousand words instead of one more good picture. My frustration with price guides is the way many of them trivialize historical artifacts, reducing them to "collectibles" or commercial trinkets to be peddled merely as souvenirs of the past.

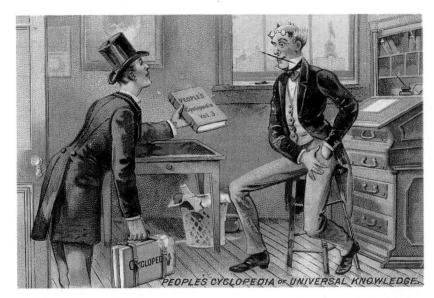

People's Cyclopedia of Universal Knowledge, drummer & clerk, $20.00.

More than any other type of historical artifact, trade cards defy such treatment. A historian would have to be blind to miss the power that trade cards have in telling their own stories, and a writer would have to be pure mercenary to catalog cards and assign prices without at least occasionally noting the historical significance of some of these cards. In attempting to combine a "Historical Reference" and a "Value Guide" into one volume, some compromises were unavoidable. I am painfully aware of the hundreds of paragraphs that I was forced to drop in order to make room for more cards, and I am equally aware of the hundreds of cards that I left out to make room for historical notes. Still, if I had to do it over, I would do it the same. Victorian trade cards demand no less.

To Use as a Historical Reference

Each reader will undoubtedly discover his or her own way to use this resource. My suggestion to researchers and armchair historians is to flip through the book a few times to get a feel for it, and then study the table of contents. Skim the "Images" section of each article, and read the "Historical Notes." Ignore the "Pricing Tips" and "Sample Prices." Most importantly, study the cards themselves, because they are loaded with details and insights on Victorian America that will intrigue and surprise you like no other source you have ever encountered. (For example, did you notice the brass cuspidor beneath the knee of the clerk in the above illustration?)

To Use as a Price Guide

For the best results, study the table of contents and orient yourself thoroughly to this resource before you begin attempting to look up specific card prices. Trade cards are a nightmare to index properly, and because of page and time limitations, I was forced to forego an index. The challenge of indexing is the same problem faced by dealers trying to decide into which album to file a card. Take for example the Marks Folding Chair card found on page 46. This card could be legitimately filed under Furniture, Brownies, Columbian Exposition, or Uncle Sam. If you were to ask dealers at shows if they had this card, most would direct you to look under each of the above possibilities. You might consider this book good training for your next show.

Once you have become familiar with this resource, you will develop a sense for how cards have been grouped by products, companies, card styles, and topical images. When you need to price a card, check the table of contents and review the pricing tips of all relevant articles. It is somewhat unlikely that your exact card will be listed under Sample Prices. Nobody knows for certain how many different trade cards were issued, but the number certainly exceeds 100,000. This resource specifically prices perhaps one or two out of every 100 known cards. That being said, you will be surprised how helpful the pricing tips and sample prices will be. I have intentionally focused a lot of attention on the common cards that most collectors encounter, trusting that advanced collectors can do a pretty good job of pricing the rare cards themselves. The values given for specific cards were provided by Russ Mascieri, who is considered the nation's top expert on trade card prices. Keep in mind, however, that with the influx of a new generation of enthusiastic collectors, card prices are becoming volatile.

Introduction   Russ Mascieri

Trade Card Prices & the Current Market

About the Prices Listed in this Book

Prices Are Based on Recent Auction Sales of Cards in Very Fine Condition.

Despite the absence of any comparable or previous comprehensive price guides for trade cards, the prices found in this book can be trusted as an accurate representation of current market values. Evaluating trade card prices today, versus five to ten years ago, has become much easier and more precise because of auctions. Market data exists on about 15,000 cards offered and sold through the ongoing Victorian Images, Inc. auctions. Prices in this guide are based mostly on actual prices realized in the past 27 auctions during the last several years. It is important to note that the prices provided in this book are for cards sold in Very Fine condition.

Determining a Card's Value

For a card in Very Fine condition, use the quoted price.

A card in Very Fine (VF) condition must be free of all defects and must have fresh colors. Cards may have some slight evidence of having been pasted into a scrap album on the reverse side and still warrant the VF grading. However, glue stains, album page remnants, scuffs, or scrapes on the reverse side will lower the grade of the card, even if the front is perfect. Mint cards in perfect, pristine condition, having never been pasted into a Victorian album, are indeed rare. Surprisingly, there is little premium placed on Mint cards over VF by the current market, probably because the front of a Mint card and a VF card are both perfect. The trade card market is totally dominated by collectors, and without the influence of investors, values tend to be about equal for Mint and VF cards.

**For Fine quality,
deduct 30% from the quoted price.**

A Fine (F) quality card is fresh, but it may have a minor corner crease or very slight edge wear, neither of which affect the image. A card that is faultless on the front (VF in appearance), but which shows traces of glue stains on the back, is reduced to a Fine overall grading.

**For Very Good quality,
deduct 60% from the quoted price.**

A Very Good (VG) card is fresh, with more than one corner crease, or a single crease that affects the image, or a tiny margin tear, or a small toning spot, or an otherwise Fine appearing card that has moderate glue stains or a reverse side with a small scuff or scrape. In all cases, the flaws must be minor and the card must present itself in an attractive condition.

**For less than Very Good quality,
deduct 60% or more.**

Cards with greater degrees of faults than mentioned will bring one third of the listed price, or less. Collectors will occasionally save a badly damaged card as a "space filler" until an example in better condition can be found, but such cards must be fresh and attractive.

When is a card so "trashed" that it is trash?

While each collector must judge for himself or herself how much wear and tear he is willing to tolerate, cards with blunted corners, stains, trimmed margins, major tears, and major creases all should be heavily discounted. Generally, the more the damage detracts, the greater the discount; the more rare the card, the more damage it will take to completely eliminate all of its value. Most dealers toss severely damaged cards into a 50¢ or $1.00 box, or simply give them away. Trade card dealers often make lots of 50 or 100 damaged cards and common stock cards which have not sold and place them in local antique auctions where they might receive anywhere from $50 to $150 per 100. The above Arbuckle Coffee card in VF condition has a value of $8. In "trashed" condition, as shown, 25¢.

Condition is NOT "just a matter of opinion."

In judging condition, use a sharp eye. Remember, condition is an absolute, and not a relative judgement. Despite the fact that a trade card may be over 100 years old, if it is not perfect, it is not VF. Because it is 100 years old, it may be hard to find a VF example, and a Fine example might be quite suitable for your collection. However, when it comes to placing a value on a card, either to purchase or to sell it, the right price will be determined by its absolute condition.

Prices quoted are selling, or retail prices. If a collector has cards to sell, after strictly grading them by the above criteria, one may expect a reputable dealer to pay 33% to 50% of the retail value for cards under $50. For cards valued at $50 or more, one may expect dealers to pay 50% to 60% of the listed price, assuming that the dealer is interested in adding to his or her inventory.

The Current Market

An Evolving Market

There has not been any significant information on trade card collecting, and trade card prices in particular, until the past couple of years. Trade card auctions started in 1992, and the Trade Card Collector's Association began publishing *The Advertising Trade Card Quarterly* in 1994. An entire generation has passed since the deaths of Burdick and Bray, which marked the end of a trade card collecting era around 1960. Leadership never passed to any dealers or collectors who were active during the late 1950s or early 1960s. The current hobby evolved from a new group of collectors and dealers dating mostly from the 1970s and 1980s. This explains the often great differences in preferences for various types of cards today versus what was in demand a generation ago. The new collectors of the 1990s are having further dramatic effects upon the hobby's continuing evolution, especially in terms of changes that are occurring in trade card prices.

Despite the fact that many thousands of trade cards are stocked in dealer inventories (one can usually find dozens of albums packed with trade cards at most of the larger paper and post card shows), finding a specific card that is not common may be a very difficult task. Even though hundreds of thousands of firms used trade cards for advertising during the 1876 to 1900 period, over 90% of all trade cards were stock images with store names imprinted. Specific product cards are much scarcer.

Take for example the cards from the H.J. Heinz Company, a well-known firm today. Their die-cut pickle shaped trade cards are very popular with collectors. As of today, there are 31 different varieties of these die-cut pickles known. The most common examples sell for $20 to $25 in VF condition, and they are commonly seen at major shows. The scarce ones, priced at $50 to $75, are very difficult to find, and they only occasionally show up in dealer stock. It takes a lot of patience and searching to find cards in this group. The rare examples, from the $75 to $150 range, are frustratingly hard to find. There are collectors who have been pursuing Heinz cards for 10 to 20 years or more who have not been able to complete the group. (There is one variety of which there is only one known example.)

Merchant's Gargling Oil, "Darwin's Grandpapa," $60.00.

*Heinz
die-cut, $30.00.*

The present state of the market can be well illustrated using the Heinz example. For the old-time collectors accustomed to paying $5 to $10 for any Heinz card they found, the 1995 price of $150 seems excessive, despite the fact that they haven't found the last few cards that they need in 10 years of searching. Compounding the problem is that today's $150 card went for $100 last year, and the long-time collector thought that price was already too high. To many of the new collectors of the 1990s, $150 seems reasonable for a lovely card that takes ten years to obtain. From our vantage point, it seems to us that the scarcity of many trade cards is very underrated, and that the current pricing is only starting to reflect a proper valuation.

As auctioneers, we draw this conclusion not so much from the actual price level as from the large amount of people bidding at these levels. With few exceptions, current prices are not created by two wealthy, crazed collectors, bidding increasingly higher prices, each determined not to lose the lot.

What trade card auctions have accomplished is to take trade cards not easily accessible and make them available to all buyers through the bidding process. Beyond the actual sale, the auction has become a price discovery mechanism for the entire market. For the overwhelming majority of cards, this is a very accurate reflection of current value. When the market establishes a price, it factors in both the card's scarcity and its beauty, which is generally measured by excellence in graphic design and printing quality.

Black and White Cards Versus Full-Color Cards

An area of the trade card market worth discussing separately is the demand for black and white versus full-color cards. Within the hobby, the bias has historically been in favor of cards produced in full color, or "chromolithographed" as they are often called. A minority of collectors consider the black and white cards to be business cards, despite the fact that they are indeed illustrated trade cards. Perhaps it is because Victorian collectors did not prize them highly. Certainly, it was the color images, the first color printing

seen by many Victorians, which so fascinated them and touched off the original trade card collecting craze. Thus, it was the color and not the black and white images that were prized and saved in the scrap albums. Since 99% of the cards we have today come from these albums, it stands to reason that the unsaved black and white cards are very scarce today. Many, and it is probably not an exaggeration to say most, are unique. Certainly all but a few are rare. Additionally, they also typically have strong graphic appeal, often being finely engraved. Even though the market is considerably thinner for these black and white cards, better graphic examples typically fall into the $100 to $300 range, and they can even go much higher.

Cliff House, Manitou Springs, Colo., engraved card, $150.00.

The Future of the Trade Card Market

We feel the future is very bright for the trade card hobby. As price guides and lists of known cards (as published in the *Advertising Trade Card Quarterly*) continue to disseminate information on trade card values and rarity, many of the observers who are currently enamored with these great Victorian advertising artifacts will undoubtedly gain the confidence needed to make the financial commitments to begin collecting with earnest. Additionally, for those who appreciate making new discoveries and doing original research, trade cards offer one of the last great frontiers in collecting. So far, very little research has been done related to trade cards, and those collectors who are interested will continue to find the field wide open for new contributions.

Many Trade Card Categories Are Still Under Collected

Although many topics and categories of trade cards are avidly collected, there are numerous other categories still very under collected. Early theatrical posters are hot in the marketplace today, yet 1880s trade cards for theatrical productions (and cards promoting and picturing the big stars of the day like Lilly Langtree) still languish. Theatrical trade cards are yet to be discovered by most collectors. Many theatrical collectors simply do not know of the existence of these trade cards. Trade cards with furniture advertisements is another area of great historical significance that is still very under collected. Some of the most ingenious advertising imagery of the nineteenth century was produced by the shoe industry, yet there are very few collectors of shoe cards outside of the general collectors who collect virtually everything. The same would apply for cards advertising stoves and ranges, as well as the trade cards issued by the manufacturers of baking products. Some of the best use of color, quality printing, and imagery are cards from the piano and organ companies, yet these, too, are very under collected. With few exceptions, genuinely rare cards from these categories seldom sell for $75 – 100 or more, and truly scarce cards that only turn up once every couple of years can often be picked up for $15 – 25.

The Collectible "Sieving Process"

Trade card collecting has made dramatic changes over the last five years. Still, in many ways, this hobby is only just beginning to catch up with the evolving distribution process experienced by many other collectible groups during the 1980s. The action of

"One hundred years hence." From rare stock card set, $250.00.
"Summer excursions to the North Pole." Maher & Grosh Cutlery imprint.

Stock card, bookseller imprint, "Great Variety of Advertising Cards for sale," $5.00.

most collectible markets is comparable to a large sieving process, whereby material filters down through various dealers and collectors until it reaches the end collector who wants it the most and who plans to keep it. The process is sometimes direct and efficient. One collector decides to sell, and when he does part with a piece, he sells it directly to another collector who finds a place for the item in his personal collection. Other times, the material has to sift through many layers to reach the end buyer. Often this process involves layers of dealers who sell to other dealers who obviously think the item is worth more than the current asking amount. The material eventually gets sold to a collector, or if the dealer has overestimated the item's value, it sits in his stock until the market catches up with his price or he sells it for a loss.

Beyond being major sources for the material that collectors desire, retail dealers also perform an important function in the marketplace. They act as sponges, soaking up all of the material that comes onto the marketplace that does not go directly into the hands of collectors. With the inception of auctions, the traditional process has been altered in that some of the best material no longer gets into this sieving process with its many layers of middle brokers. Instead, a good deal of great material goes directly from one collector to another through the bidding process, with the auction house as the only broker in between.

Most Cards Are now in the Hands of Collectors, Dealers, and Institutions

The other interesting aspect of the trade card market is what I call the "free float" of material. This is material that is not in the possession of active collectors, dealers, or institutions. It is the material that comes out of attics, like grandmas' scrap books. Like so many other collectibles, news that all of those trade cards that had been gathering dust for decades were worth something gradually became known in the 1980s. Much, if not most, of this material has made its way to the market, mostly through antique, paper, and country auctions.

Dealers have lately begun to lament that they are not making as many great finds at antique auctions and flea markets as they once did. This speaks to what I think is the end of this process. There will always be a trickle of newly-discovered material, but the market has been efficient. Most trade cards are now in the hands of collectors, dealers, and institutions. This change is having a dramatic effect on those dealers who had depended upon newly-discovered finds to replenish their stock. Trade cards are not unique in having to deal with this sort of transition. Actually, because trade cards have lagged other collectibles in terms of market development, it is still easier today to find a rare trade card at a flea market than it is to find a rare stamp or a rare cast iron bank.

Who Are Today's Collectors?

Some collectors collect trade cards purely for their historical or social content. These collectors represent a small part of the collector population. Others collect a very specific area, such as a city, company, or topic. They comprise a large segment of the current trade card collector population. Another group are those who collect for the graphic design appeal. And finally, there are "general" collectors, who collect across all fields. From the historical and intellectual side, institutions are becoming more active in adding to their collections, although at this point we estimate that they constitute less than 2% of the market. That is not to say they have less than 2% of the trade cards. On the contrary, the holdings of institutions are quite extensive. However, their active participation in the buying and selling of trade cards is quite limited. We expect this situation to change dramatically as the field evolves, both from their perspective as well as from the changes in the marketplace.

Russ Mascieri

Hires' Root Beer, "all gone," 1894, $15.00.

A Brief History of Victorian Trade Cards

The Origins of Advertising Trade Cards

Victorian trade cards, or advertising trade cards as they are often called, date mostly from 1876 to 1900. Exactly when the first trade card was issued is a matter of debate. A strong case can be made for pushing the date back to the seventeenth or eighteenth century, when businesses first began commissioning woodcut "tradesmen's" cards to advertise their goods and services, although such ads were not called trade cards at that time.

America's earliest known advertising card was issued in 1727 for a bookstore owned by John Hancock's uncle, Thomas Hancock. Paul Revere printed a few similar items around the time of the American Revolution. Again, there is some discussion about whether such items qualify as trade cards, business cards, handbills, or as something else. Whatever they are called, these early black and white advertising "freebies" blazed the trail for the Victorian trade cards so popular with collectors today.

Prang's Christmas calendar card, issued for Clark's Thread in 1880, $15.00.

An early (1863) Prang album card from a set entitled "Winter Landscapes," $15.00.

Besides the early woodcut and engraved tradesmen's cards, several key developments in the printing industry also contributed to the emergence of the Victorian trade card industry. Around 1800, Alois Senefelder devised a technique for drawing images on carefully prepared stones that could be used as printing plates. Because the images were drawn, as opposed to etched or engraved on copperplate, fine details and solid colors could be produced quickly and easily. Further innovations made it increasingly simple for lithographers (literally, "stone-writers") to produce beautiful color prints using as many stones as required. Each stone contributed one color to each print. The best lithographers were able to carefully line up ("register") their prints with as many as a dozen or more stone plates to create a full spectrum of chromolithographic ("chromo" means color) effects. The other major breakthrough in lithography came in the form of steam presses. Once steam presses had been perfected, large lithographic firms with dozens of employees were able to begin cranking out lithographic prints, commercial documents, and advertising items at the rate of thousands of copies a day.

Currier & Ives and Louis Prang were America's most famous early large-scale lithographers. Both firms built their reputations on their affordable prints for middle-class families. Prang quickly began releasing additional products besides wall prints, and he eventually earned the distinction as the Father of the American Christmas Card and the developer of the stock trade card. Prang never claimed to invent either item, but few question that it was he who popularized both. Another item popularized by Prang was the album card, which in some ways served as a critical link between black and white engraved tradesmen's cards and the color trade cards popularized at the Centennial Exposition. Album cards were miniature art prints that were printed without advertising and sold in sets for anywhere from a half cent to a couple of cents each.

Stock card, "Stop and think a minute Before you drop this card." Reverse ad for a Waterbury, Conn. clothier, $20.00.

The "Golden Years" of Trade Cards

Color advertising trade cards were seldom produced prior to the Centennial Exposition. For the most part, consumers were very surprised and quite delighted to receive free color cards at the Exposition in Philadelphia in 1876. Of course, not all of the cards given away at the Expo were in color, and in fact, it is estimated that 75% or more of the cards distributed there were still of the black and white variety. Exhibitors did note, however, which cards were drawing the greatest interest.

Within a short time, nearly all serious advertisers began ordering chromolithographed cards. The established advertisers that switched to color cards — plus the thousands of upstart companies that ordered cards to alert consumers about new goods and services — fueled and rode the Victorian card collecting craze to its end. The golden years of trade cards lasted from 1876 to 1900. Handbills, posters, and ads in publications were also used during this period, but chromolithographed trade cards ruled the day.

Trade cards became so popular and cheap that some firms began distributing them by the tens of thousands. A Philadelphia printer by the name of David Heston claimed that for $20 he could provide 10,000 trade cards imprinted with a firm's name and address. One dry goods chain in New York bragged of their intention to distribute 100,000 advertising cards in a single season. Charles Hires once claimed that he had issued four million root beer cards in a single year. Trade cards were sent in the mail, piled in stacks on store counters, handed out on sidewalks, stuffed into packages, and if one trade card image is to be trusted, dumped like WWII propaganda leaflets in the streets.

Gold Soap, reverse text: "In 1876, the Centennial Year, the whole country was startled by the word GOLD stuck around on everything — on flags on horses' heads; on dead walls; on bill boards; painted on fences; on horse blankets; on small cards dropped on the streets . . ." $20.00.

The Victorian Card & Album Culture

By the mid-1880s, chromolithographs (or "chromos" as they were often called) had saturated society at all levels. One cultural observer went so far as to cynically dub America "a chromo civilization," which in E.L. Godkin's opinion was not to be taken as a compliment. In Mark Twain's *A Connecticut Yankee in King Arthur's Court*, the Victorian hero laments that one of the things that he missed the most from back home was all the chromos. In describing his New England home, he recounted a nostalgic inventory of all the chromos spread throughout his house, concluding his list with mention of the nine chromos in his parlor alone. Period photographs of Victorian rooms incidentally document that chromo prints and calendars could be found everywhere, including advertising trade cards that were tucked between the glass and wooden frames of bedroom mirrors.

Advertising trade cards were by no means the only cards popular during the late nineteenth century. Calling cards were extremely popular with "cultured" men and women who used them to announce and record their visits. An elaborate calling card etiquette developed, complete with formal "card receivers" and complex rituals dictating the manner of presentation and styles of cards to use for various occasions. Advertisements can be found for dealers boasting of "thousands of holiday cards and calling cards to select from" in addition to their "advertising cards at retail prices." One 1878 stock card specifically promotes "Children's Valentines," while another draws attention to "Card and Scrap Albums" offered at the "Cheapest Prices."

Collectors who were too impatient to gather trade cards one-by-one from merchants could purchase packaged assortments of advertising cards from local dealers or firms that marketed their services mail order. Reward of merit cards were very popular as gifts for children who did well in school, as were Sunday School cards with religious images and scriptures. Post cards from the nineteenth century, although scarce, can also be found in some Victorian albums.

Victorian card albums were generally of three types. The first was the manufacturer's or lithographer's album, which was often designed for specific sets of cards that typically came pre-mounted or printed directly onto the pages. The second was the "decorated" album, such as those produced by Marcus Ward, which was composed of pages with fancy printing and pre-set boxes into which scraps and cards trimmed to size were intended to be glued. By far the most common type of album is the eclectic scrap book.

Scrap albums came in various sizes and were composed of blank pages that could be filled with anything and everything that caught the owner's fancy. Some owners carefully arranged well-coordinated pages of calling cards and holiday scraps. Others filled their scrap albums with advertising cards grouped in similar styles or themes. But as often as not, scrapbooks were filled with a hodgepodge of paper that included everything from fair tickets to trade cards. Many of these albums can be found with sentimental inscriptions inside their covers, and some even include the

Chase's Liquid Glue, ". . . will hold fancy cards in scrap books without wrinkling, showing through, or discoloring," $20.00.

dates the album was begun and finished. Tastefully arranged albums were often displayed in parlors as evidence of good taste.

The Decline of the Victorian Trade Card

The high-water mark in trade cards is generally considered to fall on Chicago's Columbian Exposition of 1893. A generation of master lithographers had emerged through two decades of experimentation, and the number of breath-taking cards that were turned out in that year is staggering. Some of the earlier masters were never surpassed in their patience and technique, but by 1893 there were so many more craftsmen in the field that their output in fine cards, cigar labels, calendars, and advertising posters dwarfed the output of any earlier years.

Only near the end, when magazines and newspapers loosened their advertising policies during the cut-throat years of "yellow journalism," did the trade card begin to lose its luster.

Edison Phonograph, trade card reproduced from a 1905 oil painting during the waning years of trade card advertising, $40.00. This same image was also used for an Edison advertising post card issued after 1907.

Newspapers and magazines began boosting their circulations through sensational serial pieces written by participatory journalists like Nellie Bly and "muckrakers" like Lincoln Stevens. Newspapers hired advertising representatives to promote display advertising and to work with clients on tailoring their pitches to the daily medium. Magazines appropriated new printing technologies and started selling expensive full-page back cover ads that were justified on the basis of circulations that began running into the hundreds of thousands, and even millions.

The postal service didn't help matters any when it adjusted its regulations to accommodate the growing popularity of penny-stamp post cards. By 1901, advertising trade cards were considered old fashioned. Suddenly, clean albums with pre-cut slits for post cards were "in," and mother's messy trade card albums were "out." Ironically, examples of trade cards from 1879 are actually more common than cards from 25 years later. By the close of the St. Louis Exposition of 1904, advertisers had virtually abandoned trade cards in favor of other marketing ploys. Few companies cared any longer to issue cards, and fewer still were the collectors bothering to paste them into the albums that would preserve them. A few industries carried on with insert "trading" cards that were packaged with their products, and few other firms like Hires occasionally issued cards for special marketing campaigns, but the trade card era was over.

Detroit Evening Journal, "Three Editions Daily," $30.00.

Collecting Victorian Trade Cards

Advertising trade cards offer some of the most exciting collecting opportunities found in any field of antiques. Because of the incredible range of images and topics captured by trade cards, collections can be uniquely tailored to fit and enhance any type of personal interest. Collectors have ventured into trade cards and built unique collections based upon interests as diverse as music, hunting, watch collecting, the oil industry, quiltmaking, local history, education, design, and professional sports.

Finding Good Cards to Buy

Collectors entering the hobby today have some advantages over the collectors of a generation ago. Back in the "good old days" when trade cards were often 50¢ or less, most dealers didn't want anything to do with them. Some dealers would buy scrap books at auctions or estate sales, but few dealers were interested in soaking the cards out for 25¢ each. If a collector wanted a card, he usually had to buy an entire album.

Antique dealers today have noticed the surge of interest in trade cards. I know one dealer whose wife almost made him walk home after he bid $500 for a scrap book at a 1993 country auction. The only thing he knew about trade cards was that a few collectors had asked for them, but he soaked them out in his bathtub, bought two notebooks and some plastic sleeves, and put them out to sell. The first time I saw his binders, they had already been picked over twice, and I still managed to find a few hundred dollars worth of good cards. Every time I went back to his shop, the cards had been marked up another few bucks, and they were still continuing to sell. The last time I stopped by, he was down to one binder and starting to worry about finding another scrap book.

That dealer was lucky. His album happened to be filled with great cards that floated off as soon as they hit water. His next album might not be worth $50, and the cards might not come off with a crowbar. Still, his story is instructive. More and more antique dealers are handling trade cards, and in some parts of the country, cards are becoming easier for collectors to find.

Trade Card Dealers, Auctions, and Shows

In addition to the many general antique dealers who have begun to carry small inventories of trade cards, there are a growing number of dealers who specialize in them. Most of these dealers also handle other paper and advertising items, but they are experts in trade cards, and they typically stock thousands of cards in carefully organized three-ring binders. Several of these dealers have experimented with selling cards through various types of catalogs, approval services, and auctions. One dealer has even begun marketing cards on the internet. The Victorian Images, Inc. auction service is by far the largest and best established source for collectors looking for high-end and rare trade cards, and they do occasionally offer group lots of common or slightly damaged cards that often sell for very reasonable prices. Some dealers advertise in collector magazines, and nearly all of them can be contacted through the membership directory published by the Trade Card Collector's Association.

Regional paper shows have become popular, and most of the major trade card dealers set up at several or more of these events each year. Calendars with the dates and locations for shows are printed regularly in publications like *Paper Collector's Marketplace, Barr's, Post Card Collector, Ephemera News*, and *The Advertising Trade Card Quarterly*. Attending paper shows is one of the most fun and efficient ways of finding cards, and there is no better way to learn than spending a day talking with dealers and other collectors while looking through thousands of cards. Post card shows are also beginning to draw a few trade card dealers, and many post card dealers themselves now carry a small supply of trade cards. If shopping at a post card show, ask each dealer specifically for advertising trade cards. Some dealers keep their trade cards beneath or behind their tables, and you could be walking past the bargain of the century and never know it.

The most important trade card show each year is sponsored by the Trade Card Collector's Association in conjunction with their annual national convention. The convention and show are conducted in a "beginner-friendly" spirit designed to put people at ease. In addition to the hundreds of thousands of cards available on the sales floor, each convention is packed with optional activities, educational seminars, trade card auctions, meetings, and educational exhibiting.

Managing a Trade Card Collection

Some collectors keep the focus of their collecting tight and narrow, while others have rambling collections numbering thousands of cards. The larger the collection, the more important it is to develop a systematic method for card management, but even small collections must be well managed, because cards can be easily damaged or misplaced.

Organizing and Preserving

No two collections are alike, and no two collectors process information in the same way. If it makes sense for you to file your Heinz pickles next to lawn mowers because they both make you think of green, fine. Just make sure that your system is one that you can remember. The last thing you want is a lost pickle the day your mother-in-law stops by to check your Heinz cards because she thinks she spotted a stack of them at a garage sale. For a few ideas, examine the organization of this book.

Part of organizing a collection (or a dealer's inventory) is selecting supplies for storing and protecting cards. Before transparent plastic sleeves, storing cards was a problem. Today it is not. Archival (no PVC, acid free) plastic pages with pockets are affordable and easy to find. They enable front and back viewing and keep cards safe. Sports card shops carry styles to accommodate any size of card, with prices running 15¢ to 25¢ per page depending upon the quantity and number of pockets. These pages come hole punched for three-ring binders, which makes them easy to snap in and out and shuffle around as a collection grows. If you have difficulty locating archival pages, sleeves, rigid holders, or other supplies, contact: Trade Card Collector's Association, P.O. Box 284, Marlton, NJ 08053

Some collectors use stiff plastic "rigid holders." Rigid holders come in standard sizes, and they protect cards better than any other method. Once a card has been slid into a holder, it can be filed in a box or drawer like those used for card catalogs in libraries. Holders allow viewers to pull items and examine them closely front and back without touching cards or risking damage. One drawback to these holders is their expense, as they run 30¢ to $3.00 each. Another disadvantage is that a spilled stack must be completely reorganized, whereas a dropped album leaves cards in order. The biggest concern is over the long-term effects of plastics on trade cards. Document experts warn plasticizers (softeners) in plastics will damage paper over time.

Caution: Never use "magnetized" photo albums with gummy pages and pull-up transparent sheets. These albums can destroy cards in five years or less. Avoid storing cards loose in boxes. Corners *will* bend, and you will reduce the value of your cards by 30% or more.

Soaking and Salvaging

Most dealers (and some collectors) eventually purchase a scrap book. Before soaking a scrap book, keep in mind that the number of intact Victorian albums is rapidly declining, and the number of collectors considering adding one authentic album to their collection is growing. Some albums are worth more than the sum of their parts, especially if they are filled with inexpensive items or cards that are likely to be damaged when removed.

Soaking one's first album can be a nerve-wracking ordeal. We've all seen what rain does to newspapers, and we fear the same for our cards. Fortunately, most trade cards have as much in common with blue jeans as they do newspapers, because rags were a part of the original recipe for good card stock. Cards can often soak for hours, or even days, without a trace of damage except to the ink. The best approach to soaking is to go slowly and carefully, keeping in mind that no technique is foolproof.

First, remove the least valuable page from the album. Never dismantle an entire album until you are certain that you can finish the job.

Next, submerge the page in clean, room-temperature water. Be careful. Wet cards easily tear. If you are lucky, cards will begin drifting loose from the page within a half hour. After 30

minutes, test the glue by gently lifting the page away from a card. Never pull cards from pages, as this increases the risk of damage to the card's back. If the card resists, you are dealing with serious glue. Re-submerge the card for another hour. If the card still sticks, switch to hot water, but keep in mind that hot water is tougher on ink. Watch your reds, as they will be the first to run. If hot water doesn't work, try soaking overnight. If cards still stick, soaking is probably not going to work.

Once you've freed a card, gently remove the glue from the card's back by rolling your fingers over the slick areas. (Traces of glue can leave stains, wrinkle cards, or re-adhere to other surfaces.) Change your water often, and use several tubs or trays if you can.

After rinsing the card, set it on a flat surface to dry. If you set the card on an absorbent towel, never pat the card dry with another towel. Cards tear under uneven pressure.

When the card is mostly dry, but still damp, lay it on blotting paper or several sheets of typing paper. Cover the card with more paper, and then stack books. Caution: books with embossed covers or cards stacked on top of each other without adequate buffers can leave creases. If this happens, or if traces of glue cause a card to re-adhere during the pressing and drying process, re-soak the card and try again.

Depending upon humidity, cards should remain pressed for one to five days. I like to press cards for several hours, and then to check and re-press them using dry paper. Generally, the more weight used, the better the end product.

Final Collecting Tips

When buying cards, be certain to carefully consider the issues involved with damaged cards. Many leaders in the hobby disagree with me, but I don't mind picking up a $25 card for $5, because I can live with a few creases, stains, or trimmed edges. But be careful in your haste to save money that you don't kid yourself into believing that $10 is a good deal for a $25 card that is trashed. Be sure to study Russ Mascieri's discussion on page 5 about conditions and values.

Watch out for items that appear complete but that are pages from booklets, panels separated from folders, or square cards cut to look like die cuts. Buying such cards is like buying an antique bottle with the neck broken off.

Buy a good 8x magnifier. For less than $20, you can buy something even stronger with a built in light. Study a few cards with your magnifier, and compare what you see with pictures in magazines and color photo copies at your local copy shop. Then carry your magnifier when you go shopping, and don't worry about buying reproductions. Good chromolithography is virtually impossible to fake.

Angels, Demons & Devils

(See also: Cupids & Cherubs; Brownies.)

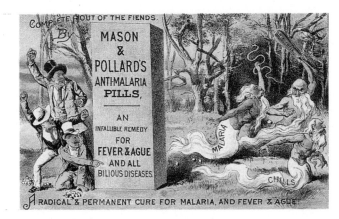
Mason & Pollard's Anti-Malaria Pills, $50.00.

Celestial & Demonic Images

Trade card images with celestial characters can be fun and challenging to collect, but it is often difficult to determine whether the winged figure in an image should be interpreted as an angel, a Cupid, or a cherub. This lack of specificity in the image was probably intentional on the part of the lithographer, as such distinctions were generally irrelevant to the purpose of these figures in Victorian advertising. There are collectors who try to limit their purchases to only angels, but such collectors may become frustrated with dealers who are as uncertain about an image as they are, so such collectors will have to learn to decide for themselves into which group a borderline image falls.

The demon and devil images are usually easier to identify, but some cards do occasionally stump collectors. This is especially true with cards depicting ghoulish apparitions that are tormenting humans. Some collectors include these cards with their demon and devil cards, while others do not. There are so few Grim Reaper cards that most collectors lump them in with their demon and devil cards as well. Trade cards with angel images are generally more colorful and more common than cards with demonic figures, although there are several wonderful full-color devil cards that do occasionally turn up.

Historical Notes

Belief in supernatural beings took a beating from science during the Victorian age. The Enlightenment had chipped away at such belief amongst the educated upper crust of society, but it wasn't until the mid-1800s that certain habits of "scientific thinking" began to impress themselves upon the down-to-earth masses. Traditional Christianity, and other religions to a lesser extent, fell under direct attack from the faculties of a number of prestigious American universities, and men and women of common faith were left to sort out the pieces as they watched their churches crumble.

Many Victorians wanted to retain their biblically-based belief in angels, demons, and the devil. But this was an age when status and social acceptance ruled people's lives, and to profess belief in supernatural beings was to risk ridicule. The Victorian caricatures of celestial beings that were produced by advertisers during this time were popular, partially at least, because they allowed consumers to ponder these images safely, without ridicule, and to struggle in their own hearts over the extent to which they believed that such creatures were real.

Wheeler and Wilson Sewing Machine, $20.00.

Nearly all images in advertising are selected and refined to accomplish two things. First, they try to grab a potential customer's attention; and second, they try to channel that attention towards the goods or services being offered. Images of supernatural beings were "sensational" in the truest sense of the word, and they grabbed the consumer's attention. Directing that attention towards where the advertiser wanted it was easy. Most angels in trade card ads are shown as the bearers of salvation, usually in the form of a new model or brand. Demons are typically shown in Victorian advertising as being driven off by the latest miraculous concoction of American industry. Most advertisers whimsically romanticized their angels and demons, and then absurdly subjected them to the goals of corporate America. Advertisers exploited the curiosity and inner struggle of the masses, and got away with it, because they were not, after all, treating the angels and demons seriously.

Pricing Tips & Cards to Watch For

Images of cherubs and Cupids are common in Victorian trade cards, but cards with angels, demons, and devils are far fewer in number. Expect to pay $10 – 20 for the most common of these cards, but plan to pay far more for the rare ones. The brightly-colored devil cards are particularly "hot" with collectors, and most of them are scarce, so they can easily run $75 or more. The most affordable angel cards were issued by sewing machine and thread companies. Also watch for celestial figures when flipping through patent medicine albums, as angels of hope and mercy frequently appear to dying patients with a bottle of the doctor's best snake oil, while the demons of malaria and cramps are often chased off with the same.

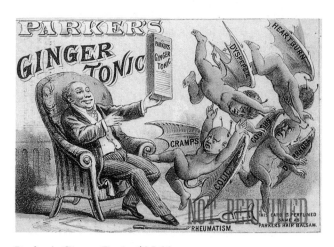

Parker's Ginger Tonic, $25.00.

Akron Rubber Works
1881 fireman squirts arsonist demon over shoulder $200.00

Arbuckles' Coffee
pretty girl face in wings, clouds $8.00

Arbuckles' Coffee
"A Happy Christmas" 6 little angels, pine boughs $15.00

Brewer Emery Wheels
Devil sharpening his tail, cupid sharpening arrow $350.00

Clark's Thread
1881 calendar, angel hands woman thread $15.00

Davis Sewing Machine
angel with trumpet & wreath, sewing machine $15.00

Dr. Fitzgerald's Invigorator
grave scene, corpse talks, Dr.'s house behind $40.00

Dr. Kermott's Mandrake Pills
angel with trumpet, banner, in cloud $20.00

Dr. Wm. Hall's Balsam
Dr. with patient, bottle, angel "Star of Hope" $20.00

Dunbarr Shoes
Black angel with shoes visits sleeping man $25.00

Girondin Medicine
hand pouring bottle, demons run, angel, 2 cherubs — folder $40.00

Jackson Wagon
angel blowing trumpet, ghosts rise to wagon in sky $50.00

Keystone Watch Cases
Devil sits with hand on cheek, die-cut keystone $12.00

La Sanadora, Romero Drug Co.
"Virgen De Guadalupe" angels, crown (from Las Vegas, N.M.) $30.00

Lancaster Watch
skeleton/Grim Reaper riding watch like bicycle $60.00

Liberty Bell Brand Jelly
demons ring big bell, ship on water $40.00

Mrs. Potts Sad Iron
"In De Colored Folk's Heaven" 3 Black angels $30.00

Sapolio Soap
"Terra-Cotta Statuette 'Ange Dechue'" premium $15.00

Sea Foam Yeast
2 panels, "with/without" green monster on belly $6.00

Davis Sewing Machine, $15.00.

Singer Sewing Machine
"Devil Sewed Tares" horned devil, sewing machine, bum $15.00

Solar Tip Shoes
Devil with fork, frightened cat, "Shoddy Insoles" — folder $60.00

Stock Card — Sawyer's Soap imprint
little demon "Pan" playing pipes for cherub $5.00

Theatre du Chatelet
French theater card, "Seven houses of the Devil" $12.00

Wheeler and Wilson Sewing Machine
angel with trumpet, cherub, parade, lions, machine $20.00

La Sanadora, Romero Drug Company, $30.00

Animals

(See also: Bears; Birds; Cats; Cows; Dogs; Elephants; Frogs; Horses; Pigs; Entertainment; Exploration & Travel.)

Animal Images.

Images of animals were extremely popular in advertising a century ago, and trade cards with good animal illustrations continue to be popular with collectors today. Exotic creatures like monkeys and parrots are almost as common in trade cards as dogs and cats. Animals were used so pervasively in Victorian advertising that one is hard pressed to find any trade card category where animal images cannot be found. In some cases, an animal will be central to a card's design, while in others, an animal will be used merely as a prop, perhaps positioned off to one side of the central activity of the card's focus. By today's standards, a few of these cards appear brutal, or even sadistic, especially in images where a monkey or a cat is tormenting another animal. Fortunately, most animal cards are delightful, or eccentric at worst. Many collectors pick several animals to watch for, largely ignoring all others in order to keep their collections down to a manageable size.

Historical Notes

Pets, especially unusual ones, were popular during the Victorian period. People could afford them, and they made for good conversation pieces. Pets frequently served the same pur-

Colburn's Philadelphia Mustard, $20.00.

David's Ink, 35.00.

Scott's Emulsion, $20.00.

Merrick's Thread, $20.00.

pose as ferns, imported tapestries, oriental vases, and all of the other bric-a-brac that cluttered Victorian homes; they contributed to what was then considered an overall appearance of cultural sophistication and economic achievement. Children and their pets were often shown in advertising in an attempt to pull a mother's heartstring, or to make her smile, so that she would be favorably disposed towards the goods or services offered.

Exotic and untamed animals are also common in Victorian advertising, partially as a result of two developments in American culture. The first development was an increase in exposure of the public to exotic animals through the tours of traveling circuses. Railroads enabled circus entrepreneurs to service even small and remote towns all across the continent. When the circus rolled in, sensational advertising immediately sprang up hyping the animal acts and exhibits, until everyone in town was convinced that tigers, monkeys, and elephants were the most amazing things they would ever have an opportunity to view. Trade card lithographers exploited the groundwork laid by circus advertisers, giving consumers another — this time free — look at the animals that people wanted to see.

Colburn's Philadelphia Mustard, $12.00.

J. & P. Coats Thread, $15.00.

J. & P. Coats Thread, $8.00.

Comstock's, stock card, $12.00.

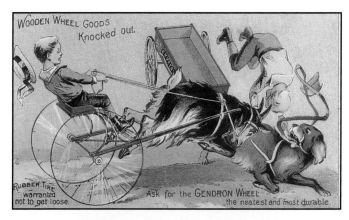

Gendron Iron Wheel Co., $60.00.

M. Shwartz Manufacturing Clothier, stock card, $4.00.

A related development that contributed to the Victorian animal-mania in advertising was the emergence of the municipal-park movement. Between 1880 and 1900, nearly every community experienced a barrage of local activist writing and soap-boxing on the subjects of fresh air, "pleasure gardens," wooded groves with foot paths, boating ponds, community bandstands, museums, art galleries, and city zoos. Municipal parks became the talk and pride of even such unlikely places as Minneapolis and Kansas City. As citizens listened to the debates and studied the arguments reproduced in their favorite magazines, many became convinced that parks, including zoos, were essential to a community's mental, physical, and cultural health. Zoos further increased public awareness of exotic animals, and advertisers exploited this freshly-nurtured curiosity by providing trade cards with colorful images of the most extraordinary creatures in the world.

Pricing Tips & Cards to Watch For

A wonderful collection of animal images can be assembled entirely of very inexpensive cards. Because so many animal cards are available, stock cards, or ones in less than full color, can often be purchased for $5 or less. Cards with clever illustrations of unusual pets like goats or monkeys are often popular with collectors. Sweet images of innocent children with animals are also among the most collected. Watch for cards with bright colors and striking images, or cards advertising products like canned meats, patent medicines, or tobacco products, as these cards will often bring $15 or more. Anthropomorphic cards, where animals are dressed up and put into humorous human situations, are also pursued by many collectors, but many of the ones that are stock cards or sewing related can still be found for under $10.

Arbuckle Coffee, $15.00.

Challenge Corn Planter, $60.00.

Page Fence, $35.00.

Alden Fruit Vinegar
lion defends barrel from animals "Too Good To Divide" **$20.00**

Arbuckle Coffee
"Giraffe" from series of 50 lovely , 1890 . . . .**$8.00**

Brook's Thread
goat on spool, 8 men play tug-of-war **$12.00**

Chicago Yeast Powder
2 goats eat flower from can, boys watch, 1887 . . . .**$15.00**

Clark's O.N.T. Thread
4 boys racing racing goats like horses, Prang 1878 . . . .**$12.00**

Frank Miller's Shoe Dressing
monkey teasing crying boy in tree **$25.00**

J. & P. Coats Thread
4 white mice eating cheese, square card **$8.00**

J. & P. Coats Thread
monkey torments parrot with thread **$10.00**

James Pyle's Pearline Soap
boy in hat teases dog with crab, cat watches **$5.00**

Luncheon Beef
fancy rabbit couple, fan, handkerchief **$8.00**

Old Crow Sour Mash Whiskey
2 rats on bottle, Old Crow barrels in background **$30.00**

Stock Card "Alligators Teeth" imprint
fox with duck in mouth, rabbit diving in hole **$10.00**

Stock Card — dry goods imprint
zoo scene, woman with umbrella fends off giraffe, seals **$8.00**

Stock Card — sewing imprint
"Our Neighbor's Pets" — boy at window, birds, dogs, cat **$10.00**

Stock Card — store imprint
lion, artist easel & brushes, windmill, sunset **$5.00**

Zoo-Zoo Brand Tobacco
tiger in circle, giraffe, monkeys, etc. **$100.00**

Dr. Kilmer's Prompt Parilla Liver Pills, $30.00.

Huntley & Palmer Biscuits, $25.00.

Brockmann's Monkey Theatre, $30.00.

Arctic

(See also: Bears; Exploration & Travel; Soaps.)

Arctic Images

Images of the Far North intrigued collectors during the trade card era. Many Victorian readers followed captivating accounts of Arctic exploration in the periodicals of the day, but they had to rely on trade cards for full-color illustrations (romanticized as they were) to see what the Arctic looked like. Trade card advertisers supplied images of everything from wild polar bears and winter nights to salty whalers and timid Eskimos. Some of the best of these images were issued by stove and meat companies, who often printed their cards in colors ranging from the rich deep blues of Arctic seas and skies to the bright contrasts provided by warm campfires and polar ice. Stock cards with Arctic scenes, as well as a number of one or two-color private issues, were distributed in large quantities that can be found advertising a wide variety of products.

Historical Notes

Private whaling fleets ventured farther and farther north throughout the Victorian period, plotting coastlines as they went. Whalebone was used in corsets, bustles, and collars. Whale oil was used as a lubricant and as a fuel for lamps. Whale oil also became an essential ingredient in nineteenth century soap making. One of the most aggressive of all advertisers in the 1800s was a soap manufacturer that used a whale for its trademark.

The closing decades of the nineteenth century saw an explosion of interest in the Arctic regions. As American affluence and literacy increased, exotic expeditions and sensational travel adventures seized the public's imagination and burst into popular culture. Cashing in on the public's fascination with the international race for the North Pole, Victorian advertisers of the late 1800s pitched everything from wood stoves to sewing threads through their often whimsical depictions of life and adventure in the Arctic.

Arbuckle Coffee, $15.00.

Exactly when the North Pole was finally attained has been a subject of historical debate. Both the Royal Geographical Society and the National Geographic Society of Washington took Robert Peary at his word and credited him with a 1909 successful march to the North Pole. Today, many historians doubt Peary's account and question his documentation, as well as the shear logistics of traveling the many miles he needed to in the little time that he had.

The other late-Victorian contender for North Pole was a very popular American by the name of Dr. Frederick Cook, who convinced many that he had made it to the pole a year ahead of Peary. Experts eventually discredited Cook's claim, and it now seems unlikely that either man made it all the way to the Pole as they had claimed.

Pricing Tips & Cards to Watch For

Cards with Arctic scenes are popular, and often expensive, particularly when they feature striking images of polar bears, whaling, or specific historical figures. Some of the Arctic cards fall in the $10 – 20 range, but plan to pay a good deal more for the scarce and beautiful stove, soda water, and meat cards. A good place to begin collecting Arctic images is with the fairly common 3-color set of six 1882 Bufford stock cards, which can be found with imprints for everything from "Chest-Shield" undershirts to patent medicines. Arbuckle Coffee issued a good number of colorful but affordable cards that featured nations of the far north. Watch for one of their rarest cards, a vertical "Greenland" variant of their Alaska card from their "Sports and Pastimes" series. The Greenland variant, like the Alaska card, shows a baby polar bear sitting on its mother's stomach, but the variant sells for $35 instead of $15. Also keep an eye open for the rare soap cards that have "Soapine" printed in a black arch over the whale, as these cards can bring $100 or more.

Libby, McNeill & Libby's Beef, $30.00.

Arbuckle Coffee, $15.00.

Soapine Soap, rare version, $250.00.

Gold Coin & Gold Medal Stoves, $50.00.

Arbuckle Coffee
"Esquimau" dog team, caribou, seal hunter, 1893 ....**$8.00**

Arbuckle Coffee
"Lapland" reindeer, blindfolded boy playing tag, 1893 ....**$10.00**

Brook's Thread
3 whalers, whale's tail, distant ship **$15.00**

Colburn's Mustard
polar bear watches ship from iceberg **$20.00**

Esquimaux Rubber Boots
native hunter stabbing polar bear, dog teams **$150.00**

Garland Stoves and Ranges
stove and range in Arctic, explores warm, bear, ship **$35.00**

Jewett's Fancy Base Burner
stove, Arctic explorers, sled dogs, flag **$50.00**

Merrick's Thread
"In Search for the North Pole" hot air balloon (Andree's) **$20.00**

Mrs. Potts' Sad Irons
Uncle Sam's Expedition to North Pole, ship, melting ice **$35.00**

Shaker & New Tariff Ranges
"Greeley Arrives at the North Pole" big card, dead bear **$50.00**

Singer Sewing Machine
"Archangel" Samoyed family by skin hut with machine **$10.00**

Soapine Soap
"You will find it at the North Pole" Uncle Sam, flag, whale **$40.00**

Soapine Soap
"Soapine is Useful Everywhere" dog team in Arctic **$30.00**

Stock Card
"Preparing for a Journey" dog team, Bufford, 1882 ....**$8.00**

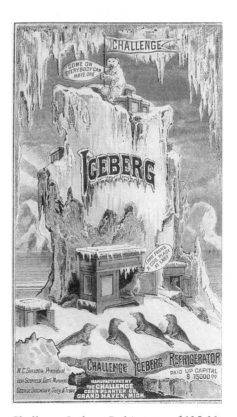

Challenge Iceberg Refrigerator, $125.00.

Baseball

(See also: Sports.)

Baseball Images

Almost all trade cards with baseball images were originally issued as stock cards, often in sets of four to six each. Privately issued cards with baseball images are rare, but they can occasionally be found with advertisements for sports publications, equipment manufactures, or specific teams and events. Additionally, there are a few private issues that satirize baseball while promoting a non-baseball related product.

Historical Notes

The first baseball cards were trade cards, which were issued a full decade prior to the more familiar tobacco insert cards of the

Modern baseball cards have taken thousands of fans and long-time collectors on a roller-coaster ride. In many cases, prices for cards were driven up by speculators who didn't care for the sport or enjoy the cards. Investors were buying mass-produced cards by the case, then packing them away unopened on the advice that factory-sealed assortments fetched better prices when resold. In response, card manufacturers increased their production. The market became artificial, because the real supply and the actual collector demand became confused. When investors began unloading, they discovered that everybody who wanted their cards already owned them, and that there weren't enough new speculators coming into the hobby to keep baseball prices from collapsing. Not all modern card prices fell, but enough did to severely rattle the industry. Unlike the readily available cards of recent years, Victorian trade cards are truly scarce. In some cases, only one or two examples of a card are known to exist, and that puts these cards in a league of their own.

Merchant's Gargling Oil, $25.00.

Tetley's Tea, stock card, $25.00.

Downs & Webster Coal Dealers, stock card, $35.00.

late 1880s. Sports card reference books have basically ignored trade cards for two reasons. First, trade cards seldom have the uniformity of size and design that is characteristic of "modern" trading cards. And second, trade cards have been considered too rare to mention in guides targeted for those who deal in readily available cards. In fact, trade cards are so rare among sports collectors that even many of the hobby's leading figures have never owned one. But trade cards are an important part of sports history. Trade cards give evidence of baseball's penetration into Victorian popular culture, even as early as the 1870s. These cards also document specific aspects of the pastime, particularly in the realm of sports equipment (i.e. no gloves in early trade card images), uniforms, grandstands, etiquette, etc.

Pricing Tips & Cards to Watch For

Even the most common stock cards with baseball images are now selling for $20 and up. Stock cards with good color illustrations of baseball games in progress start at $30, but can bring several times that amount when the image is strong or the imprint is desirable. Cards with the names of actual players and teams bring $50 or more. Watch for privately issued cards with good baseball scenes, and especially for cards with sports-related advertising, as these cards are rapidly disappearing from the market.

Arbuckle Coffee
"United States" card #1 Sports Series, baseball (and others) **$50.00**

Enameline
die-cut baseball player, gray uniform, orange stripes, "P" **$75.00**

Marshall & Ball
pitcher winding up, second baseman off left elbow **$50.00**

Nelson Morris Lard
pigs playing baseball, grandstands, flag **$50.00**

Stock Card
"Home Run" 2 players carry third off field **$35.00**

Stock Card — druggist imprint
"Barometer... good for Base Ball" boy, hand up, ball **$15.00**

Stock Card — Maher & Grosh imprint
"Chance for a kick" argument at home plate, 1888 . . . .**$75.00**

Stock Card — bitters imprint on back
young girl, Christmas stockings, toys, bat & ball **$15.00**

Stock Card — hatter imprint
small size, batter hits player with bat (1881 Tobin card) **$30.00**

M. W. Eastman Boots and Shoes, stock card, $30.00.

McLaughlin's Roasted Coffee, $25.00.

Vogel Brothers 1882 Fashions, $75.00.

Dan Brouthers, stock card, $75.00.

Maher & Grosh, stock card, $75.00.

Bears

(See also: Animals; Arctic; Cowboys.)

Bear Images

Bear images are plentiful in trade cards, and they can be found in advertisements for a wide variety of products. About half of the illustrations with bears depict bears in a humorous light, often dancing with hats or dressed up and acting silly. Trade cards

Woolson Spice Co., $15.00.

mostly pre-date Theodore Roosevelt and the teddy bear craze, so images of stuffed bears are probably nonexistent. The other half of the bear cards depict a bear in some sort of confrontation, usually with a human. Sometimes the bear is humorously shown surprising a hunter, but in many cases, the conflict is violent and life-threatening. Bears are particularly common in stock card images, many of which were mass produced in only two or three colors of ink.

Historical Notes

American Victorians were far more aware of wild animals than were their European cousins. Bears had been chained and trained for traveling shows in Europe for hundreds of years before the first white American ever had to go face-to-face with a truly wild grizzly bear. An ironic contrast runs through the nineteenth century images one finds of bears. On the one hand, one finds evidence of the European tradition, where bears are seen as comical animals to be dressed up in skirts and made to dance for Saturday nights' entertainment. On the other, one finds in many of these images evidence of a deep respect, even fear, for North America's most dangerous animal.

Legends of frontier encounters with bears form an integral part of the American identity. Part of the Davy Crockett mystique was rooted in his claim to have personally killed 105 bears in his first seven months in the wilderness of western Tennessee. While there is no way to substantiate Crockett's bear-killing boast, the record is unmistakable about Crockett becoming one of the most popular "backwoods frontiersmen" ever elected to the United States Congress. Crockett died at the Alamo in 1836, but bears were by no means through scoring their claw mark on the American character.

As the frontier moved west, so did the legacy of the bear. Rocky Mountain fur traders added their own legends to the growing body of American bear folklore, as did the trappers, miners, and settlers of California. In fact, when the American "patriot" William Ide led a rebellion declaring California free from Mexico in 1846, the uprising was labeled the "Bear Flag Revolt" because of the image of a grizzly bear that they had sewn onto their banner. California has stuck with that bear now for over 150 years.

For the "civilized" Victorian consumers targeted by most trade card lithographers, wild bears were no longer a threat. But such bears were still potent enough in their collective awareness to have a power that is all but lost on Americans today. Smokey the Bear has put on pants and learned English, and he has stepped out of the forest to tip his hat and share a helpful word. Certain images in trade cards remind us, however, that there was a day when, in the minds of many people at least, "Smokey" had claws.

Pricing Tips & Cards to Watch For

Some collectors prefer trade cards with images of bears that are cute and huggable. Such images can be found mostly in stock cards, series of cards with fairy tale themes, and in several thread ads. Images of bears in nature, or in conflict with humans, can frequently be found in Arbuckle Coffee ads, tobacco cards, and in several of the more rare thread card illustrations. Many of the "cutesy" bear cards can be purchased for under $15, whereas the "dangerous" bear cards tend to bring over $15. Watch for affordable but striking bear images on the fronts and backs of "Pettijohn's California Breakfast Food" cards, as they used a bear for their trade mark. Also keep an eye open for a scarce set of Van Haggen soap cards with bear images that brings over $50 each.

Dean Brothers Grocery and Meat Market, stock card, $5.00.

Arbuckle Coffee
Greenland, map, polar bear skin, 1889 . . . .**$10.00**

Belding Thread
sitting hunter looks at lunging bear, thread around neck **$50.00**

California Silk Manufacturing
2 vaqueros lasso grizzly bear with thread **$100.00**

Dr. Morse's Indian Root Pills
Indian on horse stabbing bear **$35.00**

Famous 'Bearskin' Stockings
family of 6 dancing bears, boy and girl holding socks **$20.00**

Hassan Cigarettes
"Peace offering to spirit of bear" (1910 insert card) **$5.00**

J. & P. Coats Thread
"Native Daughter of Golden West" 2 bears, gold pan, pick **$40.00**

National Tubular Axle
"Happy New Year" 3 dancing bears, "in Barnum's big show" **$30.00**

Pettijohn's Breakfast Food
"'Bear' in Mind Wur Trade Mark" black bear, mountaintop **$15.00**

Stock Card
"Golly, I'se a Dead N... " bear traps Black man, honey, cave **$25.00**

Stock Card
bear killing mountain man, other man with knife, dogs **$20.00**

Stock Card — Alaska Compound imprint
polar bear killing seal on ice flow **$20.00**

Stock Card — clothing imprint
black bear and polar bear caught hugging in moonlight **$10.00**

Stock Card — Denver Fur imprint
bear with gun scares hunter from lunch **$20.00**

Stock Card — dry goods imprint
2 polar bears at zoo, "Dive in Billy! Ladies a'comin" **$12.00**

Stock Card — medicine imprint
black bears watches wilderness artist paint, gun **$5.00**

Stock Card — medicine imprint
"Teeth Extracted Without Pain" black bear hurts white one **$15.00**

White Ceylon Soap
polar bear on rock scares 2 people on skates **$8.00**

Woolson Spice Co.
"Rose Red and Snow White" dancing with bear **$15.00**

J. & P. Coat's Thread, 20.00.

W. Duke, Sons & Co. Tobacco, $25.00.

Gold Medal Coffee, $15.00.

Neptunite Dyed Umbrella, $35.00.

Beer, Whiskey & Wine

(See also: Root Beer, Sodas & Waters.)

Alcoholic Beverage Images

Trade cards advertising beer, whiskey, and wine are among the most popular of all advertising items. These cards are frequently of a very high quality, with good color, fascinating text, and compelling images and designs. Many images in this grouping include an attractive depiction of a company's bottle, complete with a minutely detailed facsimile of their label to insure that consumers would recognize the brand on the shelf amongst the bottles of their competitors. One also finds generic stock cards in this class, usually imprinted by a local brewery or bottler during the holiday season. The reverse sides of some beer cards have fabulous illustrations of the breweries that produced the product, or, in a few cases, the portrait of the company's founder.

Historical Notes

There are two very different and equally colorful histories with respect to production and consumption of alcoholic beverages. The first is the history of the industry and the people that have produced these beverages; the second is the history of the movements and individuals that have opposed them. Advertising trade cards and Victorian abstinence "pledge" cards are invaluable artifacts for collectors and students interested in either aspect of the alcoholic beverage history. Both types of cards were mass distributed in order to alter alcoholic consumption patterns during the rising heat of the debates that ultimately resulted in national prohibition. Advertising trade cards encouraged alcohol consumption, while pledge cards forbade the use of intoxicating beverages in any form.

Breweries, distilleries, and wineries have been an important part of American history from the beginning. One of America's earliest domestic enterprises dates back to 1630, when Governor Peter Minuet established New Amsterdam's first public brewery. One of America's first social crusades dates back to 1639, when Puritan ministers raged against drinking, and the General Court of Massachusetts enacted a law prohibiting public toasts. Distillers of Bourbon County (Virginia/Kentucky) began producing corn whiskey in 1746. Farmers of Litchfield County (Connecticut) began pledging to abstain from alcohol in 1789. The tension between those who produced or used alcohol and those who condemned it ran through local and national politics from our very first elections on down to today.

The debates over alcohol became passionate, and even violent, during the golden years of trade cards. Louis Prang & Company, one of the most respected chromolithographers in America, produced a beautiful pledge card in 1876 that reads: "I _____ solemnly promise to abstain from the use of all Intoxicating Liquors as a beverage, including Wine, Cider, and Malt Liquors." For the next 30 years, similar pledges were imprinted on stock cards that were available for use by both temperance societies and alcohol manufacturers alike. One must sometimes do a double-take to catch whether a stock card that mentions alcohol is for or against its use.

The energy and media attention that was generated by the prohibitionists and temperance unions was unabashedly exploited by a number of American entrepreneurs. Hires Root Beer boldly labeled itself a "Temperance Drink," and dozens of imitators tried to outdo themselves in their "healthful" claims for their own version of a "stimulating temperance beverage." The Atlantic & Pacific Tea Company distributed a set of six cards relating the tragic tale of a fine young man going to alcoholic ruin as a "Result of Not Using" their teas and coffees. Ironically, several of the major breweries themselves capitalized on the temperance crusade by developing "Malt Extract" products that they marketed as "safe" and "non-intoxicating." Pabst and Anheuser Busch each used images of innocent young girls hugging their malt extract bottles to convey the safety of their products, while at the same time the text of their ads promised that their product (much like the stuff they put in their other bottles) would cure "irritability" and induce sleep.

Pricing Tips & Cards to Watch For

Alcohol-related cards tend to be more expensive than cards from other industries, especially when the trade card promotes a firm that has widespread name recognition, as with Anheuser Busch, Tivoli, or Pabst cards. Stock cards with alcohol imprints can be found for under $15, but privately issued cards can rarely be found for under $25. Expect to pay $50 or more for nice cards with bright colors and strong images. The alcohol industry invested heavily in advertising, so watch for expensively produced novelty cards in this category, including mechanicals, metamorphics, hold-to-lights, and numerous die-cuts.

Vieux Cognac, Flli Branca: Milano, $30.00.

H. Clausen Brewing, NY — Lager, $75.00.

Dole Brothers Hops & Malt, $40.00.

Degenkolb, brewery stock card, $50.00.

H. Clausen Brewing, NY — Lager, $75.00.

Anheuser-Busch Brewing, St. Louis, $35.00.

Gibson's Whiskey, Phila., $35.00.

Duffy's Malt Whiskey, $30.00.

Moerlein's National Export Beer, $350.00.

Moerlein's "National Export,"
$60.00.

Hermitage Sour Mash Whiskey, $30.00.

Palest Brewery, New York, die-cut, $60.00.

Mount Vernon Whiskey, $20.00.

Pabst Malt Extract, $35.00.

Pledge Card, $8.00.

Old Times Distillery, Louisville, die-cut, $30.00.

North Western Brewing, Chicago, die-cut, $75.00.

Atlantic & Pacific Tea Co.
"Brandy Smash" saloon brawl, "Result of Not Using" **$10.00**

Charles A. King Lager Beer
happy man, bottle in hand, glass on table **$80.00**

Dr. Underhill, On the Hudson, Wines
grapes, wine vault, 1870s testimonials, varnished folder **$60.00**

Franz Falk Brewing, Milwaukee
2 bottles of beer, girl cries as 1 bottle spills off tray **$30.00**

H. Clausen Brewing, N.Y. — Ale
harvest scene, hunting scene, bottle with label **$75.00**

Large Whiskey, Pittsburg
die-cut of a half full whisky tumbler, "Drink a little Large" **$40.00**

Siegel's Extra Dry, New York
6 men in wine cellar, champagne prices on back **$35.00**

Stock Card — Champagne imprint
fan die-cut shape, "Eclipse... The Wine of the Elite" **$5.00**

Stock Card — Falk's Milwaukee Beer
couple under moon, concerned mother **$15.00**

Stock Card — Family Wine & Bottling
fairy girl on snail, Brooklin bottling imprint **$8.00**

Stock Card — wine imprint
Irondequoit Wine Co., N.Y., horseshoe, red ribbon,1880 . . . .**$8.00**

Tivoli Export Beer, Phila.
pretzel die-cut, Poth Brewing **$40.00**

Tnadzai's Russian Beer, stock card, $5.00.

Anheuser-Busch Brewing, $125.00.

Bicycles

(See also: Sports; Entertainment.)

Bicycle Images

A high percentage of the bicycle images found in trade cards treat wheelmen and the bicycling craze lightly. The bumps and spills that occur in many of these illustrations are rarely depicted in a way that elicits concern. Unlike the participants in cards from other sports, bikers are seldom if ever presented as intentionally violent or mean-spirited. They are often shown bumbling themselves into terrible collisions that come off humorously because of the way that the artist has portrayed them. Stock cards and private issues with bicycle scenes are both plentiful, with most of the private issues coming in full color. Admiring women show up in many of these images, often adding a wonderful touch to the overall effect.

Historical Notes

Victorian wheelmen took their wheels seriously, even if trade card lithographers did not. By some estimates, in 1890 there were over 300 manufacturers turning out some 10 million bikes a year. The classic Victorian "high-wheeler" was by no means the only style of cycle available, but serious challengers failed to emerge until the late 1880s, when tricycles and "safety" bicycles began "rapidly coming into favor with Ladies and elderly gentlemen" (according to the ad on the back of one trade card). Safety bicycles, with their equally-sized wheels and dropped frame, allowed women to participate in a nation-wide recreational fad that rivaled any similar outdoor activity before or since. Cycle clubs sprang up everywhere, with Chicago alone boasting of some 500 clubs. A good Columbia

Columbia Bicycle, $200.00.

high-wheeler was running over $100 at the height of the craze, so most wheelman thought little of spending a few bucks more to outfit their entire club in matching hats and uniforms for cross country touring.

James Starley patented the first vehicle under the name "bicycle" in 1873. Albert Pope geared the industry up in 1878 by abandoning his sewing machine production in favor of the country's first bicycle factory. In less than a decade, Pope's "Columbia" bicycles, plus countless imitations, were bouncing down country roads and city streets from coast to coast. Bicycle sprints and endurance contests invaded horse racing tracks to the point where even a cowtown like Caldwell, Kansas, was sponsoring a high-wheeler race as a special feature of its 1885 fair.

Pricing Tips & Cards to Watch For

Many fascinating stock cards with bicycle images are still available for under $15. Bicycle images on stock cards printed in only one or two colors can often be found as low as the $5 to $10 range. Expect to pay more for privately issued cards, especially when the colors are vibrant and the image is compelling. Watch for trade cards advertising specific models of bicycles or special biking races and exhibitions, as the historical value of such cards increases their demand and price several fold. Bicycle cards become even more valuable when the image includes features that catch the interest of even non-bicycle collectors, as with a Pan-American Exposition card that was issued by the National Cycle Company picturing Uncle Sam with one of their bikes ($150).

Clark's Thread, $15.00.

Reid's Seeds, $15.00.

Boss Watch Cases
wheelman with long nose, big watch case $15.00

Columbia Bicycle
wheelmen at night, hats, trumpet, reverse: "Pope M'F'G Co." $60.00

Gendron Velocipede & Tricycle
mother and 3 children ride 2 cycles, all wearing hats $60.00

Hampden Park, Bicycle Club
Springfield, MA, race track, wheelman, Milton Bradley Lith. $40.00

J. & P. Coats Thread
4 brown rabbits running away from home on high-wheelers $15.00

Love Button-Hole Sewing Machine
wheelman waves hat, red shirt, blue pants $40.00

New Home Sewing Machine
naked cherubs racing bikes at track, machines for seats $10.00

Standard Sewing Machine
wheelmen on machines, women watch, "Clear the Track!" $25.00

Star Braid
2 wheelmen, web braid for bikes, 1 falls, girl watches $15.00

Stock Card — clothing imprint
"Bucked" boy with hat on high-wheeler falls, 1881 . . . .$15.00

Stock Card — clothing imprint
2 boys stand next to early highwheelers, straw hats $20.00

Stock Card — dry goods imprint
boy with hat on bike, eggs for wheels $15.00

Stock Card — organ imprint
cyclist chased through woods by 2 bulls, distant boats, 1884 . . . .$15.00

Stock Card — piano imprint
woman racing on early tricycle, beating 2 men $30.00

Stock Card — reverse fertilizer ad
"Cupid's Work Is Done" couple & baby on bike, Cupid sleeps $25.00

Stock Card — shoe imprint
4 frogs as wheelmen, two collide, flowers $15.00

White Bicycle & Sewing Machine
phone call "My papa has a White Bicycle" reverse bike ad $75.00

Lautz Soap, stock card, $15.00.

Grand Casino Race, $150.00.

Columbia Bicycle, $60.00.

Birds, Chickens & Owls
(See also: Animals; Patriotic.)

Bird Images

Birds and flowers are the most common subjects found in Victorian trade cards. In some cases, the birds depicted are of an identifiable species; in others, the artist took license and let his imagination fly. Images of song birds and parrots are popular with many collectors, as are depictions of chickens and owls. Several popular sets of humorous stock cards with owls in anthropomorphic situations were used by the Atlantic and Pacific Tea Company, but some of these cards were imprinted by other firms as well. Birds are usually treated with respect in trade card images, except for parrots. In some illustrations, a parrot is shown in a flurry of feathers as he tries to escape from the paws of a monkey or cat. While a few bird cards are rather dull in their one and two-color depictions of birds, other cards with bird illustrations feature some of the most breathtaking colors and intricate embossings found in trade cards.

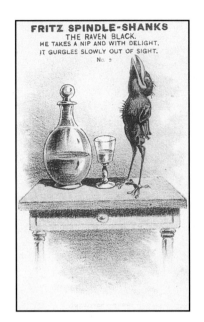

Fritz Spindle-Shanks, stock card, $5.00.

Historical Notes

Given what we know about Victorian fashions and taste, it comes as no surprise that birds were extremely popular in American culture during the final decades of the nineteenth century. Like the Oriental fans, embroidered tapestries, and gilded statuettes of the classic Victorian parlor, birds were beautiful, delicate, and superfluous. It was that "non-essential" quality of birds that made them so attractive to Victorians, who flocked to pet stores and bird exhibitions in search of a perfect expression of their supposed sophistication and cultural refinement. Elaborately gilded cages could be found with colorful songbirds and talking parrots in the homes of leading citizens in every community. Middle-class Victorians found both pleasure and prestige in showcasing their prize birds in some of the most prominent places of their homes.

In an 1879 Palmer's advertising "Manual of Cage Birds," one finds tricks for catching and taming birds, advice on cages, breeding, diseases and their remedies, and helpful hints for training birds to eat food "from your outstretched tongue." The birds that are discussed in the greatest detail are canaries, mockingbirds, nightingales, parrots, skylarks, redbirds, and crows. Of mocking birds, it is said that the "best singers are reared in the country where they hear the songs of all other birds," and that "a good singer is worth $3 to $150." Of parrots, it is said that they are "uncleanly in habits, and their cage must be cleaned daily," and that "some do not talk." And finally, the booklet notes in its discussion of the crow (and raven) that "he learns to distinguish all the members of the family, screams at the approach of a stranger, learns to open a door by alighting on the latch, attends regularly at the table at meal-time, learns to speak some words..." and that a crow "will eat anything, animal or vegetable, that you may give him, from a lump of sugar to a piece of putrid flesh."

Chickens also had their place in Victorian culture. As with caged birds, some Victorians took great delight and pride in breeding and showing their prize poultry. In addition to the poultry found on farms, chickens were also kept in the back yards of many families as a source of eggs for food and barter. (It only took one hen house in each neighborhood for chickens to make an impression upon an entire culture.)

Pricing Tips & Cards to Watch For

When looking for cards with images of birds, chickens, or owls, always check under sewing and coffee/tea cards. A nice collection of beautiful cards can be assembled from very inexpensive stock cards as well. Expect to pay $5 to $10 for sewing and beverage cards with bird images, and $5 or less for stock cards with images of birds. Exceptional cards from these groupings will sometimes bring $10 to $15, but very rarely $20 or more. Watch for farm-related products with chicken images, as cards advertising poultry foods, equipment, and medicines are in demand and often sell for $20 or more. Also check the imprints on stock cards, as an advertisement for birds, bird cages, bird seeds, bird medicines, bird exhibitions, etc. can increase a card's collectability and value considerably. For the best in parrot cards, look for cracker ads in food albums and expect to pay anywhere from $15 on up, depending upon the card's rarity.

English Song Restorer, stock card, $15.00.

H. W. Vahle, stock card, $8.00.

Moore's Throat & Lung Lozenges, $10.00.

Ayer's Cherry Pectoral, $10.00.

Boraxine Washing Soap, $8.00.

Reliable Incubator & Brooder, $50.00.

Wells Tea Co., stock card, $5.00.

Conkling & Chivvis, stock card, $10.00.

Lion Coffee, $12.00.

New Home Sewing Machine, $15.00.

Improved Egg Food of San Fransisco, $100.00.

Singer Manufacturing, $20.00.

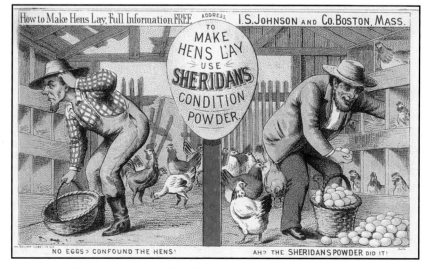

Sheridan's Condition Powder, $25.00.

Clark's Thread
"The Tomtits" 2 yellow & black birds, pine cones **$6.00**

Domestic Sewing Machine
2 "Prize Brown Leghorns" **$15.00**

German Food For Mocking Birds
1879 turkey stock card, "Premium Quality Mixed Seed" **$10.00**

Hoyt's German Cologne
girl with bird on shoulder, bird in flower basket, 1894 cal. **$20.00**

Imperial Egg Food
chicks, hen chases rooster, "Steal My Egg Food Will You!" **$25.00**

J. &P. Coats Thread
red bird with thread spool hanging from beak **$10.00**

Pond's Bitters
henhouse, "Easter Eggs... Wait Till I Catch that Peacock" **$20.00**

Stock Card — "Bee Hive" imprint
red/black bird & green/yellow/blue bird in blossoms **$4.00**

Stock Card — beer garden imprint
rooster, beetle, fancy border **$5.00**

Stock Card — clothing imprint
"The Original Hen-Pecked" hen chasing scrawny rooster **$5.00**

Stock Card — Partridge's Cafe
13 partridges at edge of wheat field, 1885 . . . .**$5.00**

Stock Card — shoe imprint
owl, boot, 2 mice **$5.00**

William's Poultry Food
girl feeding chickens, turkeys, boy with horn, ...**$20.00**

Wright's Indian Vegetable Pills
6 swallows on limb, "Elixir of Opium" on back **$6.00**

Rutland Stove Lining, $12.00.

Grand Bird Exhibition, stock card, $20.00.

Murray & Lanman's Florida Water, $12.00.

Clark's Thread, $8.00.

Blacks
(See also: Ethnic.)

African-American Images

Victorian trade cards with illustrations of African Americans are perhaps the most collected, fascinating, and controversial of any advertising collectible found in America. Images in this grouping range from harmless humor to mean-spirited joking and malicious racial stereotyping. In some images, Blacks are depicted in dignified roles with realistic features and typically Victorian demeanors. In others, Blacks are presented as bumbling fools with distorted features and brutish dispositions. The language used in the captions of some of these ads is highly offensive, and the dialect attributed to those who speak is often pathetically exaggerated for "comic effect." Images range in quality from very poor to very fine. Illustrations depicting African Americans can turn up in nearly every category found in trade cards.

Historical Notes

A study of African American images in advertising offers somber insights into some of the grimmer aspects of Victorian culture. Because Victorians judged the purchasing power of the Black community to be extremely limited, very few cards were designed with Black consumers in mind. In the first place, many trade cards advertised items that were a financial stretch even for middle-class whites. And secondly, even those trade cards that marketed basic "necessities" (soap, clothing, patent medicines, etc.) were of little relevance to those who often bartered, made their own, or went without.

Most advertisers operated on the assumption that there was little to be gained financially by stroking the Black community's vanity the way their ads so often did that were targeted at the white middle class. Nor were advertisers particularly concerned about economic, political, or legal backlash from ads that insulted the Black community. On the other hand, they saw something to be gained from producing ads with racially prejudiced images and slanderous text. The white community of the North often fretted over migrating Black workers, who were seen as threats to wages or as laborers who would fill positions that could be used by young whites and European immigrants. The whites of the South tended to resent Blacks for their own political and historical reasons, and whites everywhere viewed Blacks as a threat to white culture. By ridiculing Blacks, advertisers gained the approval of many of their customers, and customer approval is everything when it comes to sales.

The Blacks that appear in trade card images are generally shown in one of two ways. The first way that they are shown is as domestic servants, often mellow and compliant as they serve the whims of their white employers. A classic card of this sort was commissioned by the Spicers & Peckham Stove Company. The card shows a very white Uncle Sam (the supreme symbol of the WASP middle class) requesting his dinner of a very Black and subdued domestic servant. The other images of Blacks in trade cards are comprised mostly of "comical" scenes. These cards typically show clumsy, dancing, dishonest, or lazy characters, often with distorted features and an insatiable appetite for melons and some white farmer's chickens. Racial slurs are common in the text of these cards, as are dialect and dialogues that present Blacks as incredibly childlike or stupid.

Such cards apparently resonated well with white consumers, because the later into the trade card era one goes, the more of them one finds. In some cases, an earlier card was modified at a later date, with the reissued card boasting even thicker lips and broader smears against the Black community. Images of white men aiming or shooting guns at Blacks appear frighteningly often, but one almost never finds an image of a Black person intentionally doing harm to a white. That was one of the very few areas in Victorian culture that advertisers felt was nothing to joke about.

Pricing Tips & Cards to Watch For

Cards depicting African Americans are in demand among collectors, with most cards running $15 and up, depending upon the card's quality, scarcity, and the product advertised. As with all ethnic cards, the ones with the most racially inflammatory images and language often bring the highest prices. The most affordable images are found on one-color stock cards, which can sometimes be found for under $10. The best values are found in thread cards, with many of these cards having great designs and striking colors, yet rarely selling for over $20. Watch especially for tobacco cards with Black images, as these will often bring $50 or more when found in good condition. Also watch for cards with special historical significance, as in cards that allude to sports figures or that advertise minstrel shows and "Uncle Tom's Cabin" productions.

Williams & Clark Bone Fertilizers, $35.00.

Rising Sun Stove Polish, $15.00.

Sollers & Co's Minstrels shoes, $40.00.

Magnolia Ham, $35.00.

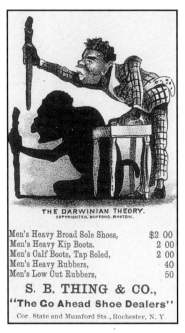

S. B. Thing & Co., stock card, $20.00.

Sapolio Soap, die-cut, $12.00.

Duchess & Princess, $60.00.

Rices Musk Mellon, $20.00.

J. & P. Coats Thread, $12.00.

A. L. Foster & Co., stock card, $8.00.

Gold Dust Washing Powder, die-cut, $40.00.

Pillsbury's Best Flour, $30.00.

Clarence Brooks Varnish, $25.00.

Wooldridge Bone Phosphate, $30.00.

Arbuckle Coffee, $15.00.

Kangaroo Komplete Kompound (KKK), $50.00.

Ayer's Cathartic Pills, $8.00.

St. Louis Beef Canning, $50.00.

Alden Fruit Vinegar, $50.00.

Dr. Haas' Horse & Cattle Remedies, $90.00.

Andes Stove, stock card, $15.00.

Selz Rock Bottom Shoes, $20.00.

Arbuckle Coffee — #48
"American Negroes" dancing, cake walk, 'possum hunting $25.00

Biliousine Sure Cure
man holding stomach, watermelon rinds $20.00

Briggs Bros. Seeds
man stuck on barbed wire, melon, farmer with gun $40.00

Clark's Thread
man, white horse, woman in wagon "Ef Dat Mile End..." $20.00

Clark's Thread
fishing man sits on spool, "I reckon dis yere's strong..." $8.00

Clark's Thread — Industrial Series
"Cotton Picker of the South" large card $15.00

Collins' Fever & Ague Cure
raft, flood, alligator biting man, 2 mules $30.00

Czar Baking Powder
shocked mother and son, huge bread on table $15.00

Dixon's Stove Polish
Black woman scrubs naked girl on table $10.00

Domestic Sewing Machine
billboard, Black driver, 2 horses, 3 white women, dog $15.00

Domestic Sewing Machine
billboard, Black family, old wagon, 1 horse, sick dog, 1882 . . . .$15.00

Dunham's Coconut
2 monkeys pelt 2 pickers with coconuts $12.00

Fairbank's Golden Cottolene
girl with arms full of cotton, tin bucket, label $15.00

Hi Henry's Premium Minstrels
"Uproarious Skating Carnival," 6 skaters falling $30.00

Higgins's Soap
"Whoa! Dar Sambo!" mother, 4 children, wash tub $10.00

Jas. S. Kirk Soap Makers
boy with hat marches, red carpet, 2 big cotton balls $15.00

Kendall's Spavin Cure
"Dat hoss can jist fly now," rider hangs on in air, boot flies $12.00

Kerr's Thread
fancy indoor cakewalk, 4 men carry spools $15.00

Lautz Bro's Soap
white man scrubs boy's face at wash tub $20.00

Liebig "Scenes d'Afrique"
racing giraffes, zebra, camel, alligator $5.00

Merrick Thread
"Fooled dis time...," fishing man hangs above alligator $12.00

Merrick Thread
2 Blacks eat melon, string white man from tree $25.00

Stock Card — church series
"Sister Snowball, You Am A liar," riot in church, 1882 . . . .$15.00

Stock Card — Seaweed Tonic imprint
boy in straw hat, torn clothes, at fence $15.00

Stock Card — Sovereign's Association
Black cook in ship's galley, white girl watches, doll $15.00

Vacuum Harness Oil
"No mo' hard work for old Uncle Ned" can with wings $20.00

Sanford's Ginger, $25.00.

Sure Catch Sticky Fly Paper, $125.00.

Brownies, Elves & "Little Folks"
(see also: Angels; Santa Claus.)

The "Little Folks" Images

Images of brownies, elves, fairies, and various other little imps of the imagination and folklore are abundant in Victorian advertising. Collectors are often frustrated in trying to determine whether an artist meant for a given character to be interpreted as an Irish leprechaun, a forest sprite, a mischievous cupid, or something else. Further complicating the situation is that Santa Claus was often depicted by early trade card artists as an elf, sometimes dressed in red, but just as often in brown, green, or even blue. These artists must be forgiven for their lack of specificity, however, since most legends have it that the little folks are not ones to stay put for artistic posing. Some collectors specialize in a particular type of imp, with the Brownies of Palmer Cox being among the most popular. While collectors may disagree over whether a particular card belongs in a Santa collection,

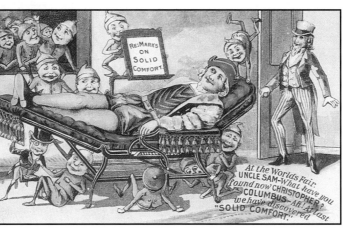

Marks Adjustable Reclining Chair, $30.00.

an elf collection, or someplace else, most collectors will agree that these wonderful images are among the most delightful of any that are found in advertising.

Historical Notes

Legends of supernatural little folks go back thousands of years. According to some traditions, these imps are dangerous, or at best, mischievous. Other traditions hold that the little people are helpful and kind. Because of immigration, throughout the Victorian period America experienced a wonderful convergence of colorful folklore from a wide variety of traditions. Additionally, with the rise of technology and scientific thinking, American immigrants often lost the faith in magic that had once led their ancestors to tremble over stories of little folks and the unknown.

By the time of the trade card era of the late nineteenth century, Americans were ready for an invasion of whimsical — if not nostalgic — little folks. More than any other entrepreneur, Palmer Cox provided the little people that millions of Victorian children and adults were yearning to chuckle over and embrace. Cox introduced his "Brownies" to the public through the pages of *St. Nicholas* magazine in 1883. Within only a few years, his Brownies had overrun the culture, showing up everywhere from toys, board games, and books, to trade cards. Cox continued peddling Brownie adventures well into the twentieth century, inspiring hundreds of imitators all along the way.

Pricing Tips & Cards to Watch For

Only a few of the Palmer Cox trade cards have his signature or the word "Brownies" on them. Watch for imitations. Early Palmer Cox scenes depict a band of near look-alike imps; by the mid-1890s, the Brownies had taken on the clothing, props, and features of such characters as Uncle Sam, an Irishman, an Indian, a Chinaman, a capitalist, and a host of others. Most Brownie cards, as with many of the little folks cards, are still abundant enough for prices to remain affordable. Expect to pay $5 to $10 for stock cards with little folk images, $10 to $40 for the majority of the private issues.

Liebig's Meat Extract, $5.00.

Confections, stock card, $10.00.

Beals, Torrey & Co Shoes
  7 elves pulling shoes out of drawer $35.00

Diamond Polishing Powder
  woman washing outside window, elf scrubbing sign $15.00

Eldorado Engine Oil
  "Listening to the Fairies" black & white $25.00

Estey Piano and Organ
  Brownie parade, banners, shows products $15.00

Hinds Honey and Almond Cream
  Brownies filling bottle, Uncle Sam $25.00

J & P Coats Thread
  fairy and woman sewing, before & after, two panels $25.00

McLaughlin's Coffee
  elves giving child ride on coffee box, small card $25.00

Montgomery Ward & Co
  "Where the Brownies get their supplies." $30.00

New England Mince Meat
  "The Fairy's Pie" large card, pie, many fairies $40.00

Stock Card — Clothing Imprint
  little folks using coat as a tent $15.00

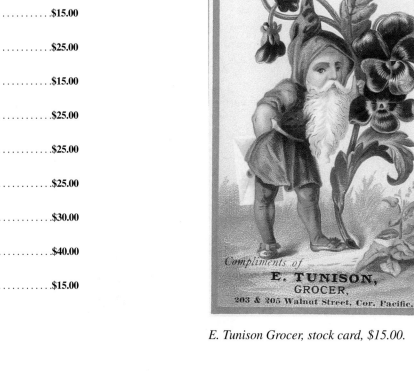

E. Tunison Grocer, stock card, $15.00.

Dixon's Stove Polish, $20.00.

Besse, Besse & Co., $15.00.

White Sewing Machine, $12.00.

Cats

(See also: Animals.)

Cat Images

Nostalgic illustrations featuring cats are fairly common in trade cards that were targeted at women, especially in advertisements for domestic products like toilet soaps and threads. Cat cards within this class are often attractively designed, typically in soft colors with sentimental scenes of girls (housewives when they were young) hugging kittens or, in some cases, of cute cats in heart-warming anthropomorphic scenes. When cats appear in stock card images, they do not always receive such sweet and gentle handling. Some stock cards show cats being tormented, while others show nasty cats on the giving end of the abuse. The cats that appear in privately issued cards for non-domestic products also received mixed treatment, sometimes coming off as adorable pets, while other times coming off as ill-bred creatures of back allies

Scott's Emulsion, $8.00.

and dark streets. Most collectors prefer the nostalgic images of cats, and, fortunately, there are plenty of them to be found.

Historical Notes

The lithographic industry that produced Victorian trade cards was dominated by male artists. These artists often worked directly from the recommendations, notes, and even sketches provided by the firms that purchased their services. These artists sometimes worked through several water color drafts of an image before getting the final nod of approval to put a card into full production on the presses. But again, these were mostly male artists who were trying to please mostly male-owned and managed firms.

Bon Ami Cleanser, $20.00.

Subtle hints of the male bias of the industry are detectable if one carefully studies enough trade card images. This is perhaps the most noticeable in a comparison of the treatment of cats verses dogs in advertising illustrations. Dogs appear far more often in trade card images than cats, and they are generally shown as pure bred animals faithfully fulfilling their role as "man's best friend." They are often presented as loyal "working" animals, quietly at their master's side. When shown as household pets, dogs are typically portrayed as attentive and alert to the needs of the children that they guard. Mean dogs occasionally appear in trade card illustrations, but rarely in scenes other than when lunging at the end of their chain in an attempt to defend territory in their master's back yard.

Cats, on the other hand, are allowed to suffer more than dogs in trade card images. While it is true that many flattering images of cats were produced to win the favor of female consumers, it must also be added that there is a large group of cards where cats are the subject of terrible abuse. Besides the scenes that one might expect of cats being chased over fences, there are a disturbing number of additional images where the tails of cats are run through wringers, pulled by monkeys, or pecked by birds. Cats are also shown dripping wet from wells or children's pranks, and are frequently depicted themselves in the sadistic light of their own abuse of other animals. One gathers from such images that Victorian lithographers often thought more highly of dogs than cats.

Pricing Tips & Cards to Watch For

Many attractive images of cats are found among trade cards advertising soap, sewing products, insurance, and patent medicines. The soap and sewing cards are usually very affordable, with many fine cat images still selling in this group within the $5 – 10 range. Stock cards with cat images are also typically priced well under $10, but the illustrations found among stock cards are sometimes distasteful to collectors. Watch for nice illustrations of purebred cats, as some collectors prefer specific breeds, and such cards are hard to come by. Also watch for cards with anthropomorphic and "Puss in Boots" images, as these are another favorite with many collectors. Because of the products typically advertised using cat images, very few cat cards sell for over $30, which makes them one of the most affordable categories of trade cards.

Handy Box Shoe Blacking, $35.00.

Household Sewing Machine, $12.00.

J. & P. Coats Thread, $15.00.

Standard Java Coffee, $15.00.

Woolson Spice, $20.00.

Brook's Thread, $20.00.

Domestic Sewing Machine, $8.00.

Ryeninjun Flap-Jack, stock card, $10.00.

Dr. Thomas' Eclectric Oil, $10.00.

Lautz Bro's Gloss Soap, $8.00.

Dr. Isaac Thompson's Eye Water
   girl applies eye drops to cat on desk, bottle in her hand **$15.00**

Glenwood Ranges & Heaters
   girls with stripped cat in tree **$8.00**

Heminway & Sons Thread
   girl in white nightgown, 4 kittens, one on her nightcap **$15.00**

J. & P. Coats Thread
   girl in red dress on bench, kitten in lap, cat rubbing shoulder **$5.00**

J. O. Draper Toilet Soaps
   girl, 3 kittens in basket, straw **$8.00**

James Pyle's Pearline Soap
   girl with no shirt hugging cat with pink bow, same eyes **$8.00**

James Pyle's Pearline Soap
   girl on red carpet holds calico cat **$6.00**

Larkin Soap
   white cat sharing bowl with 7 ducklings **$10.00**

Merrick Thread
   "Ding, dong, dell! Pussy's in the well!" cat, spool over well **$12.00**

Merrick Thread
   "Mamma Uses Merrick's Thread" girl in nightcap hugs cat **$8.00**

Shawmut Soap
   "An Armfull" girl in straw hat holding 3 kittens, mother cat **$10.00**

Stickney & Poors Mustard
   2 girls in hats, baskets, white cat with blue ribbon **$15.00**

Stock Card — from a set of 6
   "Did you see me get the best of him?" bandaged cat, 1881 . . . .**$5.00**

Stock Card — bitters imprint
   white kitten on desk, spilled ink bottle, quill pen **$8.00**

Stock Card — stove imprint
   cat with medal, "1st Prize at International Cat Show" **$8.00**

Stock Card — studio imprint
   "Three Little Maids are we" 3 cats with fans mimic theater **$20.00**

Rough On Rats, $25.00.

J. & P. Coats Thread, $8.00.

Hoyt's German Cologne/Rubifoam, $25.00.

Lavine Soap, die-cut, $15.00.

Children

Children Images

Collectors enjoy images of children as much today as consumers did a century ago when advertisers discovered the power of these images to capture attention and sell merchandise. Children appear in ads for every product imaginable, including such seemingly unlikely products as farm implements, alcohol, and tobacco. Some collectors prefer cards picturing children with angelic faces, while others prefer images of girls with dolls or of mischievous boys at play. For an extra challenge, some collectors search for trade card illustrations copied from the prints of famous children's authors like Kate Greenaway or Maud Humphrey.

The quality of child images in trade cards varies widely, but within this grouping one finds many examples showcasing the finest artistic techniques of the Victorian age. The quickest way to identify images of exceptional quality is to check the eyes and cheeks of the children illustrated. In cards produced by master lithographers, eyes will appear bright and natural, and cheeks will typically shade smoothly down from a robust pink to a pale white at the temples and chin.

Historical Notes

Trade cards regularly depict healthy children in happy, prosperous homes. The adults targeted by most of these cards were reasonably affluent Victorians who dreamt of providing for their children the innocent and carefree life that these cards offered as the ideal. In many cases, advertisements suggested that the ideal childhood could be attained simply through an investment in their product. Trade cards hinted that the timely purchase of the correct brand of "Worm Destroyer," or "Cough Killer" could keep a child healthy, and that the holiday purchase of a new doll, pair of roller-skates, or bicycle could keep a child happy. In reality, few Victorian children had it nearly as good as the "good life" portrayed in these ads.

It wasn't until 1916, during the closing months of the Victorian era and at the brink of WWI, that the federal government was finally able to find enough support to pass its first child labor laws regulating the exploitation of children. Ironically, some of the industries that were the most guilty of child exploitation (cotton mills/threads and mining/light manufacturing) were the very ones quickest to depict children at home basking in lives of ease. Sadly, the too-late laws of 1916 were barely enforced, and then were struck down only two years later. Children were sent back into dangerous mines, were scheduled for nights shifts in mills, and returned to 14-hour days in sweat shops.

Besides the one million or more children who were pressed by necessity into sometimes slave-like service, there were tens of thousands of others who ran the streets unsupervised while both parents trudged off to work. A few cards capture this side of childhood, but such scenes are usually treated humorously, as if laughing about them would make them more palatable to the middle class. Trade card images of ragamuffin boys shining expensive boots and underfed children staring at hams are rare, but they can be found. Even more rare are the images of the children who were beaten and abused by over-stressed parents who just barely got by themselves. Such images failed to evoke the positive responses that advertisers sought for the increases in sales that trade cards were distributed to assure.

Pricing Tips & Cards to Watch For

Hundreds of cards with wonderful images of children can be found for under $10. Check in albums for soaps, threads, and stock cards for the best buys. Great "oversized" cards that are suitable for framing and usually priced under $20 can be found in numerous coffee series. The most lovely and detailed illustrations of children are often found on cards advertising canned milk and patent medicines, where impressions of beautiful and healthy children were essential. These cards generally sell for $15 to $30, partially because of their superior artistry, but also because of the special demand for patent medicine advertising.

Keep an eye open for a set of five stock cards with images from Kate Greenaway's *Under the Window*, as some dealers price these cards around $5, not recognizing this artist's unsigned work. J. & P. Coats Thread issued a set of 17 cards with Greenaway illustrations taken from her early book of Mother Goose nursery rhymes. Watch also for early unsigned images by Maud Humphrey and Richard Outcault. Very few dealers file children cards as a topical category, so the best approach may be to find a dealer that one feels comfortable with, and then to take the time to flip through every album that looks promising.

Hall's Vegetable Sicilian Hair Renewer, $12.00.

Muad Humphrey, stock card, $15.00.

Ayer's Cherry Pectoral, $12.00.

Hires' Root Beer, $20.00.

Dr. Hand's Remedies for Children, $30.00.

Mrs. Winslow's Soothing Syrup, $20.00.

Dr. Kilmer's Indian Cough Cure, $20.00.

Shaker Family Pills, $35.00.

Johnson's Anodyne Liniment, $15.00.

Dr. Hand's Remedies for Children, $20.00.

McLaughlin's Coffee, $10.00.

Warner's Safe Yeast, $25.00.

Quaker Bitters, $15.00.

Terry's Scissors and Shears, $35.00.

Highland Evaporated Cream, $20.00.

Perry Davis' Pain Killer, $15.00.

Kate Greenaway, stock card, $8.00.

Diamond Dyes, $15.00.

Fairbank's Cottolene, $20.00.

Hall's Vegetable Sicilian Hair Renewer, $20.00.

Hoyt's German Cologne, $15.00.

Gendron Iron Goods, $60.00.

Metropolitan Life Insurance, $10.00.

Acme Soap
  "Oh dear, Willie will be drowned!" boy falls in well with soap . . .$4.00

Acorn Stove & Ranges
  Black girl with doll, acorn leaves, holding arm of white girl $30.00

Andes Stoves and Ranges
  "His Name is Andes" boy with lamb $8.00

Ayer's Sarsaparilla
  "My Jewels" mother with 3 children $20.00

Celluloid Collars, Cuffs & Shirt
  boy in father's suit demonstrates celluloid in dipped in water $10.00

Colegate & Co. Soap
  ragged newspaper boy rests in alley, dog, ad on paper $15.00

Goshen Carpet Sweepers
  girl with sweeper points to boy with doll, toy horse $25.00

Hall's Vegetable Sicilian Hair Renewer
  faces of 8 lovely children around bottle $25.00

Household Sewing Machine
  boy & girl with fancy hat in speeding "Household" wagon $12.00

Hoyt's German Cologne
  die-cut book marker, girl, glasses, red cap $15.00

Kate Greenaway stock card
  "Walking by the Sea" 2 girls, umbrellas, fruit tree $8.00

Kate Greenaway stock card
  "Going Fishing" 2 children on stone bridge, Clark's Thread $8.00

Magnolia Ham
  5 poor children ride ham like horse, 4 shoeless, 1 Black $30.00

Muad Humphrey style stock card
  boy picks flowers, girl with fan, Standard Sewing Machine $15.00

Stickney & Poors Mustard
  2 girls, white cat, 2 baskets, hats, picket fence $20.00

Stock Card — clothing imprint
  2 poor children stare at window display, boy shoeless $8.00

Stock Card — confectioner imprint
  "Nice dogie... poor pussy" naughty boy with firecrackers $8.00

Stock Card — confections imprint
  girl with flowers, box, hat, in adult's shoes $8.00

Stock Card — dentist imprint
  girl in gloves, cap, holds lip, pouting $15.00

Stock Card — Frear's imprint
  2 boys in hats tricking woman with string, man smiles $6.00

Stock Card — insurance imprint
  boy and girl under umbrella, Grace Drayton style faces $10.00

Stock Card — insurance imprint
  boy in red cap with St. Bernard dog $12.00

Stock Card — medicine imprint
  mother with stick, boy by ear, caught skinny dipping $8.00

Stock Card — shoe imprint
  Black girl with clothes pins at fence, hand on chin $8.00

Stock Card — smelling salts imprint
  2 shoeless shoeshine boys eating melon, grapes $10.00

Stock Card — stove imprint
  blonde infant in hanging fern basket, white gown $4.00

Van Houten's Cocoa
  blue eyed boy in blue sailor outfit, red scarf $20.00

Scott's Emulsion, $12.00.

Borden's Condensed Milk, $15.00.

Chinese

(See also: Ethnic; Irish.)

Chinese Images

There are dozens of trade cards with Chinese images. Most of these are linked to chores like washing and ironing, which were often associated with Chinese labor. Chinese people are often depicted in offensive ways in trade cards. There is a confusion in some images between the cultures and features of Chinese and Japanese people. Images that exploit white disgust over the supposed Chinese diet are abundant, with the two most common themes being a face-off between a hungry man and a large dog, or an illustration of an Oriental diner contemplating a rat. Most of these cards were cheaply done, with their chief value resting in their historical significance rather than any graphic or artistic merit they might have.

Historical Notes

The devastation of the Opium War and a series of droughts left many communities in nineteenth century China in waste and famine, so when rumors of "Golden California" arrived, there was no shortage of young men willing to leave home. But when they arrived in America, their long pigtails (queues), strange shoes, and peculiar hats drew many stares. As their numbers increased, the unfamiliar clatter of their Asian tongues began unnerving many whites, who were suspicious of the way the Chinese kept to themselves and refused to "fit in." As racial tensions grew, the Chinese drew tighter together, thus becoming even more conspicuous and less understood.

Bret Harte penned an immensely popular poem in 1870 that circulated in papers across the country. His poem, "The Heathen Chinee," told the story of a card game between an Irishman and a Chinaman named Ah Sin. After Harte's poem, the phrase "Heathen Chinee" fell into common usage in America, and with the phrase came an open prejudice against Chinese immigrants. Dennis Kearney built an entire political career around the hostile slogan, "The Chinese Must Go!" America wrestled with "The Chinese Question," which involved the problems raised for illiterate American laborers by the continuous influx of of Asian immigrants.

If the Chinese immigrants of this period were guilty of anything, it was their willingness to tackle the dirtiest work without complaint. As they withdrew from mining towns and railroad camps, they continued to take on jobs that others hated. Cooking, cleaning, and above all else, laundry work became their standard fare. Many middle-class families even began to prefer the Chinese over Irish and Blacks as domestic servants. And because a laundry business required little initial capital, it became the favorite arena for Chinese enterprise.

Pricing Tips & Cards to Watch For

Like other ethnic cards, those with Chinese images command premium prices. Look for them especially among soap, ironing, sewing, clothing, and food-related advertisements, where privately issued cards with Chinese stereotypes often bring $20 or more. The most infamous Chinese image was produced on a large "Rough on Rats" card. The image is of a man eating a rodent, and the card sells for $400 or more. Also keep an eye open for Chinese figures appearing in patriotic scenes, especially where Uncle Sam is sharing a product with people from around the world.

Imperial Chinese Magic Polish,
$25.00.

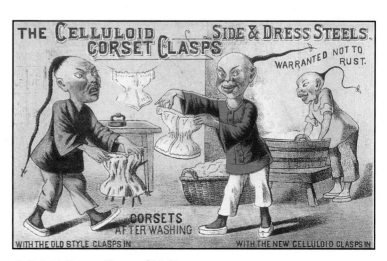

Celluloid Corset Clasps, $35.00.

Magnolia Hams, $35.00.

Paragon Dried Beef, $40.00.

Agate Iron Ware
Chinese man in pot boat, "For China," bird in teapot $20.00

Beymer Bauman Lead Paint
Chinese man painting fence, painters from states dancing $100.00

Celluloid Waterproof Collars & Cuffs
men in water, white shirts, "Off for China" on sails $25.00

Domestic Sewing Machine
3 impish Chinese in tree, coffin "Run Out" cemetery $12.00

Lavine Soap
7 Chinese men dance around soap box in laundry $15.00

Mrs. Pott's Sad Iron
Uncle Sam leads Chinese from Calif. back to China $90.00

Mrs. Pott's Sad Iron
"Dennis Kirney No Goodee" Chinese man dances, iron $30.00

New Process Starch
Chinese laundry worker, old process — woman New Process $15.00

Peerless Wringer
Dennis Kearney runs "Ah Sin" through wringer, metamorphic $50.00

Stock Card
2 Irish boys torment Chinese boy on box $10.00

Stock Card — clothing imprint
Chinese man with chop sticks mad at cat taking his rat $15.00

Stock Card — clothing imprint
"Chinee Man No Cheatee" cards fall from sleeve, silouhette $12.00

Stock Card — jewelry imprint
"John Chinaman he eatie dogie," dogs scare men $15.00

Stock Card — Telephone Soap imprint
"Two hearts that beat as one," dog & man eye white rats $15.00

Waterproof Linen
man cheats Chinese laundry man, metamorphic card $40.00

Wilson's Corned Beef
2 men dance with can, "Offee to Yang tse kiang" $30.00

Celluloid Waterproof Collars & Cuffs, $15.00.

City Views
(See also: Expositions; Hotels; Statue of Liberty; Transportation.)

City View Images

City views of specific Victorian skylines, main streets, buildings, bridges, or monuments are relatively scarce and are typically in high demand with trade card collectors. Most city views fall into one of six groups: generic street views, specific exposition buildings, the Statue of Liberty, specific company sites, the Obelisk in Central Park, or the Brooklyn Bridge. Advertisers tended to stick with city views that were generic enough to appear relevant to consumers in any part of the country. When lithographers were forced to commit to images of specific sites, they typically produced an illustration of a firm's actual (or embellished) facilities, with the surrounding cityscape conveniently omitted. Other city views tend to be scarce, and they are generally found only in black and white illustrations or in the photo-lithographic views of major cities that were distributed by several coffee, thread, and patent medicine companies. The attention to detail is often remarkable in city and building views, but the use of colors is generally quite limited.

Historical Notes

Expositions, the Statue of Liberty, the Obelisk in Central park, and the Brooklyn Bridge all received enough national publicity to make their way into trade card images for national distribution. Beyond those attractions, specific city and building views are somewhat scarce, unless one also counts "Corporate Headquarters" illustrations as "city views."

The Industrial Revolution blackened the skies of every major city that participated in its arrival. In fact, the views in most major cities are visibly crisper today than they were a century ago. Factories once stoked their boilers with coal, and houses once "kept the home fires burning" with coal and wood all night and for every meal. Incredibly enough, this was also a day when consumers judged a company's prowess by the number and size of its smokestacks, lethal as those smokestack were.

In trade card images, it is not uncommon to find companies boasting of their success through the number of smokestacks they portrayed belching black soot into skies over the cities that they served. In some cases, artists were encouraged to add smokestacks that were never built, or to exaggerate the size and output of the ones that were there in order to enhance the image of the firm in the minds of consumers.

Pricing Tips & Cards to Watch For

City views are rarely found for under $10 in Victorian trade cards. For affordable views of interesting cities, one should start with the photo-lithographic sets that were mass-distributed by Jersey Coffee, Clark's Thread, and Hood's Sarsaparilla, which can still be purchased on occasion for $5 – 10 each. Also watch for cards from sets of 50 issued by Arbuckle Coffee, particularly their "Pictorial History of the United States and Territories" set and their "Views from a Trip Around the World" series, some of which can be found for under $10 each. Watch for views depicting "The Residence of...," as these views are often in demand with collectors who reside in the region of the homes featured in such cards. Also check the backs of stock cards, where one occasionally finds a wonderful building illustration that by far eclipses the color stock image on the card's face.

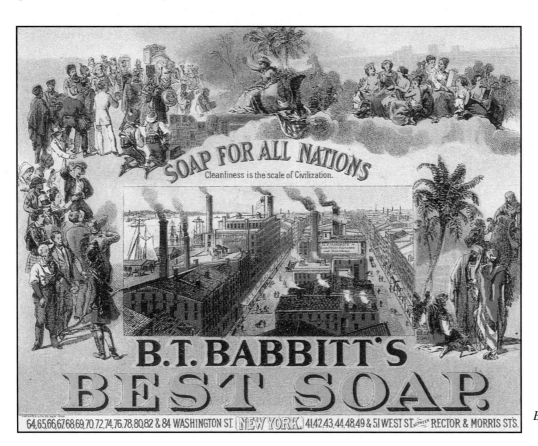

B. T. Babbitt's Best Soap, $15.00.

Arbuckle Coffee
Boston Commons, Old South Church — one of 50 world views **$10.00**

Arbuckle Coffee
Melbourne, Australia — from set of 50 world views, 1891 . . . .**$4.00**

Boraxine Cleanser
The Boston Museum of Art — Larkin Soap **$20.00**

Branson & Bro., Coal
winter view, snow, horses, wagon, Branson depot & offices **$40.00**

Chesebrough Vaseline
"Egyptian Obelisk in Central Park New York" **$15.00**

Clarence Brooks Coach Varnishes
"The New St. Patrick's Cathedral," Am Bank Note Co Lith **$15.00**

Clark's Thread
"Harper's Ferry, W. VA.," valley, town & water below **$10.00**

Clark's Thread
Pike's Peak from Colorado Springs, Col. — hotel at end **$20.00**

Grand Mardi-Gras & Display
hold-to-light, Uncle Sam over Galveston & harbor **$120.00**

Jacoby & Hidson, Syracuse, NY
"New West Shore R.R. Depot," Syracuse, NY, 1883 . . . .**$35.00**

Jersey Coffee
"Photo-Lithographic View" of San Francisco, Golden Gate **$10.00**

Johnson's Anodyne Liniment
City Hall, Halifax, N.S. **$20.00**

Lydia Pinkham's Vegetable Compound
Brooklyn Bridge with advertising sign hanging below **$15.00**

Manitou Mineral Water & Bath House
photo view of downtown Manitou, Colo. **$30.00**

Mica Axle Grease
Garfield Monument, Cleveland, Ohio **$15.00**

New England Cough Remedy
Hartford's Soldier Memorial, dimensions **$15.00**

Royal Baking Powder
"Great Suspension Bridge between New York and Brooklyn" **$25.00**

Singer Sewing Machine
Brooklyn Bridge, ships **$20.00**

Stock Card — shoe imprint
Washington Monument, compares height to other buildings **$15.00**

Syracuse Wall Paper
green & red residence of Syracuse, NY, mailman at porch **$40.00**

The Jersey Coffee
Chicago, LaSalle St. from Board of Trade, from set of 100 . . . .**$10.00**

Warner's Safe Yeast
"Safe Yeast Building" woman at window, container **$12.00**

Wright's Indian Vegetable Pills
"The Bowery, New York" photo, elevated track **$25.00**

Chilicothe Colleges, $35.00.

Willimantic Thread, $15.00.

Stock card, $15.00.

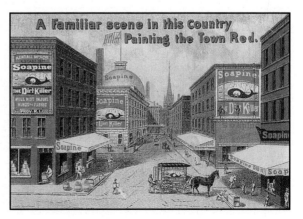

Soapine Soap, $25.00.

Clothing & Dry Goods

(See also: Corsets; Food; Furniture; Shoes; Stock Cards.)

Clothing & Dry Goods Images

Most trade cards with ads for clothing and dry goods stores are of the "stock card" variety, which can be found with images of everything from children and animals to military scenes and natural wonders. Some of these stock cards are beautifully embossed or cleverly designed, while others are quite unremarkable. The black and white imprints found on the backs of these cards are often of more interest to collectors and local historians than the color stock images found on the fronts. Privately commissioned cards with illustrations of actual stores, local attractions, or proprietors are relatively scarce. Privately issued cards promoting specific brands of clothing, linen, hooks, etc. also tend to be scarce and in demand.

Historical Notes

The average shopper of the early nineteenth century bought a wide variety of bulk goods from a local general store, then prepared and tailored those goods to their own ability and taste. Those who could afford well-trained domestic servants (or private tailors) dressed and ate consistently well, while others reserved their best homemade clothes and meals for special occasions. Expensive specialty shops that catered to the elite were only sustainable in major cities and wealthy neighborhoods. People of lesser means bartered for better workmanship as they were able. Racks of manufactured dresses and suits of standard sizes were unheard of, as were products with clearly marked and uniform prices.

The Civil War played an important role in "kick starting" a number of manufacturing industries that had geared up for the mass production of military items in standard sizes and styles. After the war, aggressive dry goods entrepreneurs began expanding to make room for dazzling new inventories of affordable,

Foster's Hook Gloves, $35.00.

mass-produced articles that they grouped in departments, often on multiple floors. More laborers were hired as factories increased their production to keep such stores filled. As more workers were paid on a regular basis, more consumers were created, and the cycle picked up speed.

Advertising trade cards played an important role in the emerging culture of Victorian consumption. Local stores purchased and imprinted inexpensive stock cards to announce the arrival or clearance of merchandise. Once inside a store, customers were exposed to additional merchandise, and then were sent home with more trade cards to remind them of the irresistible nonessentials that awaited their return. Trade cards forced competitive marketing and uniform pricing within communities, and they sealed the doom of marginal stores that lacked the resources to maintain affordable and up-to-date inventories. Nationally issued trade cards also influenced the products and brands that local stores carried by exposing purchasing agents to the latest models and by planting seeds of interest directly in the minds of consumers, who then went to stores with requests for demonstrations.

Pricing Tips & Cards to Watch For

Most stock cards with clothing and dry goods imprints sell for under $5. Watch for such cards that "slip through" with imprints for historically significant stores like Marshall Field, Lord and Taylor, and John Wanamaker. Also keep an eye open for cards from the hometowns of one's own family and friends, as these cards make wonderful and inexpensive gifts. Local museums, libraries, and historical societies typically have members who deeply appreciate these cards and who value them more highly than most collectors. Privately issued cards for nationally distributed brands of shirts, pants, gloves, etc. generally sell for over $20, with cards for familiar companies like Levi Strauss often bringing many times that amount.

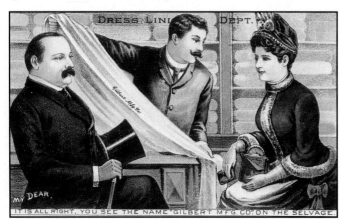

Gilbert's Fabrics, $35.00.

Gordon's Store, stock card, $20.00.

Continental Clothing House
"Special Sizes for Tall Men," clerk hooks tape on cane $20.00

De Long Hook and Eye
"Eclipses Everything," Indians worship invention/eclipse $30.00

Feder's Pompadour Skirt Protector
"For the binding of every skirt that I make." 3 women $20.00

Kamo Baking Powder
riddle: Bear in Dry Goods Store (ans. — Muzzlin' — muslin) $10.00

Koch & Shankweiler Clothing
stage coach with painted ads, 4 horses, trumpet, banner $20.00

Marshall Field & Co., Chicago
design like box, "Linen Department" girl, flowers, linen $25.00

Montgomery Ward — mail order promo
"Where the Brownies Get Their Supplies," emptying catalog $60.00

Orr's Pantaloon Overalls
salesman supervises tug-of-war demonstration with pants $60.00

Pearl Shirts
wife to man reading paper: "George, I have just bought..." $8.00

Prang Stock Card — Wanamaker
"General Dry Goods House," well-dressed family, 1877 . . . .$15.00

Stark's "Unique" Waist Band
boy suspended by pants from Brooklyn Bridge, cop, hat $40.00

Stock Card
father, son, clerk, mom, Johnny's new suit, Tobin — 1883 . . . .$10.00

Stock Card — A.W. Walker
"Dry & Fancy Goods," 2 boys, holiday turkey, rose $4.00

Stock Card — Gould's Hat Store
"best $1.00 Hat in town — $2.00 Derby," clerk, jockey in cap $8.00

Stock Card — Haskell Hats, Furs
2 men, hats, canes, umbrellas displayed, stuffed game $20.00

Stock Card — J. Morgenstern
"Manufacturer of Fine Furs" boy under big hat, 1871 . . . .$50.00

Stock Card — Jacob Reed's Sons'
"Oldest Clothing Store In America — Established 1824" $5.00

Stock Card — Leigh & Prindle
"Ready Made Clothing," girls feeding winter birds $4.00

Stock Card — Morris Gross
clerk strokes chin, well-dressed man in derby, dog $12.00

Stock Card — Union Clothing Co.
1888 presidential candidates "Sunday Suites" at Week-Day $30.00

The Old South Clothing House
Boston's Old South Church, ad on roof $15.00

Womrath Ladies' Fine Furs
woman in blue coat with seal fur hat, muff, trim $15.00

White Labor Shirts, San Fran., Cal., $75.00.

Celluloid Waterproof Collars, $10.00.

Coffee, Tea & Cocoa

(See also: Food; Root Beer.)

Hot Beverage Images

Thousands of delightful trade cards were commissioned by the Victorian firms that marketed coffee, tea, and cocoa. These companies also produced dozens of paper advertising toys, die-cuts, and paper dolls that have made their way into the collections of many trade card enthusiasts. A major marketing ploy in the industry was to insert attractive advertising cards (usually one per package) into containers of the product, and in this way to lay a foundation for repeat business as consumers tried to complete sets of these cards.

Arbuckle Coffee issued about ten wonderfully designed adult oriented sets (mostly 50 cards per set) that are rapidly growing in popularity with collectors. Woolson Spice (Lion Coffee) and McLauglin Coffee each issued attractive sets of oversized cards with seasonal and topical themes that appealed especially to children. Jersey Coffee produced several fascinating "instructive" sets with American and foreign views, while Dilworth's released an interesting assortment of under-sized cards that are easy to spot because of the large golden coffee urn that appears in most of their images. Cocoa cards are also popular with collectors, with Van Houten's being one of the favorite firms collected. Outside of the many cheaply produced stock cards that were used by the Atlantic and Pacific Tea company, most of the trade cards that are found with imprints from the hot beverage industry are above average in quality and design.

Historical Notes

The story of the Boston Tea Party is one of the most familiar of all patriotic legends in America. Behind the folklore, however, is a cultural reality. Colonial Americans took their tea very seriously, consuming an estimated million or more pounds of it a year. The rumor back in Europe was that Americans overdid it with their tea, drinking too much of it, chugging it too fast, and brewing it far too strong. This misuse of tea was even offered as a partial explanation for the restlessness of the American character. Coffee and cocoa were overshadowed by the tea industry until after the Civil War.

In 1870 when Hartford and Gilman expanded and renamed the Atlantic & Pacific Tea Company (the new A&P name having been shrewdly selected to piggyback the media hype surrounding the completion of the transcontinental railroad), coffee beans still comprised a relatively small part of their business. By 1882 there were 120 A&P stores in the United States, and the company was copyrighting its own cards for "Sultana" coffee that boasted of "Air-tight Trade-Mark Caddies" that assured freshness. Innovations in packaging and marketing had boosted A&P coffee and cocoa sales everywhere, but especially in their more remote outlets where inventory turned over at a slower rate. Chase and Sanborn improved its market share with refinements in canning coffee in 1878, while other firms advanced the industry through innovations of their own. In addition to their heavy marketing through trade cards, Arbuckle's "Ariosa" Coffee endeared itself

with many rural and western communities by dropping a peppermint stick into every bag. Legend has it that cowboys would sometimes fight over who could make the "Arbuckle's" and get to the candy first. Cocoa sales increased as affluent Victorians developed a taste for it at breakfast, and as health-conscious consumers began looking for invigorating "food" alternatives to coffee and tea "brews."

Pricing Tips & Cards to Watch For

Historically, coffee, tea, and cocoa cards have tended to be very inexpensive, often $5 or less each. As more collectors have begun to notice the beauty of cocoa cards, prices for many of the better cocoa cards have begun to move up. The best Van Houten, Runkel Bros., and Blooker's cocoa cards are currently bringing $25 and up. Coffee and tea trade cards have experience uneven appreciation, with many of these cards still selling for less than $5, while others from the same set may command $50 or more. This is especially true with Arbuckle cards and their "History of the Sports and Pastimes of all Nations" series. Watch for their Scotland (golf) and United States (baseball, bicycling, photography, circus) cards in particular, which now bring $50 or more with some sports collectors.

Reeves & Parvin Mountain Coffee, $20.00.

Bennett Tea House, stock card, $15.00.

Chase and Sanborn, $12.00.

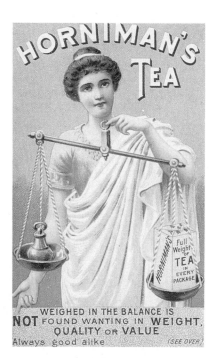

Horniman's Tea, $25.00.

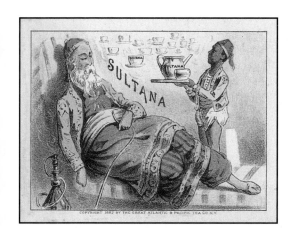

Sultana Coffee, $12.00.

Van Houten's Cocoa, $15.00.

Runkel's Cocoa, $15.00.

Chase and Sanborn, $15.00.

Van Houten's Cocoa, $15.00.

Phillips' Digestible Cocoa, $15.00.

Oriental & Occidental Teas, $8.00.

Genuine Franck Coffee, $30.00.

Dilworth's Coffee, $5.00.

Arbuckle Coffee
"She Bought a New One," umbrella, 2 women in rain — by Puck . . .$15.00

Arbuckle Coffee
Massachusetts, map series of states, 1889 . . . .$10.00

Arbuckle Coffee
California, history of states series of states, 1892 . . . .$10.00

Arbuckle Coffee
Virginia, history of states series of states, 1892 . . . .$10.00

Arbuckle Coffee
Mexico, history of sports & pastimes series, 1893 . . . .$10.00

Arbuckle Coffee
Munich, Bavaria, views from around the world series, 1891 . . . .$6.00

Jersey Coffee
Hall of Mines, Columbian Expo, 1893, color photo-lith $12.00

Lion Coffee
die-cut "River Steamboat" rev. "Paper Toys for Children" $15.00

Lion Coffee
die-cut "Old King Cole" on throne with pipe, bowl $10.00

McLaughlin's Coffee
"Gypsy" little girl with cards, ace of hearts, wagon $10.00

McLaughlin's Coffee
Confederate Ram Manassas Attacking USS Brooklyn, 1889 . . . .$10.00

Morning Joy Coffee
die-cut of brown pony, reverse: Atlanta Exposition $20.00

Scull's Champion Rio Coffee
2 Black men loading coffee bags on cart, small dog for horse $20.00

Stock Card — "Jamova Coffee"
"The Sunny South," large Black woman, pot, cup $12.00

Union Pacific Tea Company
Uncle Sam sits with Chinese man "get so fat like me" $25.00

Woolson Spice — Lion Coffee
"Midsummer Greeting," woman picking cherries from ladder $8.00

Levering's Roasted Coffee, die-cut, $20.00.

Reeves & Parvin Mountain Coffee, $20.00.

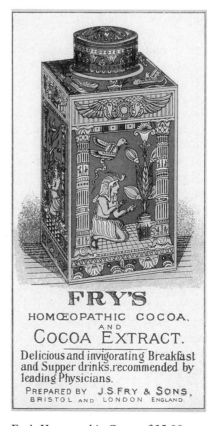

Fry's Homœpathic Cocoa, $35.00.

Columbia

(See also: Expositions; Statue of Liberty; Uncle Sam.)

Miss Columbia Images

Patriotic images are popular with collectors, and some of the best of these images include depictions of Miss Columbia. Uncle Sam appears more often on trade cards, but when Columbia is shown, she is usually presented as the most attractive of all ambassadors of American business. Columbia is seldom found in black and white images, as she is usually draped in a red, white, and blue flag. She is frequently identifiable through her association with other American symbols like Uncle Sam, eagles, flag shields, a cap, crown, or wreath with stars, American maps, etc. She is often shown presenting goods to the world in trade cards that were produced for expositions. In several cases, the product itself may be called a "Columbia" brand, and she may even be part of a company's trade mark.

Historical Notes

The history of America's Miss Columbia goes back thousands of years. She has her origins in classical goddess figures and the powerful female deities of primitive religions. In numerous wood cuts and engravings from the sixteenth to nineteenth centuries, a female figure is used decoratively in maps and literature about America. These early personifications of America often dress this woman in feathers and place her in the midst of dense foliage to create the mystique of an Indian queen in the fertile New World wilderness. Her name, Columbia, was drawn from the name Christopher Columbus, and in many early cases the word Columbia was synonymous with the New World as well as with the female symbol.

While in some images Columbia appears almost indistinguishable from her allegorical female cousins, Liberty and Justice, several American touches can usually be found to confirm that this is America's own special lady. The Indian feathers, bow, buckskins, etc. were an American touch, as were the post-Revolutionary War additions of stars and stripes to her classical toga or robes. Americans also preferred placing her beneath a patriotically colored cap, or to add stars to her classical helmet, crown, or wreath. Columbia is further distinguishable from other female symbols by the context and activity in which she is typically presented. Her context is often unquestionably American, whether it be a in "modern" Philadelphia kitchen or on a rock overlooking an American town. Around her one invariably finds a flag, a flag shield, an eagle, or some other clue that she is a distinctly American figure. In some cases, the illustration of a product itself is done in a way to indicate Columbia's American identity. And finally, one can spot Columbia by what she is doing. Victorian capitalists turned her into an heroic peddler, a role which would have seemed trivial to Miss Liberty and one which would have been intolerable to the blindfolded Miss Justice.

Pricing Tips & Cards to Watch For

Columbia is one of the most expensive and difficult topical images to collect in trade cards. Outside of a few soap cards, very few of these cards can still be found for under $15, with most selling in the $30 to $100 range. Watch for cards where Columbia is shown at an exposition, with Uncle Sam, with ethnic figures, or is depicted selling "romantic" products like alcohol, tobacco, and farm equipment. Collectors tend to converge on such cards and snap them up quickly, often paying $50 or more without blinking an eye when such cards are offered for sale.

A. Werner "America" Champagne, $50.00.

Enterprise Meat Chopper, $50.00.

Arbuckle Coffee
> United States map, eagle, flag, Columbia — from set of fifty **$15.00**

Bixby's Shoe Polish
> Columbia holds shoe, women of all nations, flagshield **$25.00**

Boston Daily Globe
> Columbia, globe, paper, flag drape, wreath & red cap **$40.00**

Celluloid Cuffs & Collars
> Columbia, Chinese, Uncle Sam, flag drape, cap, flag shield **$100.00**

Challenge Corn Planter & Ice Box
> Columbia in classical martial garb, 2 swords, products **$75.00**

Great American Tea Company
> Columbia in red cap, flag drape, 1865 calendar (early A&P) **$250.00**

Highland Evaporated Cream
> die-cut of can, 6 — panel folder, Columbia, scales, flag shield **$100.00**

Jas. Kirk Soap — "American Family"
> Columbia & Uncle Sam as eagles, flag dress, flag shields **$8.00**

Jas. Kirk Soap — "Columbia" brand
> Columbia, eagle, flag, flag dress, feathers, top of globe **$8.00**

Keystone Wringer
> Columbia, big wringer on table, wreath, draped in red **$25.00**

Keystone Wringer
> Columbia presents wringer, classic red drape, star wreath **$25.00**

Libby McNeill & Libby's Meat
> Columbia, flag drape, eagle, capitol building, star crown **$50.00**

Libby McNeill & Libby's Meat
> Columbia, classical style, red ribbons, cow, Columbian Expo **$20.00**

Loyal Soap
> Columbia, box, red star cap, eagle, flag drape, flag shield **$40.00**

Mrs. Potts' Sad Irons
> "Miss Columbia" in kitchen, "Brother Jonathan" (Uncle Sam) **$35.00**

Parisian Sauce
> Columbia gets sauce, Statue of Liberty, eagle, flag shield **$50.00**

President Suspender
> Columbia holds product to McKinley & Bryan, 1900 election **$75.00**

Stock Card — druggist imprint
> "America," Columbia, flag dress, torch, broken chains, 1879 . . . .**$8.00**

New Home Sewing Machine, $35.00.

Standard Fashioned Shoes, $60.00.

Columbia Yarns, $30.00.

Corsets

(See also: Clothing & Dry Goods; Risque; Women.)

Corset Images

Many collectors, female and male, are intrigued by trade cards used in the marketing of corsets and undergarments. Privately issued cards are the most popular with collectors, especially when the cards feature bold, full-color illustrations of women wearing a particular brand or model. Collectors of corset cards often appreciate cards advertising products other than corsets, so long as the images on these cards contribute insights on nineteenth century undergarments, fashion, and Victorian attitudes toward the human body. Stock cards with black and white illustrated corset ads on the reverse are more common than privately issued corset cards. Many of these stock cards have portraits of famous women on the front, and occasionally the endorsement of a theater celebrity as part of the text on the reverse.

Historical Notes

Corsets helped define Victorian culture as well as any other item of the period. Trade cards that advertise corsets bring that culture back to life like no other artifact — including actual corsets — can. These cards peek into elegant boudoirs, thrusting fleeting glimpses of pretty women in their "unspeakables" before the public eye. Through the postures, facial expressions, dialogs, testimonials, and advertising claims found on these cards, one finds a fascinating peephole into the romance, extravagance, and absurdity of a culture obsessed with appearance and social status.

Some critics hold that a tightly laced corset was the supreme symbol of a Victorian woman's confined and dependent status. Corsets represented the lost freedom of childhood's short skirts and play clothes, which were exchanged at puberty for an assortment of skirts, corsets, and undergarments that were used subconsciously as armor against male intrusion. Others take a more romantic view, suggesting that corsets embraced a receptive culture. According to this view, women and men both often experienced the equipment and rituals of Victorian underclothing as exquisitely indulgent and feminine, if not downright erotic.

Corsets were essential for creating the hourglass silhouette that Victorians held in high esteem. Additionally, corsets served as a solid foundation upon which to lay the layers of bustles, petticoats, overskirts, bodices, aprons, etc. that women wore to substantiate their economic status and social sophistication. Nearly all Victorian women wore them, even if they were so poor as to only have one to save for holidays and special occasions. Early corset trade cards emphasize "skirt supporting" features. After corsets had established their place in fashion, women began developing physical problems, and advertisers shifted their emphasis to the "healthfulness" of their brands.

Pricing Tips & Cards to Watch For

Black and white stock cards with corset imprints can usually be found for under $10. Privately issued corset cards typically run $10 to $20 in black and white, $15 to $40 in color. Graphics and condition play an unusually significant role in pricing corset cards, as most collectors find plain or soiled undergarment ads unappealing. Watch for a Holmes Undergarments metamorphic card and a Coronet Corset card with Brownies, as these have sold in auctions for over $150 each.

Queen Bess Corset & Skirt Supporter, $50.00.

Alaska Down Bustles
    woman in bustle & corset, diagrams of bustle $35.00

American Lady Corsets
    Gibson girl style model, high fashion, 1905 ....$25.00

Ball's Circle Hip Skating Corsets
    2 women at skating rink, corset inset, flowers $20.00

Ball's Health Preserving Corset
    "Revolution in Corsets," woman in corset, sword, red banner $20.00

Ball's Health Preserving Corset
    corset in center, woman in mirror, nursing mother on sides $25.00

Ball's Misses Corset
    young woman in lavender bonnet $5.00

Bortree "Duplex" Corset
    metamorphic, "Mrs. Brown — perfect figure," peeping thru door $20.00

Bortree Corsets
    woman adjusts bracelet, corset, necklace $20.00

Bortree Manufacturing Co.
    corsets, sleds, dancing, buggy, etc., 1884 Ohio Expo on rev. $15.00

Cooley's Globe Corset
    metamorphic, 2 women, corset, "lived happily ever after" $35.00

Cooley's Globe Corset
    woman sits, small dog (that wears corset) on her knee $40.00

Doctor and Madame Strong's Corsets
    woman adjusts bracelet, 2 inserts showing modeled corsets $25.00

Downs' Self-Adjusting Corset
    red corset in window display, woman in gloves, purse, dog $20.00

Dr. Strong's Tampico Corset
    woman at glovebox dresser in corset, necklace $20.00

Dr. Warner's Coraline Corsets
    die-cut corset folder, cherub pokes out of bosom $12.00

Eureka Health Corset
    woman in front of full mirror, hand mirror $20.00

Feder's Brush Skirt Protector
    woman & friend in parlor discuss skirt protector, piano $25.00

Griswold Corset Parlor — Boston
    2 girls, small toy horse, cart, flowers, tree ad $10.00

Jackson Corset Co.
    woman in corset in front of mirror, brush $20.00

Royal Worcester Corsets
    blonde woman in corset, no arms, roses, Columbian Expo $35.00

Stock Mechanical — R & G Corsets
    girl walks, hat, doll in hand, bag with ad $25.00

Warner Bros. Coraline Corsets
    "Æsthetic Craze," Oscar Wilde, cupid presents corset $25.00

Warner Bros. Coraline Corsets
    "Minnie Hauk Uses...," portrait, holding hat $15.00

Warren's Featherbone Corsets
    die-cut feathers, blossoms, ...$15.00

Ball's Health Preserving Corset, $40.00.

Thompson's Glove Fitting Corsets, $30.00.

Ball's Health Preserving Corset, $20.00.

Cosmetics & Perfumes

(See also: Cupids & Cherubs; Patent Medicines; Soaps.)

Cosmetic & Perfume Images

Many collectors are drawn to trade cards advertising cosmetics and perfumes because of the high quality of the images often commissioned by this industry. Nearly all of the Victorian perfume cards employ beautiful images of flower sprays or bouquets rendered in wonderfully feminine colors. Healthy children appear in many of these ads, as do attractive women, water scenes, and tropical gardens. Additionally, these cards offer the most illustrations of winged Cupids, cherubs, fairies, and imps found in trade cards. Black and white stock cards were rarely used for these ads, but one can find a good number of color stock cards that were used by local bottlers and larger firms that were attempting national marketing campaigns on a limited budget.

Historical Notes

Perfume, as opposed to basic staples like food, clothing, and soap, is a luxury item. Perfume and cosmetics are among the first items to be removed from a shopping list when money is tight. On the other hand, expensive perfumes and pampering cosmetics are among the favorite items selected from shelves when times are good. Perfumes make the statement that all is well, and they set a mood of reassurance that life is worth enjoying. Most people agree that for pure self indulgence, or for an intimately frivolous token of love and appreciation, few items fit the bill like wine, jewels, roses, or a fancy bottle of sweet-smelling perfume.

This was never more true than during the late Victorian period in America. For the most part, the last quarter of the nineteenth century was a time of tremendous economic expansion. New products and whole new industries were born almost overnight. Young men and women who had been raised dirt poor on subsistence farms suddenly found themselves working in the city with a few extra dollars each month to burn. Meanwhile, innovations in production were rapidly making opulence affordable for nearly everyone. Even for poor immigrants and ex-farm kids who were "moving up," it felt like a good time for a materialistic binge. Among those who benefited the most from the free-spending mood of the day were the dozens of manufacturers of Florida Waters, face creams, tan removers, and ladies perfumes.

A major factor in the expansion of the perfume industry was the aggressiveness of its marketing. Victorian consumers were looking for tangible symbols to mark their upward mobility. Consumers added useless turrets, ornate cornices, and lavish wraparound porches to the exteriors of the abodes, while at the same time adding feathered hats, leather gloves, and rustling bustles to their wardrobes. Perfume peddlers made sure that a shelf of their products was seen in the same light as extravagant houses and frivolous clothing: as a litmus test for economic status and cultural refinement.

Advertising trade cards figured significantly into the success of perfume companies in convincing Victorians that fragrances like "Florida Breeze" and "Spanish Jessamine" should be wafting about their wrists and chins. In fact, as an added gimmick many of the cards of the period were actually doused in a scent just to insure that these cards would not go unnoticed. And for many Victorians, getting noticed was everything.

Pricing Tips & Cards to Watch For

Many cosmetic and perfume cards were produced in enormous quantities and distributed nationally, thereby making them readily available and affordable even 100 years later. Most of the common Austen's and Hoyt's Cologne cards were perfumed, which accounts for the slight browning found over many of these cards. These cards can often be found for $3 to $10, or even less if the discoloration is severe. The larger Hoyt's/Rubifoam for the Teeth cards are less common and more popular, especially when they carry a "Lady's Calendar" on the front or back. Collectors who are trying to complete calendar sets will often have to pay $20 or more for the more elusive of these cards. Also watch for clean examples of the many Murray & Lanman Florida Water cards, as these cards are exquisitely designed and are growing in popularity. Palmer commissioned several lovely die-cut cards, and nice stock die-cuts can be found for other firms as well.

Hoyt's German Cologne, $20.00.

Dr. Hebras Viola Cream, $15.00.

Hoyt's German Cologne, $25.00.

Palmer's Rob Roy, die-cut, $40.00.

Colgate's Soaps and Perfumes, $10.00.

Thurber's Florida Water, $25.00.

Murray & Lanman Florida Water, $12.00.

Murray & Lanman Florida Water, $12.00.

Cachous Perfume the Breath, $15.00.

Hoyt's 10 Cent Cologne, $20.00.

Palmer's Cyrano-Rose, die-cut, $20.00.

Murray & Lanman Florida Water, $12.00.

Austen's Forest Flower Cologne
  cherub with large bottle, 1887 ....$8.00

Austen's Forest Flower Cologne
  2 women, one with long brown hair & collar, roses $6.00

Austen's Forest Flower Cologne
  romantic couple on big tree swing $8.00

Corning's German Cologne
  girl with flowers in apron, hat, oval frame around image $12.00

Dr. Price's Hyacinth Perfume
  woman with umbrella and gloves on flowers $8.00

Eastmans Wild Rose Extract
  small 1880 calendar card, flower design $10.00

Hagan's Magnolia Balm
  sailor singing on deck with 5 women, bottle $12.00

Hoyt's German Cologne
  man and woman in garden, roses, 1890 ....$20.00

Hoyt's German Cologne
  2 girls dance around big bottle, 1881 ....$12.00

Hoyt's German Cologne
  girl's face in red rose $8.00

Jennings' Handkerchief Perfumes
  die-cut stock card of fan, berries, purple bow, red leaves $6.00

Laird's Bloom of Youth
  ad on woman's hat, hand at chin, roses $6.00

Mellier's High Class Perfumes — stock
  small man on knees before big lady in hat $6.00

Murray Rose Cream, Bay Run, etc.
  woman, flowers in hair, jar in hand, ...$20.00

Read's Grand Duchess Cologne
  child with long hair beneath rustic hat, feather $6.00

Tetlow's Handkerchief Perfumes
  die-cut fan, woman's portrait in center $12.00

Kaercher's Persian Balm, $40.00.

Lundborg's Famous Perfumes, $15.00.

Palmer's May Bloom, die-cut, $20.00.

Ely's Cream Balm, $6.00.

Cowboys & Indians

(See also: Ethnic; Cows.)

Cowboy & Indian Images

Artifacts that capture the mystique of the "Wild West" hold a special magic for a wide variety of collectors. In trade cards, images of the West are often romanticized or whimsically satirized, as many of these illustrations pre-date the acceptance of the "Western Realism" tradition in art that came about later as a result of the work of Charles Russell, Frederic Remington, and others. Trade cards from before 1890 often show well-scrubbed cowboys outfitted in the flashy tradition of the California vaquero, or they depict comical cowboys with distorted features getting into ridiculous sorts of trouble. Indians are typically depicted in trade cards as either "Noble Savages" or as childlike buffoons. Cowboys and Indians appearing in trade cards after 1890 are found in more "traditional" scenes, and they are usually outfitted in a recognizable style of hat, chaps, and buckskins with the familiar gear of pistols, lariats, tomahawks, and the like.

Historical Notes

News of the massacre at "Custer's Last Stand" arrived at the Centennial Exposition just as Philadelphia was winding down from its 1876 Fourth of July celebration. Sitting Bull and Crazy Horse were at their peak of power and notoriety at the very moment in advertising history that trade cards were establishing themselves as a part of American life. Cowboys and cattletowns were also thriving in 1876, as were mining camps and pioneer migrations. It is small wonder, then, that cowboys and Indians were treated differently then in advertising than they would be today. For those west of the Mississippi, the dangers and challenges of the "Wild West" were realities; for their relatives back east, those dangers translated into genuine prayers and concern. Lithographers had to be careful in their attempts to draw attention to their cards not to upset their audience and scare customers away.

Early trade card illustrations typically treat cowboys and Indians with a light touch of whimsy or humor. The West itself was depicted in many images as a romantic land of adventure and golden opportunity. Graphic images of violent encounters between whites and Native Americans seldom turn up on trade cards before 1890, after which time the last of the Indians were "subdued" and relegated to isolated reservations. Frederick Jackson Turner delivered a paper in 1893 at the Columbian Exposition in which he declared that the days of the Wild West were over, stating that the frontier was "closed." Ironically, Arbuckle Coffee was also at the Columbian Exposition. They were passing out a set of 50 trade cards featuring image after image of frontier ambushes, battles, and scalpings. Arbuckle apparently felt that it was finally safe to exploit such scenes for dramatic effect, and, in their own trade card way, Arbuckle declared with Turner that the violence of the frontier was by 1893 only a matter of history.

Pricing Tips & Cards to Watch For

Trade cards with images of cowboys and Indians generally command somewhat higher prices than comparable cards with other images, regardless of the product advertised. Many of these cards were printed by western lithographers, including some very desirable thread cards that were produced in San Francisco that bring $25 to $50 each. Some of the most interesting Indian cards were issued by the meat packing industry, so check under the "Food" category when looking through dealer albums. Expect to pay $15 and up for the meat cards with Indians. Watch for cards depicting famous chiefs like Sitting Bull and Chief Joseph, as these can fetch $50 or more.

Johnson & Field, stock card, $15.00.

Higgins Soap, $25.00.

Clark's ONT Thread, $15.00.

Kickapoo Indian Remedies, $20.00.

R. W. Bell & Co. Soap, $15.00.

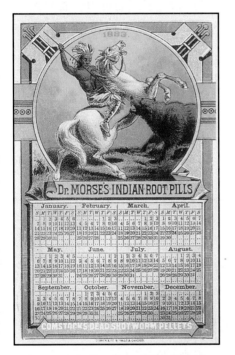

Dr. Morse's Indian Root Pills, $35.00.

Ayer's Pills, $25.00.

Indian Queen Perfume, $30.00.

Woolson Spice Co., $35.00.

Hassan Cigarettes, $8.00.

Arbuckle Coffee, $15.00.

Wilson's Cooked Corned Beef, $25.00.

Wilson's Beef, $15.00.

Arbuckle Coffee, $5.00.

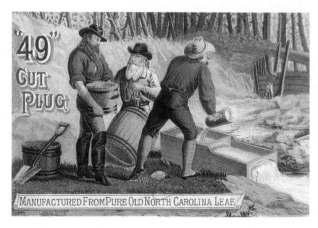

"49" Cut Plug, $225.00.

Dr. Kilmer's Indian Cough Cure, $20.00.

Page Fence, $75.00.

Boss Pat. Watch Cases, Jewelry
  Indian with gun, tomahawk, tepee **$10.00**

Clark's ONT Thread
  sunset over tepees and Indian camp, large card **$15.00**

Gale M'f'g Co Sulky Plows
  "Big Injun" holding weapon, scalp, folder **$40.00**

Lavine Soap
  Indians dancing around salesman on big box **$10.00**

Sholes Insect Exterminator
  two cowboys, sick and healthy longhorns **$35.00**

Sitting Bull Tobacco
  metamorphic — "savages" become "civilized" when open **$75.00**

Stock Card — 1888 Westfield Fair
  cowboy and Indian racing on turkeys **$20.00**

Royal Hams, $45.00.

Beals Torrey Shoe Company, $40.00.

St. Louis Beef Canning, $25.00.

Hassan Cigarettes, $8.00.

Cows, Oxen & Dairy

(See also: Animals; Cowboys; Farm; Foods; Meats.)

Cow & Dairy Images

The are several basic types of cattle, oxen, and dairy images found in trade card advertising. The first is the straight forward depiction of a cow or bull standing, posed in effect, to illustrate the size and health of a specific prize animal or to offer a representative illustration of a particular breed. Dwight's Cow Brand Soda was the most prolific producer of cards of this type. The second type includes humorous or dramatic scenes where these animals are used as an element of a card's story. The story may be of a young couple's carelessness as they are charged by a bull, or it may be of a cowboy's tenacity as he faces a herd of stampeding longhorns. The third group of images is comprised of cards that are cow or dairy related, but that in some cases do not actually show a cow. Within this group one finds advertisements for items like cream separators, milk buckets, and cattle remedies. While these cards don't always show a cow, they are often of historical importance, and they do frequently make their way into many cow card collections.

Historical Notes

The Industrial Revolution completely disrupted America's "traditional" agrarian culture, where fresh milk and meat had been readily available for each family. Because citizens were migrating further away from farms and deeper in sprawling urban centers, a new opportunity arose for entrepreneurs who had the vision to meet this fresh demand with a packaged supply of dairy and meat products. Rapid changes occurred within the cattle industry based upon its ability to do two things. The first was to increase the size, health, and efficiency of its herds. The second was to innovate new ways to process milk and beef into products that could be packaged, transported, stored, and marketed in cities. This was also the era in which sanitary glass milk bottles evolved, which in some ways revolutionized the dairy industry more than any other single innovation.

Firms like Nestle's and Borden built impressive factories and promoted their milk products as more sanitary and "progressive" than the sometimes dirty or sour milk distributed by milk wagons. They also stressed the convenience, inexpensiveness, and healthfulness of their canned goods. With infant mortality rates as they were, Victorian mothers were open to the suggestions of any respectable company that could present itself as sanitary and modern. Trade card advertising proved critical in introducing consumers to these new products and in altering American purchasing habits and lifestyles to support these new industries.

As the beef and dairy industries grew, so did the size of farms and ranches. Hundreds of fascinating patents and new products emerged as Victorians rose to meet the challenges involved in the transition from an age of subsistent family farming to the era of profitable agribusiness. The headline on one "before and after" trade card is instructive: "Money saved by watering stock as shown below." The "before" scene shows a mother and son struggling with a traditional well while a farmer hauls buckets of water to restless cattle, his plow unattended in the distance. The "after" scene (with the new B.S. Williams Windmill) depicts the same farm. This time, the mother darns a sock while her son plays with a dog. The cattle in the "after" scene now low contentedly unattended while the farmer plows and increases the farm's profitability.

Pricing Tips & Cards to Watch For

Cards with cow-related advertising and images vary widely in prices. Stock cards with cow illustrations are often acquired very inexpensivly. Unless the card advertises a particularly popular product or has an especially attractive and colorful image, these stock cards can usually be purchased for around $5. The small (aprox. 2" x 3") baking soda cards are popular with many collectors, but they seldom command more than $5 each. The larger cards from these series typically sell for $8 to $15. Watch for any of the Dr. Haas' Cattle Remedy cards, as these can bring $50 and up when found in great condition. Also keep an eye open for De Laval advertising, because this company is a favorite with many dairy collectors.

B. S. Williams Windmills, $50.00.

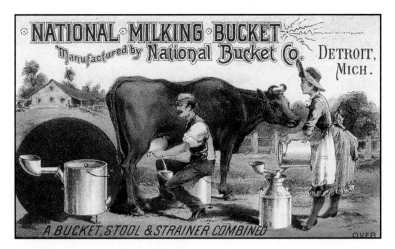

National Milking Bucket, $75.00.

Highland Evaporated Cream, $30.00.

De Laval Separator "Alpha B," $40.00.

Libby, McNeill & Libby Beef, $20.00.

Dwight's Cow Brand Saleratus, $15.00.

United States Cream Separator, $35.00.

PALATABLE,
HIGHLY NUTRITIOUS,
EASILY DIGESTED,
INEXPENSIVE.

KUMYSGEN

PURE AND STRAIGHT.

PREPARED BY
Reed & Carnrick,
NEW YORK.

Reed & Carnrick — Kumysgen, $20.00.

U. S. Wind Engine & Pump Co., $40.00.

To all interested in securing ABSOLUTELY Pure, Fresh Milk either for Infants or Family Use.

WHY

Use milk (so-called) from Swill-fed cows when you can obtain Borden's (unsweetened) Condensed Milk, which has maintained its high reputation for over a quarter of a century, for 7 cents per half pint, which, when diluted with water, makes the cost for pure, rich milk only 7 cents per quart.

OR

When you can ob- tain strictly pure milk from the same Company, direct from selected dairies, delivered to you in steam- cleaned bottles, hermetically seal- ed in Orange County at 8 cents per quart.

Borden's (unsweet- ened) Condensed Milk is simply pure milk, with nothing added and nothing but water removed Boiled water should be used in all cases where this milk is diluted for nursery pur- poses.

Orders or inquiries sent to the following ad- dresses will receive prompt attention.

NEW YORK CONDENSED MILK CO.,

98 TO 106 STIRLING PLACE, BROOKLYN.
942 TO 946 DE KALB AVE., BROOKLYN.
306 TO 310 EAST 117TH STREET, NEW YORK.
221 TO 229 EAST 34TH STREET, NEW YORK.
642 TO 644 MONTGOMERY ST., JERSEY CITY.

COPYRIGHT, 1891.   DONALDSON BROTHERS, N.Y.

New York Condensed Milk Company, $75.00.

De Laval Separator, die-cut, $50.00.

Arbuckle Coffee
Kansas state map, oxen "Breaking the Raw Prairie," 1889 . . . .**$8.00**

Arbuckle Coffee
"Zebu" cow from 1890 interesting animals series **$8.00**

Arbuckle Coffee
"Beef" from 1889 cooking series of 50, cow slaughtered **$8.00**

D.W. Williams Soaps
"This is the Cow...," charging dog that barked at maiden **$10.00**

Domestic Sewing Machine
"Prize Jersey Bull Pedro," black bull in pasture **$12.00**

Domestic Sewing Machine
successful farm scenes, house, bull, cow, distant riverboat **$12.00**

Domestic Sewing Machine
"$30,000 Jersey Rarity," brown cow in pasture **$12.00**

Dr. Haas' Cattle Remedy
milk maid "before" — cow overflows pail "after" 1883 . . . .**$80.00**

Dr. Haas' Horse & Cattle Remedies
broken toy cow, girl cries, boy promises Dr. Haas', 1883 . . . .**$80.00**

Dwight's Cow Brand Soda
"Simmenthal" Swiss cow, soda box, "A.D.T." signature **$15.00**

Dwight's Cow Brand Soda
"Yak," shaggy Thibet cow, soda box, "A.D.T." signature **$15.00**

Dwight's Cow Brand Soda
calendar card, 1891, cow in center, months surround **$20.00**

Dwight's Cow Brand Soda
"Polled Angus — Good milkers...," from set of 30, small A.D.T. . . .**$4.00**

Grandmother's A&P Condensed Milk
cow watches calf lap from can, ad inset on fence, 1899 . . . .**$15.00**

Lactart Acid of Milk
milk maid steps over fence, rocks, pail on head, cows, 1884 . . . . .**$12.00**

Pitts Agricultural Works
"Cloak Feat" bull fighters, red cape, areana — Land Roller ad . . .**$20.00**

Stock Card
artist on ground, cow face on canvas, cow running away **$5.00**

Vermont Farm Machine — Separator
barefoot boy turns crank in cow pasture, 2 children play **$35.00**

Standard Food — ". . . flesh and milk," $20.00.

Standard Food — ". . . flesh and milk," $20.00.

Holt's Lightning Hay Knife, $25.00.

Cupids & Cherubs

(See also: Angels; Brownies; Cosmetics.)

Cupid & Cherub Images

Whimsical images of Cupids and cherubs are abundant in Victorian cards of all types. Cherubs are generally defined by collectors as the plump, huggable little children that appear in Victorian images with feathered wings. Cute children without wings are sometimes referred to as "cherubs," but to collect these images as cherubs would run a person's collection up into thousands of Victorian cards. Collectors usually consider Cupids to be the cherub-like boys with wings that appear in love scenes, often with a bow and arrow. Cupids and cherubs are usually shown naked. The childish imps with butterfly or gossamer wings are frequently called fairies, and the adult-sized figures with wings are generally defined as angels. It all becomes confusing in scenes where the imp's wings are hidden and its face and body are less chubby and more mature. In those cases, it's each individual collector's call whether to consider the character a Cupid, a cherub, a fairy, or an angel.

Part of the attraction of these images comes from the warm colors that were frequently used. Additionally, these cards often convey a tranquil, pure, and transcendent mood that encourages the viewer to smile, and even drift into flights of fancy, when viewing them. In that sense, these soft trade card images are quite different from the many ads that attempt to grab attention through splashy sensationalism or crisp, high-energy designs. Many of the Cupid and cherub cards were originally perfumed with sample scents, which also contributed to overall agreeable effect they had on consumers.

Historical Notes

Cupid came down to the Victorians through Greek mythology. According to Greek tradition, Eros, the god of love, was the winged child of Ares and Aphrodite. He was typically pictured as a chubby little guy who flew around armed with a bow and arrow that could do a person more good than harm. It was the Romans who started calling the little fellow Cupid. Cherubs have a culturally mixed heritage, but they were baptized by the Judeo-Christian tradition through the mention of winged cherubim in the Bible. As these biblical cherubim brushed wings with pagan Cupids, a bit of blurring occurred, and the two cherub traditions merged in Western art to give us the characters that became so popular in Victorian advertising.

There are few symbols more synonymous with "Victorian" than the naked little Cupids and cherubs that popped up everywhere during that period. They were carved on cornices, embossed on products, stamped on Valentines, and printed on advertising of every sort. As symbols, Cupids made for perfect little quintessential Victorians: they were conspicuous, frivolous, and eccentric. In other words, Cupids were not farmers, and most of the Victorians who shaped the culture that we find reflected in trade card images were very concerned about not being mistaken for farmers.

The changes that took place during the Victorian period were enormous, and they effected nearly every aspect of life. Driven by huge steam-powered engines, the traditional industries of construction, transportation, manufacturing, and agriculture were all revolutionized. Mechanized farms released young people from their farm chores and sent them into cities in search of good-paying jobs. Once these ex-farmers adjusted to city life, they often became eager to distance themselves from their rural backgrounds by "putting on airs" and acting as urbanized and refined as possible.

That shift from an agrarian society to an urban culture was reflected in the fashions and fads throughout the nation. The days of being practical, modest, and plain were out. All sorts of Victorian eccentricities, including winged Cupids and clean-scrubbed cherubs, were definitely in.

Pricing Tips & Cards to Watch For

In spite of the wide interest in Victorian cards with Cupids and cherubs, such cards are so abundant that most of them remain affordably under $20. Perfume companies issued dozens of these cards in huge quantities, so be careful when paying over $10 for one of their cards. Some of the perfume cards are quite valuable and rare, but with a little looking, many can be found in good condition for $10 or less. Stock cards with these images are also an affordable way to build a collection, as delightful examples can often be found down in the $1 to $5 range. Cupids and cherubs can show up on cards advertising everything from corsets to farm implements. Expect to pay over $15 for the ones that advertise things like tobacco, patent medicines, alcohol, and industrial products.

Ball's Corsets, $20.00.

Fairbank's Lard, $20.00.

Welcome Soap, $15.00.

Mason & Pollard's Anti-Malaria Pills, $50.00.

Merrick Thread, $15.00.

Merrick Thread, $15.00.

J. M. Hill, stock card, $5.00.

Domestic Sewing Machine, $15.00.

Hoyt's German Cologne, $12.00.

Maltine Medicine, $15.00.

Murray & Lanman's Florida Water, $12.00.

Hagan's Magnolia Balm, $40.00.

Sapolio Soap, $15.00.

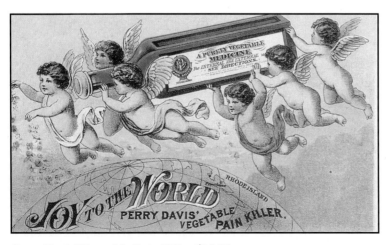

Perry Davis' Vegetable Pain Killer, $15.00.

American Machine Co.
7 cherubs making ice cream with freezer $15.00

Austen's Forest Flower Cologne
Cupid holding bottle under woman's nose, sachet border $10.00

Austen's Forest Flower Cologne
girl cherub with flower basket, perfumed card $5.00

David's Prize Soap
cherub bringing prizes to woman doing wash $10.00

Dr. Buckland's Scotch Oats Essence
3 cherubs help woman mix medicine $25.00

Edwin C. Burt Shoes
tiny cherub measures woman's foot, 1881 . . . .$8.00

Fernet — Branca Bitters
woman and bottle by water at Columbian Expo, 2 cherubs $35.00

Hall's Hair Renewer
8 cherubs prepare woman's long hair, 2 bunnies $10.00

Higgins T & C Compound
boy and girl cherubs, bottle, pine tree, vines $30.00

Pearline Soap
2 cherubs, woman holding back at washboard $12.00

Pond's Extract
girl cherub at side of boy, beach, sea gulls, parasol $8.00

Ridges Food for Infants
2 cherubs cook over fire, mother feeding baby, children $8.00

Stock Card — imprint for shoe store
girl cherub in flower wreath, hat, skirt $5.00

Stock Card — Charter Oak imprint
Cupid strums music to swooning woman $8.00

Tarrant's Seltzer Aperient
fancy woman, man drinking, 3 cherubs, red curtain $20.00

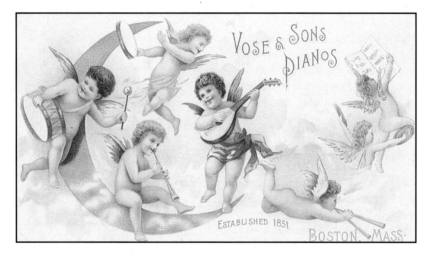

Vose & Sons Pianos, $20.00.

Hauthaway's Peerless Gloss, $20.00.

Dogs

Cards with Dog Images

Trade cards with dog images are especially popular with animal lovers, and, in general, are both abundant and affordable. Some collectors search for cards by dog breed or type (i.e. St. Bernard, hunting, pug, etc.), while others look for nostalgic pet views or humorous anthropomorphic scenes. The quality of these cards is evenly spread from low-end monotone stock cards to beautifully designed full color private issues.

Advertisements for dog food and pet supply firms can be found on numerous trade cards. Additionally, one occasionally runs into ads for pet soaps, flea and tick powders, specific pet breeders, dog shows, and other pet related odds and ends. Far more common than these, however, are the thousands of stock cards and non-pet private issues that simply throw dogs into illustrations to create warm, generic but effective vignettes.

Historical Notes

One of the many interesting developments that emerged from the new wealth of the Victorian period was a preoccupation with pure bred and exotic pets. In more primitive times, animals were judged by their usefulness around the house or farm. But the Victorian middle class latched onto a fad of expensive, "well-bred" family pets, partially, at least, because through these animals they could flaunt their material success and social status. The emphasis shifted from animals that were practical to animals with impressive pedigrees, eccentric appearances, or exotic histories.

The late nineteenth century saw an explosion of kennel clubs, pet literature, and animal shows of all kinds. People had the leisure time to make a hobby of animal breeding, grooming, and showing, and they had the money to follow their whims. Many of the trade cards of the day reflect a Victorian obsession with cats and dogs that had been "refined" through "scientific breeding."

This is not to suggest that "the family dog" was an innovation of the Victorians. But in leaner times, when one could hardly afford to feed one's family, people would certainly not spend the equivalent of a month's worth of grocery money to purchase a fluffy little poodle with a pedigree. Nor in earlier years could many people spare the time that it took to keep a pure bred animal in top-notch show condition. Many trade cards do a delightful job of colorfully capturing this emergence of pet status in American culture.

Pricing Tips & Cards to Watch For

Generally speaking, trade cards with dog images command no special premium simply for depicting a dog. Most stock cards featuring dog scenes sell for around $5, but expect prices around $10 for cards of exceptional detail, color, or creative design.

For a card with dog image to bring more than $10, there will usually have to be some additional attraction to the card. Cards selling for over $10 will usually include desirable advertising for exotic products, or will be imprinted from special cities or by collectible firms. In some cases, dog cards sell for more based upon anthropomorphic scenes, as when they depict dogs playing golf or billiards.

Many of the best sets of dog cards were produced by thread companies, so be sure to check sewing albums when picking through a dealer's stock. Watch for cards with clearly identifiable dog breeds, or better still, cards that name an actual historical dog. Also watch for cards depicting dogs in interesting scenes (i.e. rescuing children, hunting game, acting like humans, etc.).

Spencer Optical, stock card, $10.00.

Colburn's Mustard, die-cut, $20.00.

J & P Coats Thread, $8.00.

Uncle Tom's Cabin Play, $25.00.

Merrick Thread, $8.00.

Willimantic Thread, $5.00.

Stickney and Poors Mustard, $25.00.

Buchan's Carbolic Disinfecting Soap, $15.00.

Libby, McNeill & Libby's Meat, $25.00.

Mansfield's Capillaris for Hair, $10.00.

Chadwick's Thread, $15.00.

Hood's Sarsaparilla, $12.00.

Acme Soap, $8.00.

James Pearline Soap, $12.00.

Dr. Seth Arnold's Cough Killer, $10.00.

Brown's Iron Bitters
two puppies in barrel, kitten taking bone **$8.00**

Dr. Charcot's Tobacco Cure
dogs looking over fence, boys gambling **$60.00**

Dr. Sawtelle's St. Bernard Galaxy
"Roland" shown, 1885, ten dog exhibition **$125.00**

Hire's Root Beer
collie lapping drink from sad boy's glass **$15.00**

Hold Fast Tobacco
3-fold metamorphic, dog bites thief on ankle **$40.00**

Merrick Thread
girl on swing, dog barking at legs **$6.00**

New Home Sewing Machine
girl dressing white dog in green pants **$10.00**

Spratt's Fibrine Dog Biscuits
dog in autumn hunting scene, bird falling **$20.00**

Stickney Poors Best Vanilla
girl sitting next to dog, fruit, large box **$25.00**

Stock Card — Master and Dog
dog and owner at window, they look alike **$12.00**

Wistar's Balsam of Wild Cherry
girl reading book to boy and dog **$8.00**

Woolson Spice
"Midsummer Greeting" dogs flush birds **$20.00**

Dr. Seth Arnold's Cough Killer, $15.00.

Medford, stock card, $8.00.

Hoyt's German Cologne, $35.00.

Willimantic Thread, $5.00.

Elephants

(See also: Animals; Entertainment.)

Cards with Elephant Images

Because elephants are such remarkable creatures, they show up in a wide variety of collectible items, including a wonderful assortment of Victorian trade card images. These cards range in quality from poorly executed black and white cards to elaborate, full-color private issues. The most popular of the elephant trade cards are those with "Jumbo" images, but there are many others, including a number of outstanding "White Elephant" cards that rival many of the Jumbo cards in scarcity, quality of printing, and novelty of design.

Historical Notes

One can not collect elephant items from the Victorian period without running into an incredible assortment of souvenir and advertising items somehow linked to Jumbo, who remains one of the most famous and commercially exploited animals of all time. P.T. Barnum purchased Jumbo in 1881 from London's Zoological Society for $10,000. Jumbo brought in over two million dollars for Barnum in less than two years, drawing children eager for rides and fascinated crowds wherever he toured. At over twelve feet tall and 14,000 pounds, Jumbo ranked as one of the largest elephants ever measured, thus explaining the origins of the word "jumbo" in American usage as a way of describing things that are extra large. One of the most famous Jumbo trade cards ("Jumbo at the Bar") was drawn from the rumors that Jumbo was kept happy on the road through daily rations of whiskey and beer. Jumbo was struck by a train in Canada, and he died in September of 1884.

Pricing Tips & Cards to Watch For

Jumbo images are popular with collectors outside of the normal trade card circles, but a number of the Jumbo cards are common enough to still be available for less than $20. For fanciful scenes of Jumbo, watch for cards from two fairly affordable sets. The first set was issued by Bufford in 1882, is usually found printed in blues, browns, and black, and typically sells for $10 to $15 per card. The second Jumbo set was produced in tan and black by Buek & Lindner, is typically imprinted for Clark's Threads, and sells for around $15 per card.

Additional Jumbo and elephant sets were issued for thread and soap companies, but these cards tend to fall in the $20 to $50 range because of their attractiveness and relative scarcity. Keep an eye open for the Jumbo "Arrow Brand" die-cut oyster cards, as they bring over $100 each.

Castoria Medicine, $15.00.

Hartford Sewing Machine, $10.00.

Soapona — Bell Soap, $30.00.

Ivorine Washing Powder, $40.00.

Clinching Screw
"Jumbo on His Travels" in boots, banner, smiling sun . . . **$35.00**

E.B. Mallory Oysters, Arrow Brand
"Jumbo Entertaining His Friends With..." **$150.00**

Forepaugh's White Elephant of Siam
white elephant in jungle, flag, trainer **$75.00**

J & P Coats Thread
Jumbo tied in threads **$12.00**

Lavine Washing Soap
elephant with rider and box racing tribesman **$12.00**

McLaughlin's Coffee
devotees throwing themselves beneath elephant's feet . . **$25.00**

Stock Card — "Afghan Warriors"
5 soldiers riding elephant, one man walks **$10.00**

Stock Card — Clark's O.N.T. imprint
"Jumbo Æsthetic" daisy, stands with Oscar Wilde **$15.00**

Stock Card — furniture imprint
"Jumbo Leaving England" on barge, flag, big cage **$12.00**

Clark's ONT Thread, $20.00.

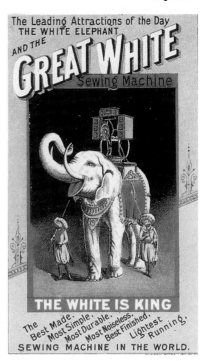

White Sewing Machine, $15.00.

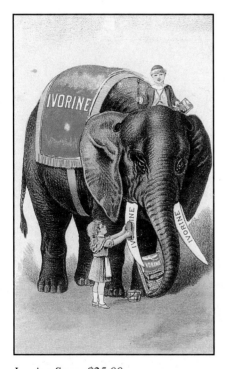

Ivorine Soap, $25.00.

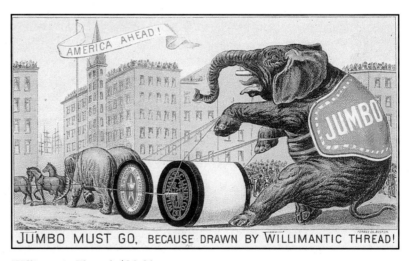

Willimantic Thread, $20.00.

Ivorine Soap, $25.00.

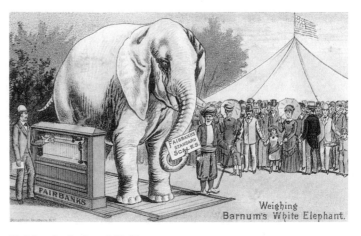

Fairbanks Scales, $40.00.

Enterprise & Mrs. Potts' Sad Irons

(See also: Expositions; Political & Patriotic.)

Enterprise Images

Trade cards issued by Enterprise Manufacturing are among the most popular of any single company collected. The quality of these cards in terms color, design, and card stock covers the spectrum. Many of the Mrs. Potts' Sad Iron cards fall on the low end, often produced in only one or two colors and typically printed on very flimsy 4¼" x 3" paper. Slightly better in quality is a set of Enterprise cards printed in brown and blue on heavy 3¼" x 6" stock. In the middle one finds the better Mrs. Potts' cards, which used a wider range of colors in more intricately designed illustrations printed on durable card stock. Most of the Enterprise grinder, chopper, and mill cards also fall into the middle range in terms of quality, including a set of Columbian Exposition Enterprise cards featuring rewritten historical events and views of many of the most famous buildings of Chicago's 1893 World's Fair. Finally, there are a small handful Enterprise cards that are of above-average to premium quality. All of these cards experience heavy collector demand, as do the scarcest of the more cheaply produced cards.

Historical Notes

There was a time when ironing was one of the most dreaded of all domestic duties. Prior to the invention of the "cold handle sad iron," burns and blisters were as much a part of the ironing ritual as sorting and folding. The ironing routine began the day before, usually Monday, when clothes were hand washed and hung out to dry. In the early days, and even until recently for the poor, dirt and stains were worked out of clothes on a washboard with boiled water, a tub, and lye soap. Women who were washing for large families suffered swollen and battered knuckles every week. On Tuesday, the dried clothes were pulled from bushel baskets and sprinkled lightly to ease the stiffness and prepare them for ironing. Nearly every article would require hand attention, as the synthetic fabrics and wrinkle-free blends that help clothes hold their shape today had not yet been invented.

Sad (flat) irons were then heated on top of the kitchen stove, often three or so at a time so they could be rotated as they cooled down. Sad irons were foundry cast (or made as a wedding gift by the local blacksmith), often weighing four pounds or more each. Women would wrap thick rags around the handles to pick them up, and then spit on their finger and touch the irons to check if they were hot enough to use. Women often worked all day, a hot stove behind them, a hot pad in their hand, and a heavy iron swinging back until their fingers, hands, and wrists were numb. Special irons like the "hand flutter" were used for ruffles, ribbons, and laces. When the Enterprise Manufacturing company began sending drummers (traveling salesmen) out with Mrs. Potts' Sad Irons equipped with "a Cold detachable Walnut Handle" that promised not to "Burn the Hand" and that was "Double Pointed" to iron on both strokes, many women sighed in relief.

Pricing Tips & Cards to Watch For

Enterprise and Mrs. Potts' cards start at $15 and go up rapidly from there. Watch for images that have special historical significance, as with cards referring to things like polar expeditions, Chinese labor issues, and Jumbo the Elephant. The cards showing people with irons for heads generally sell in the $30 to $50 range. The scarcest Mrs. Potts' cards typically run $40 to $75. Enterprise cards with historical scenes and building views from the Columbian Exposition generally sell in the $15 to $25 range. Watch for high quality Enterprise cards with good color and strong graphics, as these cards can sometimes bring $50 to $200 or more.

Mrs. Potts' Sad Irons, $30.00.

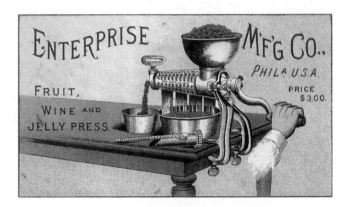

Enterprise M'F'G — fruit/jelly press, $60.00.

Enterprise M'F'G — meat chopper, $35.00.

Enterprise — coffee, spice, drug mill
grinder on edge of table, bowl, coffee beans & leaves $75.00

Enterprise Bone, Shell & Corn Mills
Columbian Expo, William Penn's Treaty, Indians, Elect. Bldg. $15.00

Enterprise Fruit, Wine & Jelly Press
Columbian Expo, Bunker Hill, pressing together, Gov't Bldg. $15.00

Enterprise Lawn Sprinklers
2 panels, tennis player punster gets soaked by maiden $40.00

Enterprise M'F'G — smoked beef shaver
shaver on right, sliced beef resting on paper $50.00

Mrs. Potts' Sad Irons
"Our Drummer's Solid Tune" salesman, music, drum $30.00

Mrs. Potts' Sad Irons
"Yours Truly" signed portrait of "Inventress" F. Potts $15.00

Mrs. Potts' Sad Irons
"It was a darling, so it was," family, infant with iron head $40.00

Mrs. Potts' Sad Irons
"The Hearts of the People," man, boy, shooting cannon, target $30.00

Mrs. Potts' Sad Irons
"Scene Just Outside Cowville," man runs for train, conductor $30.00

Mrs. Potts' Sad Irons
"And the Raven Answered 'Nevermore,'" lady ironing, raven $40.00

Mrs. Potts' Sad Irons
"The Ladies Favorite" women grab "New Style" iron man $50.00

Mrs. Potts' Sad Irons, $30.00.

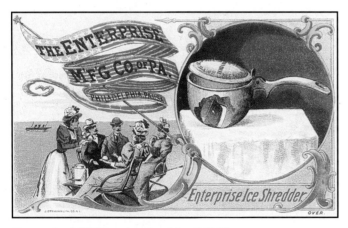

Enterprise M'F'G — ice shredder, $60.00.

Mrs. Pott's Sad Iron, $60.00.

The American Machine Co., $40.00.

Mrs. Potts' Sad Irons, $30.00.

Entertainment

(See also: Animals; Dogs; Elephants; Horses; Theater.)

Entertainment Images

Clowns and circuses have been popular with audiences for hundreds of years, so it is not surprising that trade cards with these images are popular with collectors today. Most of the trade cards with circus images are dominated by bright and cheery colors, often with bolder reds, blues, and greens than are typically found on other cards. Many of the cards with the best circus images were printed for products like threads and meats, with the circus or clown image used merely as a prop to promote the item advertised. Cards that were custom ordered for a specific event, a circus, or for some other type of traveling show, are often on light paper stock and of an inferior quality, although these can be among the most fascinating of all trade cards.

Historical Notes

America had some 30 traveling circuses already by the mid-1830s. In Europe there were, and had been for hundreds of years, small traveling shows with animal acts, jesters, jugglers, and other attractions, but most of these shows were low-budget affairs that often pulled together and fell apart with the seasons. American Victorians revolutionized the traveling show tradition through two major innovations. The first was the refinement of huge portable tents that allowed "the show to go on" profitably in less agreeable weather and for longer seasons. The second was the use of railroads, which cut down on road time and dangerous jostling of the animals, and which also allowed huge circuses to slip in and out of small and remote towns in a matter of hours.

When P.T. Barnum assumed control of New York's "American Museum" in 1842, the 31-year-old entrepreneur had already proven himself in the emerging business of big-time circus entertainment. Through the American Museum, he gained access to an additional stable of "freaks and oddities" that allowed his promotional genius almost unlimited opportunities. In 1850, his promotional coupe was a sensational and lucrative tour with Jenny Lind, "the Swedish Nightingale." Perhaps the best thing to happen to the circus world was the 1868 fire that destroyed the American Museum, thus driving Barnum even more out into the streets and on the road. Barnum sealed his fame and fortune in 1881 when he purchased Jumbo the Elephant, who proved on his first tour to be one of the biggest money-makers in circus history.

Buffalo Bill, much in the spirit of Barnum, entered the emerging business of "Wild West" road shows and claimed it as his own. A number of "Forepaughs" productions and the Van Amburgh Railroad Shows were also big into road shows and sensational advertising, and they left behind some of the most curious trade cards ever issued.

Pricing Tips & Cards to Watch For

One of the best values in trade cards can be found in stock cards with clown and circus images. Such cards typically sell for $5 to $10, and they are often colorful and fun to study. Watch for privately issued cards from an 1882 set of "Ryan's Menagerie of Wild Beasts" cards, as a complete set of 12 brought over $2,000 in a 1995 auction. Oddly enough, few trade cards can be found for Buffalo Bill and P.T. Barnum productions, probably for two reasons. First, both men were partial to lavish advertising posters (which they could afford), while their competitors had to settle for cards. And second, the few cards they did issue have long since found their way into museums and permanent collections. Keep an eye open for cards issued by either of these men, as most such cards bring $100 or more in good condition. The exceptions are the fairly common "Hood's Sarsaparilla" cards with a Barnum ad on the back, and the Jumbo Castoria medicine with a Barnum testimonial on the back, both of which sell for under $25.

Forepaugh's Wild West Show, $150.00.

Millie Christine, $100.00.

Clark's Thread
2 circus clowns, one pushing other like wheelbarrow $8.00

Clark's Thread
performer carries big spool, 2 kids with teeth $15.00

Hoods Sarsaparilla
several cards with Barnum ads on reverse $20.00

Lulu, The Man Bird
man flying over circus tent $100.00

Madame Clemens
profile of face, "Foretells the future, reveals the past..." $20.00

Magnolia Ham
trapeze artist, ham hanging from teeth, clown $30.00

Merrick Thread
man on high wire, flag, clock tower $8.00

Millie Christine
"The Renowned Two Headed Lady," Black version $60.00

Mustang Liniment
fallen horse and woman in circus ring $30.00

Professional Hypnotist stock card
3 vignettes, "Hypnotism Taught," "Diseases Cured..." $20.00

Quedah the Mammoth
hairy elephant — Van Amburgh Railroad Shows $80.00

Russian Gut Violin Strings
Grand Orchestra at Gilmore's Garden $25.00

Sacred Ox Rajah
growth from hump, "Born with an arm, hand, fingers" $80.00

Stock Card — rev. "Dissolving Views"
"Prof. J.S. Gould's Grand Art Entertainment" $15.00

Stock Card — Phila. imprint
circus performer breaks through hoop over frog $5.00

The Great Van Amburgh Shows
5 clowns, Irish clown in wheelbarrow $100.00

The Mc Gibeny Family
13 family members, "Musical & Sketch Entertainment" $40.00

The Mc Gibeny Family
shows train car family travels in $30.00

Universal Plow "At the Circus"
horse breaks through hoop, man & plow fly behind $25.00

Zeo The Air Queen — Ponds Extract
woman hanging from wire by hair $40.00

San Francisco, stock card, $15.00.

Forepaugh's Show — "Blondin," $80.00.

Ethnic

(See also: Blacks; Chinese; Cowboys & Indians.)

Ethnic Images

Many collectors find trade cards with ethnic illustrations fascinating. Sometimes the caption, or something in the text, clearly indicates the ethnicity of one of the characters. Other times one must infer a character's nation of origin based upon the stereotyped features, activity, clothing etc. that are part of the image. Singer Sewing issued several sets of trade cards showing (and labeling) ethnic representatives from around the world posed in native costumes with Singer Machines. Many small and large sets of stock cards were produced with captions indicating countries from around the world. Several common gilded sets from the late 1870s and early 1880s show women with national flags and cultural props. Slightly less common are similar cards with national stamps, and then from a few years later, non-gilded cards with international stamp and coin themes of various types.

Of more interest to most historians and collectors are the trade cards that capture the stereotyping of America's ethnic groups. These cards typically focus on negative stereotypes, with African Americans, Chinese, and Irish immigrants suffering the worst attacks. Many of the ads with Japanese, German, or Spanish images are neutral, or even positive, in their treatment of their ethnic characters. Images of other American immigrant groups are relatively scarce. Cards with ethnic themes can turn up in every category, but they are the most common in coffee, meat, patent medicine, tobacco, soap, and exposition advertising.

Historical Notes

Most Victorian immigrants landed and settled in crowded port towns where jobs were tight for illiterate workers with no special training. Immigrants were often viewed with hostility by those whose jobs and incomes they threatened, and with suspicion by the established middle class whose cultural dominance they challenged. The middle class tried to assume a charitable posture toward immigrants in grudging recognition of the role these hungry new workers played in maintaining the middle class lifestyle, which was built on low manufacturing labor costs and cheap domestic service wages. Affluent Victorians joked about immigrants, but they tolerated the newcomers so long as they "kept their place." However, as several trade cards illustrate, even a member of the staid middle class could come unglued when a Chinese man flirted with his daughter or an Irish coachman made advances on an Englishman's sister.

Although every major ethnic group that immigrated to America during the trade card era experienced some measure of discrimination, abuse, and ugly stereotyping, the Chinese and Irish consistently got the worst press. Depictions of ignorant "just landed" Irishmen and women show up in dozens of trade cards. Irishmen rarely appear in trade card scenes without pipes, shillelaghs, and Derbies, and they are typically shown with a bottle of whiskey or a pail of beer. Irish women are usually presented as crude in speech and manners, violent of nature, and homely in appearance.

In one sense, these ads are an indictment against Victorian consumers as much as the advertisers who produced the ads. Demeaning images with racial slurs would not have been used so often had they not proven to be acceptable, and even effective, in promoting sales. Beyond the Cupids and flowers that were so indicative of the romantic side of Victorians, there was also a cruel streak running through these people, a shadowy side that made racism in advertising seem to them "humorous." Trade cards document an ugly day from America's history in race relationships. The public nature of mass-distributed trade cards gave these cards a subliminal power to expose and promote certain cultural values. The mean-spirited jokes passed out on trade cards in respectable stores and chuckled at on boardwalks in front of churches and courthouses "gave permission" to many Victorians to publicly mock and negatively stereotype the ethnic groups around them. In today's age of legislated "political correctness," many collectors experience these unabashedly insensitive Victorian artifacts as both intriguing and unsettling.

Pricing Tips & Cards to Watch For

Trade card with ethnic themes and images generally command strong prices. The most affordable of these cards come from sets depicting ethnic groups in their native dress and homeland, few of which sell for over $10. Plainly designed stock cards with uninspiring imprints but strong American ethnic overtones typically sell for around $10 to $15. Stock cards with better imprints and striking graphics can sometimes bring $20 or more. Privately issued trade cards with harsh stereotyping are usually priced at $15 and up, with the highest prices going to scarce cards with particularly nasty messages and ads for products popular with collectors like alcohol, tobacco, and patent medicines. Watch for the large Taylor's Sure Cure cards and cards with dramatic Jewish stereotyping, as some of these cards have sold for $100 or more.

Atmore's Mince Meat, $40.00.

Pond's Extract, $15.00.

Van Schloppenberger, stock card, $15.00.

Wilson's Corned Beef, $15.00.

Keystone Improved Watch Cases, $15.00.

Dr. Haas' Hog & Poultry Remedy, $80.00.

Crescent Wash Board, $15.00.

Neal's Carriage Paints, $12.00.

*Celluloid Collars, Cuffs & Shirt
Bosoms, $10.00.*

Gilt Edge, stock card, $6.00.

Great Turkish Cough Syrup, $30.00.

Fisk Japanese Soap, $15.00.

Grand Festival & Fête Champêtre, $400.00.

Arbuckle Coffee
  Gypsy — Sports & Pastimes series, #20 of 50, cards, dance $8.00

Arbuckle Coffee
  Spain — Sports & Pastimes, #10 of 50, bullfight, bolero 1893 . . . .$8.00

Arbuckle Coffee
  couple in hall, "I saw Frenchman kissing you" — from Judge $15.00

Old German Family Soap
  contented family meal scene, 7 plump people, soap on floor $30.00

Schultz's Irish Soap
  washboard laundry scene, couple flirts, cat, shillelagh $20.00

Singer Sewing Machines
  "Wales," 2 women in stove pipe hats, man, machine, 1894 . . . .$3.00

Stock Card
  "Wild Australian Children," 2 kids hold hands, tall & short $35.00

Stock Card
  "Dawgy! Vere ish dat Tamned Dawg!," tiny dog under belly $5.00

Stock Card — "Belgique" stamp
  girl with flag, pitcher, stamp, Belgium costume $6.00

Stock Card — "Cards of the Nations"
  Haddock's Cards, advertises 12 designs, 1879, "France" $5.00

Stock Card — Bell's Buffalo Soap
  "Friend Barney's a hod-carrier," laborer, pipe, brick falls $10.00

Stock Card — furniture imprint
  Jewish-looking man, hand up, top hat, hand in pocket, beard $10.00

Stock Card — tailor imprint rev.
  "The Mail In Anam" — Vietnamese horseman, mail, stamps $8.00

Taylor's Sure Cure
  "The Italian dreams of music & art," man sleeps on grass $150.00

Taylor's Sure Cure
  "The German dreams of pretzels & beer," plump man in bed $150.00

Wilson's Corned Beef
  "My Lords... A Bumper to the Monarchs...," Englishmen toast $15.00

Pumps, stock card, $10.00.

Home Light Oil, $50.00.

Rising Sun Stove Polish, $15.00.

Exploration & Travel

(See also: Arctic; Ethnic; Sporting; Transportation.)

Exploration & Travel Images

Trade cards with depictions of far off and exotic settings were popular with Victorians, and such images remain favorites with many collectors today. The most common types of illustrations are of dramatic scenes showing white adventurers in jungles, the Arctic, in the Mideast, or climbing mountains. The adventurers are sometimes identified as specific historical explorers, like Henry Stanley of African fame or Lieut. Greeley of Arctic notoriety. In most cases, however, the adventurers are depicted in rather generic strokes as white men on safaris or as Victorian tourists taking in the sights. A few cards were produced with humorous images of Victorian salesmen trying to drum up sales in native villages. The quality of exploration and travel images is inconsistent, with most of these cards appearing with ads for food or coffee products.

Historical Notes

Steam ships, railroads, and innovations in back country equipment all opened up remote regions of the world in ways that seized the imaginations of American Victorians. Those who read adventure stories of famous explorers and who decorated their parlors with exotic furs, feathers, and artifacts from around the world often dreamed of one day seeing some of those places themselves. By the 1880s, "chartered" overseas travel adventures had become practical and affordable, and many Victorians were able to make their dreams come true through world travel. Hearty women were not immune to the adventure bug, and there are a surprising number of trade cards depicting ladies in full-length dresses leading the way up mountains and into jungles.

Nellie Bly was the most famous woman adventurer of the century, and whimsical images of her exploits appear on a set of rhyming stock cards. In 1890 she completed a sensational trip around the world in 72 days, 6 hours and 11 minutes. She had first earned fame as a journalist by faking insanity in order to write a muck-raking expose on the treatment of the mentally ill. Her spin around the planet was framed as a face-off between her and Jules Verne's character Phileas Fogg, who had gone around the world in 80 days. Miss Bly met Jules Verne in India, and spent Christmas in Hong Kong. Most of her highly publicized travel was accomplished by steamship and railroad.

Pricing Tips & Cards to Watch For

Generic views of remote locations are of little special interest to most collectors, and therefore they bring no special price. For a trade card with an exploration or travel theme to bring a premium price, the image must be dramatic and of good quality, the setting must be recognizable, or the characters must be identified as actual historical figures. Food and coffee cards with good images of exotic places or dramatic safari scenes generally bring $15 to $30. Watch for scarce images of agricultural equipment in African fields and images of Zulu warriors, as several of these cards have sold for over $100. Also keep an eye open for views of Uncle Sam visiting remote locations, as these cards typically bring $30 or more.

Nellie Bly, stock card, $10.00.

Magnolia Ham, $25.00.

Libby, McNeill & Libby's, $20.00.

Bensdorp's Royal Dutch Cocoa
"Humboldt as an explorator" in jungle, trophies, #86 of 104 ....$15.00

Chas. Counselman & Co's
"Arkansas Traveller," mountain man on horse, rifle, 2 hams $30.00

Colburn's Mustard
white hunter on safari shoots tiger in jungle $15.00

Corticelli Thread — stock card
4 mountain climbers reach peak, ad on flag, telescope $10.00

Huntley & Palmers Biscuits
native lures rhino, white hunter on safari aims $25.00

Libby, McNeill & Libby's Beef
"they Smuggle it," 2 men with guns in mts., big packs, cans $25.00

Liebig — 1 of 6, French
scenes in Africa, native couple poses, white photographer $6.00

McLaughlin's Coffee — one of 16
"Surveying Incident in India," rail tracks, tigers scare crew $20.00

Schnull & Krag's Package Coffee
white man sits offering coffee to native on beach $5.00

Stock Card — picture framer imprint
sailor with barrel encounters timid tropical island native $8.00

Swayne's Ointment
"Stanley in Africa," 6 weird monkeys, he sleeps, hammock $40.00

Wilson's Canned Ham
"For the North Pole," Captain must wait for ham to be loaded $20.00

Wilson's Cooked Meats
"Tourists should always be provided...," hot man, wife, boy $30.00

Woolson Spice Co. — Lion Coffee
portrait of Stanley, "African Explorer" story on back $15.00

Zig-Zag Journeys in Europe, $15.00.

Jackson's Best Chewing Tobacco, $40.00.

Magnolia Ham, $25.00.

Fairbank's Soaps, $15.00.

Outward Bound — Mediterranean Cruise, $20.00.

Expositions & Fairs

(See also: A History of Trade Cards; Columbia; Uncle Sam.)

Exposition & Fair Images

The trade cards that were freely passed out by exhibitors at expositions and fairs were often cherished by their recipients as souvenir items to take home and save. These cards were typically designed with delightful images to insure that potential customers would remember the company's exhibit as part of the visitor's exciting day. The care and craftsmanship that went into many of these cards continues to keep them popular with collectors today. The major exhibitions inspired privately commissioned cards and numerous sets of stock cards with views of notable attractions and exceptional buildings. Regional exhibitions and fairs gave rise to fewer cards with custom designs, but they did inspire hundreds of stock cards with interesting images or imprints relating to the events. Exhibition and fair cards can be found with advertising for nearly every type of product sold during the Victorian period.

Historical Notes

Because trade cards were known to enhance depictions of products for effect, many consumers felt that the best way to judge merchandise was to view it personally. Exhibitions and fairs allowed companies to market goods and consumers to examine merchandise at a single, convenient location. This meaning of exhibition is captured in numerous trade card imprints like: "Don't Miss Our Fall Exhibition of New Goods."

Early exhibitions and fairs had far less of the carnival atmosphere associated with these events today. Promoters only added glitz and glamour to guarantee their exhibitors increasingly large crowds, or, when the community got involved, for the

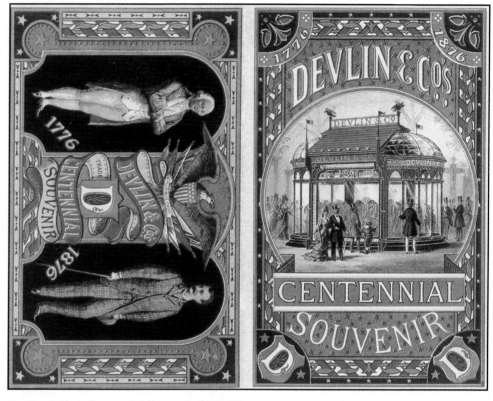

Devlin & Co.'s Centennial Souvenir, $150.00.

sake of pride. The 1893 World's Columbian Exposition (WCE) of Chicago is the best example of an event defined by its desire to outdo any previous exhibition regardless of the cost.

In the name of education, WCE promoters expanded their agenda to include things that had never appeared before at such an event. Billed as an "Illustrated Encyclopedia of Civilization," the WCE offered attractions that ranged from learned lectures, rare art displays, and elaborate manufacturing exhibits to fireworks and flashy electric lights, exotic foods, and the earliest and largest Ferris Wheel ever erected. In an effort to dodge criticisms of bawdy sensationalism, the WCE promoters neatly tucked the sideshow elements of the exhibition off on a "side street" known as "The Midway Plaisance," which for many people provided the highlights of their visit. The exhibit that caused the most stir featured "Little Egypt" and her "educated muscles." Miss Egypt was the woman who introduced Americans to belly dancing, or the hootchy kootchy as it was called. Buffalo Bill and his Wild West show were also nudged conveniently just off the edge of the official WCE grounds.

In terms of trade cards issued, the following expositions are among the most important:

1853 — New York Crystal Palace Exposition
1876 — Philadelphia Centennial Exposition
1878 — Paris International Exposition
1882 — New York's 51st American Institute
1884 – 85 — New Orleans Exposition
1885 — Montreal Winter Carnival
1886 — New York's 55th American Institute
1888 — Ohio Centennial Exposition
1888 — Buffalo International Industrial Fair
1889 — Paris International Exposition

1890 — Detroit International Exposition
1893 — Chicago World Columbian Exposition (WCE)
1894 — California Midwinter International Exposition
1900 — Paris Exposition
1901 — Buffalo Pan-American Exposition
1904 — St. Louis Louisiana Purchase Exposition

Pricing Tips & Cards to Watch For

Few categories in trade cards span as wide of a range in pricing as cards from expositions and fairs. Monotonous stock cards with exposition building views generally go for $5 to $10. The better exposition stock cards with good colors and interesting scenes often run $10 to $20, or twice that amount if they are from the Centennial Exposition of 1876. Prices become more volatile with privately issued cards, some of which are common, and others of which are rare. As a general rule, cards from the Columbian Exposition are the most abundant. Watch for cards with illustrations of actual exhibits or strong patriotic symbols, especially Uncle Sam and Columbia, as these often bring the highest prices. As always, cards for popular products or with ethnic themes tend to command premium prices.

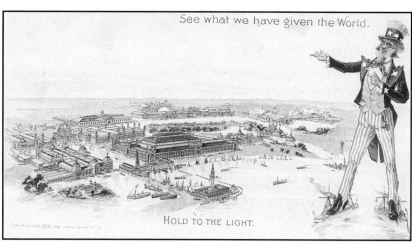

Everett Piano, $80.00.

Alston Grocery — cert. of weight
woman reads folder, Dallas State Fair, 1886 ....**$20.00**

American Institute, Nat'l Expo — NY
woman in corset reviews hats, canes, sewing, etc. 1886 ...**$50.00**

Clark's Thread
"Birdseye View" of bldgs & lagoon, Columbian Expo, 1893 ..**$15.00**

Connecticut State Fair — stock card
1888 "Peaches & Cream" vegetable people, fair of 1891 ..**$20.00**

Diamond Lustre Polish — stock card
bird eats spider, "Souvenir — Great Mechanics Fair of 1887" **$15.00**

Drown Umbrellas — stock card
book mark style, patriotic symbols, Memorial Hall, 1876 ....**$75.00**

Eldorado Engine Oil
Ice Palace, Winter Carnival, St. Paul, Minn., 1886 ....**$15.00**

Elite Bouquet — Western Perfumery
die-cut fan, flowers, Industrial Expo of San Francisco, 1883 ....**$20.00**

Enterprise Congress — Meat Chopper
Uncle Sam, Columbia, Chicago's World's Fair skyline, 1893 ......**$40.00**

Eyssell's Pharmacy — stock card
woman in chair, Kansas City Exposition, 1888 ....**$20.00**

Fairbanks' Scales
1776 — Washington weighs/modern man, barrel, scale, 1876 .....**$35.00**

Grand Duchess Cologne
woman, bottle, lists first place: 1876, 1878, 1881, 1882 ....**$10.00**

Henderson Little Red Schoolhouse Shoes
child fishing lagoon, Fisheries bldg., Chicago, 1893 ....**$15.00**

Hood's Sarsaparilla
"A Few of the World's fair," 4 children, for Chicago's 1893 ....**$30.00**

Montgomery Ward & Co. — stock card
Agricultural Bldg., lagoon, boats & pier, Chicago, 1893 ....**$20.00**

Pan-American Expo — Agricultural
2 women form map of Americas on globe, Buffalo, NY, 1901 .....**$25.00**

Paris Exposition — dry goods imprint
"Colonnade Du Trocadero," R.I. store ad on rev., 1878 ....**$10.00**

Penn. State Ag. Exhibition — stock card
man, 2 horses, rev.: "Balloons — Parachute Jumps," 1890 ....**$20.00**

Restaurant Vendrome
chef pulls goose by neck, Boston Foreign Exhibition, 1883 ....**$10.00**

Southern Expo, Louisville — stock card
Main Building view, medicinal liquor imprint, KY, 1884 ....**$40.00**

St. Louis Expo, official card
map of Purchase, back: attractions/info about expo, 1904 ....**$30.00**

Stiefel's Medicinal Soaps — stock card
photo-lith sky view of Paris Exhibition of 1900 ....**$10.00**

Stock Card — Methodist Books
5 buildings, ad shield, flowers in colors, Prang Lith., 1876 ....**$20.00**

Stock Card — piano imprint
Columbia, cherubs, 5 bldgs, by Lehman & Bolton, 1875 ....**$20.00**

Todd, Bancroft — "Kulture" Shoes
die-cut shoe, "Exposition Types," ethnic faces inside, 1901 ....**$30.00**

Underwood Typewriters
folder, Electric Tower, fountain, exhibit, Buffalo, 1901 ....**$40.00**

Walter Wood — farm machines
Black man, cabin, Souvenir of Virginia Expo, 1st Prize, 1888 ......**$30.00**

Wilcox & White — stock card
rev.: organ, highest award, Penn. & Conn. State Fairs, 1879 ....**$20.00**

Yale Locks — stock card
many Uncle Sams marching, Washington D.C. skyline, 1876 ......**$50.00**

Ohio Centennial Exposition, $130.00.

Fairy Tales, Nursery Rhymes & Literary

(See also: Entertainment; Meats; Theater; Threads.)

Literary Images, Themes & Allusions

Cards with characters, lines, and scenes from fairy tales and nursery rhymes are popular and abundant in trade cards. The best of these cards use very attractive colors and compelling designs, but these cards can also be found in cheaply done stock cards and amateurish private issues. Several advertisers issued nice sets of cards using images from Aesop's Fables with condensed versions of the stories printed on the backs. Dozens of cards reworked Mother Goose rhymes, changing key words to turn the poems into endorsements for specific products. Advertisements employing literary allusions to adult works are also abundant, with lines from the plays of Shakespeare or Gilbert & Sullivan accounting for perhaps half of these cards. Cards of the types discussed in this section are most frequently found in early ads for meats, soaps, and threads, and in later series of cards issued for baking soda, coffee, and foods.

Historical Notes

Collectors of trade cards are often puzzled by images and lines that appear in ads that seem to make little or no sense today. Several modern social critics have recently raised concerns about "cultural literacy," suggesting that the movement in American education towards "multiculturalism" has resulted in a great deal of cultural confusion. These critics hold that Americans no longer have a unifying body of substantive literature from which and to which references can be made in a way that fosters shared values, effective communication, and common goals. Such theories are debatable, but evidence that Americans did once share a rather narrowly defined type of literacy does abound.

To some extent, trade cards document an extensive level of shared literary experience in America. By choice or not, most Victorians read the same books, sang the same songs, and saw the same plays. By the time a middle class child reached schooling age, teachers could generally assume that references to certain lines from Mother Goose, the Bible, or Aesop's Fables would be understood. As schooling advanced, students everywhere would be expected to expand their control of literature to include the major works of Shakespeare, Longfellow, Byron, and a dozen others. Similarly, the adults of the period were mostly reading the same bestsellers and becoming familiar with the same plays. Beyond the evidence found in trade card, there is additional documentation that daily Victorian conversions were sometimes peppered with allusions and phrases from popular works like *Uncle Tom's Cabin*, *Patience*, or *The Mikado*.

Victorian advertisers took America's shared cultural literacy for granted, and they nurtured and exploited it in a remarkable number of ways. The rhymes of Mother Goose were kept alive through countless trade cards advertising everything from condensed milk to shoes. The sublime insights of poets like Campbell and Burns were savored on lard cards, while humorous scenes from Cervantes and Shakespeare were chuckled over in ads for soaps and cooked meats. The philosophical issues raised by Oscar Wilde were widely (though perhaps superficially) understood and mocked in dozens of ads, and the unforgettable characters created by Gilbert and Sullivan made encore appearances in trade cards for everything from pocket watches to corsets.

Pricing Tips & Cards to Watch For

Stock cards with fairy tales, nursery rhymes, or literary allusions are usually priced from $3 to $10, but they can bring more if the lithography is of exceptional quality, the imprint is especially significant, or the image is of special historical significance. Most soap and thread cards with nursery rhyme themes can be found in the $5 to $15 range. Thread cards with literary allusions and fairy tale images tend to run more in the $10 to $20 range, except for Kerr's Aesop's Fables cards, which can sometimes bring double that amount because of their scarcity and exceptionally fine graphics. Many stock, die-cut, and privately issued cards with the "Old Woman Who Lived in a Shoe" theme were used by shoe companies. Meat cards with lines and scenes from Shakespeare usually bring $10 to $25 each. For over-sized, framable cards with lovely fairy tale and nursery rhyme scenes priced in the $20 to $30 range, keep an eye open for Woolson Spice/Lion Coffee cards. Also watch for the beautifully-designed "Juvenile Shakespeare" cards that were used to promote Dr. King's New Discovery for Consumption, Coughs, and Colds.

Fairbank's Fairy Soap, $20.00.

Lion Coffee, die-cut, $15.00.

Woolson Spice, Lion Coffee, $20.00.

Nestle's Milk Food, $10.00.

J & P Coats Thread, $10.00.

Ferndell, $10.00.

J & P Coats Thread, $10.00.

Merrick Thread, $15.00.

Libby, McNeill & Libby Meat, $25.00.

Soapine Soap, $25.00.

J & P Coats Thread, $8.00.

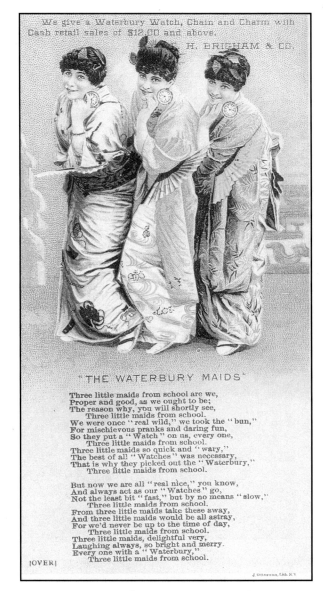

Waterbury Watches, $15.00.

Kerr's Thread, $20.00.

Ceresota Flour, Northwestern Milling, $12.00.

Wilson's Cooked Meats, $8.00.

Chas. Counselman Royal Hams, $30.00.

Cosmo Buttermilk Toilet Soap
"Little Red Riding Hood" die-cut folding purse, tale inside **$20.00**

Dobbins' Electric Soap
"As You Like It" — Shakespeare, #3 of 7, "Lover" shaving **$5.00**

Dwight's Soda
"Three Blind Mice," woman on chair, #25 of 30 small, 1900 . . . . .**$10.00**

Fairbank's Lard
"Familiar Quotations" — Byron, Corsair, pig, hat by sea, ship **$15.00**

Fairbank's Lard
"The Dog & the Shadow" — Aesop's Fable series, dog, water . . .**$15.00**

Great Atlantic & Pacific Tea Co.
"Mary had a little Lamb" — rhyme, #1 of set, Mary hugs lamb **$6.00**

Great Atlantic & Pacific Tea Co.
"Rock A Bye Baby" — child in rocker with doll, stool desk **$6.00**

Higgins' German Laundry Soap
"HMS Pinafore" — Gilbert & Sullivan, "What never?" couple **$5.00**

Mother Hubbard Soap — on stock card
Black man, red & white shirt, holds ad on sheet out window **$6.00**

Sea Foam Yeast
"Humpty Dumpty" — new rhyme, ...poor Humpty Dumpty fell . . .**$8.00**

Stock Card — clothing imprint
"Sing a song of six pence," girl in hat, fence, pie, black birds **$6.00**

Stock Card — decorator imprint
Victorian Mother Goose, gloves, top hat, flies over river **$8.00**

Stock Card — Misfit Parlors imprint
Old King Cole — rhyme image, 3 fiddlers, bowl, water pipe **$8.00**

Stock Card — music store imprint
"Patience" — Oscar Wilde, ridiculed by Gilbert & Sullivan **$10.00**

Stock Card — tailor imprint
"Jack & Jill" — rhyme, Jack falls, Jill tumbles, pail spills **$5.00**

Wheeler & Wilson Sewing Machines
"The Crow & the Pitcher" — tale, crow dropping stones in **$10.00**

Farm Related

(See also: Cows; Food; Horses.)

Farm Related Images

Trade cards with farm-related images strike a nostalgic cord with many collectors. Some collectors prefer cards with color illustrations of agricultural implements, while others have a preference for images of barns, fields, seeds, fertilizers, or livestock. As a group, these cards tend to use graphics and colors that are above average in quality. This group also includes an unusually high percentage of folders, many of which are composed of three or more panels. Broadly defined, farm related cards can include stock cards and private issues with farm scenes that never advertised agricultural products, equipment, or services. However, most collectors show a strong preference for cards that were commissioned by farm implement manufacturers or that bear imprints for products or services directly linked to farming.

Historical Notes

American farmers have always personified the tension between progress and tradition. Thomas Jefferson designed the classic American plow in 1793. By 1800 the concept had been patented in a cast iron version, but the labor-saving invention was viewed by some Yankees with suspicion. They feared that the iron might poison the soil. In most of the rest of the world, this tension between the old and the new hardly existed, because there, tradition ruled and few dared to challenge.

Not every American farmer was willing to throw away "perfectly good" equipment or practices to try out the latest innovations in farming, but America produced more than its share of risk takers. Perhaps it was the spirit of the frontier that empowered some farmers to take bigger gambles for bigger stakes, or maybe Americans were born of risk-taking stock. For whatever the reason, revolutions in farming equipment and techniques became a hallmark of the emerging American agricultural industry. Many of the most dramatic farming innovations occurred during the late Victorian period at the height of the trade card era, and these changes are delightfully preserved in the advertisements of the day. In fact, it could be argued that trade cards played an important role in ushering American farmers from traditional "back-forty gardening" to the big-time show of twentieth century agribusiness.

Pricing Tips & Cards to Watch For

Generally speaking, farm-related trade cards are among the most expensive cards to collect. A card with a farm implement ad will often bring twice the price of a similarly common or scarce card advertising a different product. Stock cards with farm-related scenes are the cheapest, with few of them bringing over $10 unless the imprint is of something special. Stock cards with line-drawn illustrations of plows, rakes, binders, etc. on the back start at $8 and run as high as $20. Privately issued cards for seeds and fertilizers usually sell for between $15 and $30. Privately issued cards with good illustrations of farm equipment rarely sell for under $25. Watch for large folders in good condition with bold colors, as these cards often bring $75 or more.

Deering Binder, $60.00.

Russell Threshers, Horse Powers, Engines & Saw Mills, $30.00.

– 112 –

American Standard Corn Planter
   boy in straw hat planting rows of corn, distant farm house $30.00

Buckeye Drill
   die-cut of 2 boy playing in huge drill (like boot), team inset $30.00

Buckeye Force Pumps
   hand pump, child cries, frog on plate, rabbit running away $20.00

Deering Binder
   salesman shows binder on table, competition piles up to see $25.00

Domestic Sewing Machine
   white farm house, livestock, farmers, hay mower $10.00

J.W.Stoddard — The Favorite Hay Rake
   man on rake, horse pulling away, house, lake in distance $20.00

Light Running Plano
   2 giant chickens pull binder, farmers marvel $35.00

Plano Harvester & Binder
   Diogenes in night with lamp, "at last I have found" $60.00

Princess Plows & Star Coulters
   "Pleasures of Farm Life," walking team to plow, child rides $30.00

Products of Arkansas
   New Orleans Expo card, peach, strawberries, grapes $35.00

Rice's Seed — Livingston Tomato
   happy farming couple in bed, huge tomato comes in window $15.00

S. R. Nye's National Rake
   3-panel folder, rake, 3 children fishing, dog, picnic basket $40.00

Star Wind Mill
   folder, windmill, farms in distance, haystacks, cattle, road $40.00

Syracuse Chilled Plow
   3 children use plow as sled with flag on ice, church $25.00

Victor Clover Huller
   "Ain't we in clover," couple at edge of woods, red huller $20.00

Yankee Swivel Plow
   red plow on green card, "Milton Bradley Co. Lith." $25.00

Lamb Wire Fence, $80.00.

Triumph Grain Drill & Seeder, $35.00.

Walter A. Wood Gear Mower, $30.00.

Buckeye Standard Mower, $35.00.

Food & Grocery

(See also: Cows & Dairy; Clothing & Dry Goods; Kitchens; Meats.)

Food & Grocery Images

The images found in advertisements for the food and grocery industries range widely in popularity and quality. Certain clusters of food-related cards experience extraordinary demand (e.g. Heinz and canned meats) while others remain largely uncollected (e.g. Fleischmann Yeast and corn starches). The quality of food and grocery images runs from the cheaply-executed stock cards common with small town grocery store imprints to the endearing images of children found on the prized Heinz pickle die-cuts. Most of the trade cards with grocery promotions are found on stock cards, while the majority of the cards with food advertisements were designed and distributed as private issues. Many of the producers of the well-designed food cards are still major players in the food industry today, including Heinz, Gold Medal, Quaker Oats, Pillsbury, Arm & Hammer, Lea & Perrins, and Jell-O. Many of the most popular of the food and grocery trade cards show detailed scenes from inside grocery stores or the kitchens in which the products were used. Also very popular are cards with facsimiles of boxes, bottles, and tins of products as they were found on grocery shelves.

Historical Notes

Until nearly the end of the Victorian period, country stores and neighborhood merchants played an important part in the average consumer's life. Nearly all purchases were made through the same establishment, often with barter and credit as part of the equation. The shelves and counters on the left side of these stores were typically devoted to canned goods and packaged foods, as well as to fresh perishables like eggs, fruits, and vegetables. Other consumable items like candy, tobacco, and patent medicines were also found on the "grocery" side of the store. The right side of the store was stocked with "dry goods" like bulk fabric, ready-made clothes, household items, tools, and the like. As department stores made their way into smaller and smaller cities, and as mail order houses like Montgomery Ward and Sears, Roebuck and Co. penetrated the rural market, customer loyalty to small local stores was severely tested.

The convenience of shopping with a local merchant was challenged by the excitement of a day trip to the nearest department store, which offered many times the selection in competitively-priced inventory, plus the stimulation of grand atriums, fabulous displays, elevators, and in some cases, even indoor gardens and fountains. Mail-order catalogs offered even better prices and more convenience, except for the wait one had to endure while the order was placed and delivered. Many local stores were able to survive in the face of such competition only by building on their strengths and evolving in new directions. The general stores that prospered often did so because they became less general, beefing up their inventories in food and redefining their services more in terms of their groceries and less in the area of dry goods. Other stores survived by associating themselves with buying co-ops and through absorption into "chains" of similar stores operating under common ownership.

Volume buying in grocery goods was possible by the end of the Victorian era because of incredible advancements in the processing and packaging of food throughout the trade card era. Many of these advancements can be chronicled in the trade cards issued by such firms as Borden, Thurber, Heinz, and Lea & Perrins. These companies discovered ways for packaging and preserving foods that made warehousing and extended shelf life possible. A close examination of food and grocery trade cards offers many insights on the bottles, tins, and boxes that were experimented with as the business of handling food was slowly taken away from local general stores and handed over to factories and grocery store chains.

Pricing Tips & Cards to Watch For

Very few food or grocery cards sell for more than $100, but below that mark there is a complete representation of prices. As always, stock cards with uninspiring imprints run in the $5 or less range. With slightly better images or imprints, these cards can bring around $10. Privately issued food cards with images of the packaged product often sell for $10 to $25, depending upon the quality of card's design, the company, and the type of food represented, as well as the card's relative scarcity. To bring over $25, a card will need to be of exceptional quality or desirability. The most desirable cards are those of companies still in business and of outstanding design, or from companies that linked their product in their ad to other highly collectible topics like African Americans or Uncle Sam. Watch for any of the Heinz cards, as even the most common of these are now bringing $20 and up. Also keep an eye open for Thurber cards, because the exceptional quality of these cards printed by the Forbes Lithographic Company is becoming common knowledge and collectors are beginning to give them a closer look.

Lea & Perrins' Sauce, $40.00.

Hecker-Hones-Jewell Milling, $15.00.

Thurber, Whyland Fruit Preserves & Jellies, $20.00.

Armour & Co. Extract of Beef, $20.00.

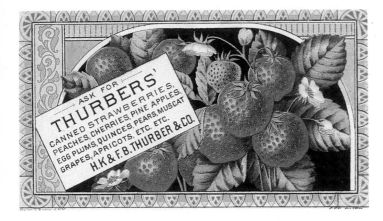

Thurbers' Canned Fruits, $20.00.

Moir English Pickles, Scotch Jams, $20.00.

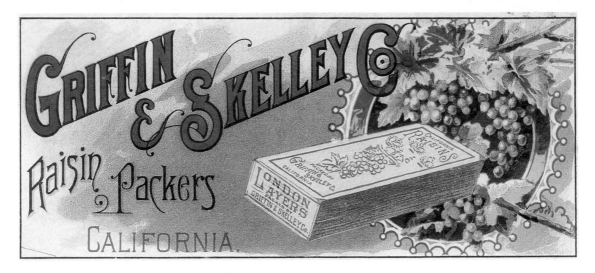

Griffin & Skelley Raisin Packers, Cal., $60.00.

Van Duzer's Extracts, $15.00.

Monticello Olives, Lilly Brand Picles, $20.00.

AMC Perfect Cereals, $25.00.

Plymouth Rock Phosphated Gelatine, $20.00.

Jell-O, die-cut, $20.00.

AMC Perfect Cereals, $30.00.

Kennedy's Vanilla Wafer Biscuit, $50.00.

Pillsbury's Best Flour, $20.00.

Mapl-Flake, Hygienic Food Co., $20.00.

Dunham's Concentrated Cocoanut, $35.00.

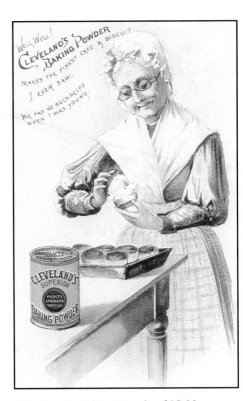

Cleveland's Baking Powder, $15.00.

Dr. Price's Baking Powder, $15.00.

H. J. Heinz Co., die-cut, $40.00.

Heinz, $40.00.

Samuel Cushman, $35.00.

Sea Moss Farine, $30.00.

Alden Fruit Vinegar
horse bucks Black man as dog bites, apple basket spills $40.00

Bremner's Eurekabread
"He gets it," boy falls snitching bread, cupboard, cracker tin $15.00

Canby's Star Baking Powder
chef in big hat, huge loaf of bread, 2 people come running $25.00

Colburn's Mustard
elephant, driver, princess, palm trees, temple $12.00

Colburn's Mustard
camel, man rides with gun, another camel in distance $12.00

Copland's Crackers, Detroit
lady with grain under arm, chef in factory, 775 barrels day $50.00

Dozier-Weyle Cracker Co.
parrot with brush says: "I'll paint this whole town red" $20.00

Dr. Prices Flavoring Extracts — stock
boy & girl flirt, fancy table cloth, hold dishes of ice cream $10.00

Fleischmann Yeast
barker on stage passes out samples to 4 people, ad on easel $12.00

Fleischmann's Yeast
boys ballooning over city, "Rises far above its imitators" $12.00

Friend's Oats — Muscatine Oat Meal Co.
paper doll, girl holds box, ad, wears hood, skirt forms ring $20.00

G. Byron Morse Dining Parlors
whimsical, soldier sword fights lady using big silver ware $10.00

Great Atlantic Tea Company
"Rotten in Denmark," 3 hold noses, grocery, Limburg Cheese $8.00

Heinz
"Mamma's Favorites" girl, hand on chin, green bench, basket $20.00

Henry Mayo Canned Goods
monkey inspects fruit & veg's, canned goods, vase $20.00

Iglehearts "White Star" Flour
mother, 2 children & infant in highchair served at table $20.00

Kenny's Ice Cream Parlor
stock card for "Delicious Ice Cream" $6.00

Log Cabin Maple Syrup
child in feathered hat, gun, pack, "My mamma says..." $12.00

Manewal Lange Cracker
girls on gilded card, bit flower on shoulder, cracker boxes $10.00

Nichol's Oats, Wheat, Flake Hominy
children dance around boxes, "Oats, peas & barley grows" $15.00

Post Toasties "are Corn Flakes"
folder, grocer delivers girl basket, boxes of cereal, factory $15.00

Quaker Oats
"We Eat Quaker Oats," 3 girls in white dresses & bonnets $12.00

Reckhow Preserving Company
"Our Packers," cherubs stuff "Mixed Pickles" bottle $50.00

Redhead's Baking Powder
"Little Redhead" girl with red hair under yellow hat $15.00

Renown Table Salt
5 children play, dog, birds "Always in tall round boxes" $12.00

Ryeninjun Flap-Jack Preparatin
stock card, Nebraska firm, boy through paper, dandelions $5.00

Stickney & Poors Spices
boy in hat with stick, dog pulls cart, boxes of product $15.00

Stock Card — confectioner imprint
blonde girl's arms full, spilling candy $5.00

Stock Card — grocer imprint
clerk spills flour on other clerk, lady gasps, barrels, scale $8.00

Stock Card — seafood imprint
table set with oysters, oranges, wine, knife, etc., 1876 . . . .$15.00

Ta-Ka-Kake Sugar Corn Flour
girl holds up a cupcake, box behind her, rev. testimonials $15.00

Thomson & Taylor Spice Co.
kitchen, Black cook holds bottle in left hand, mother, child $25.00

Thurbers' Spices
"Queen of Sheba — King Solomon," oasis scene, camels, tents $25.00

Thurbers' Spices
"The Baldwin," plumb red tomato, list of other veg's $20.00

Vienna Pudding
dog makes butler spill pudding, guests through door watch $15.00

Washburn, Crosby — Gold Medal Flour
boy rides barrel like sled, others spill, "We lead..." $15.00

Wonder Flour, Lake Superior Mills
2 girls, loaf of bread as balloon rising well $20.00

Woods Spices
exotic palms, pyramids, camel, large spice box $15.00

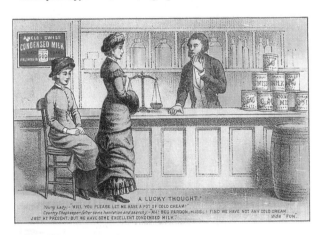

Anglo-Swiss Condensed Milk, $12.00.

Hornby's Oats, die-cut, $35.00.

Frogs

(See also: Animals; Fairy Tails; Humor; Whimsical.)

Frog Images

There are a surprising number of trade cards with delightful images of frogs. Many of these cards depict frogs dressed in human clothing and walking on two legs. Frogs are almost always used in advertising illustrations for comic effects, and they are typically depicted with expressive eyes, hands, and mouths. Despite the fact that many of these cards were printed using only two or three colors, collectors generally agree that these cards have a certain unique charm about them that causes a person to study them and smile. Many of these cards were issued as stock cards, sometimes in small sets.

Historical Notes

Most illustrators find frogs one of the easiest and most effective creatures to anthropomorphise. The naturally large, bulging eyes of frogs, as well as the ample "lips" and round bellies of frogs, are perfect for conveying emotions while staying relatively true to the creature's natural form. The long hind legs and toes of frogs are also easily exploited when the need arises to convey human awkwardness, dexterity, or vigorous activity.

The unexpected favor that frog illustrations found with sophisticated well-scrubbed Victorians is partially explainable in terms of the romantic movement's influence on nineteenth century literature and art. The romantic movement rejected "elitist" literature and art in favor of "popular" works that could be easily understood and enjoyed by all. The movement also fostered a romantic view of children, who were seen as innocent and unspoiled by the perversities of culture. Romantics urged society to learn from children, exhorting adults to rekindle free-flowing emotions, free-spirited imaginations, and child-like wonder over the curiosities of nature. The traditional conventions of literature and art fell under attack, and experimentation was encouraged. With their new-found respect for innocence, romantics revolutionized education and child-rearing. Children's stories became bestsellers, led by an invigorated interest in classic cottage tales collected into respectable illustrated works based on The Fables of Aesop, Tales of Mother Goose, and Grimm's Fairy Tales.

At the height of the romantic movement, intriguingly unconventional books with talking animals and stylized illustrations were being cranked out at an amazing rate. In addition to the new illustrated versions of Aesop's "The Ox and the Frog" and the Grimm brothers' "The Frog Prince," other stories with frog characters became popular. Randolph Caldecott's successful "A Frog, He Would a-Wooing Go" was published in 1883, and similarly illustrated stories followed. During this time, children's books were being written and illustrated by some of the same people (e.g. Kate Greenaway) who also contributed work or inspiration to the advertising trade card world. The influences of these artistic genres upon each other is apparent in numerous places. Beatrix Potter's famous frog story, "The Tale of Mr. Jeremy Fisher," was not published until 1906, but the story's illustrations were based

on drawings that she had begun in 1893, when most of the trade cards reproduced on these pages were still popular and in circulation. One can only guess what Mr. Fisher would have looked like if Larkin Soap had been less successful in distributing their Mr. Frog Goes a-Fishing series.

Pricing Tips & Cards to Watch For

Trade cards with frog images are popular with many collectors, but few collectors have become competitive enough in buying them to drive prices up above what these cards would bring with some other image. The only frog cards that sell for more than one might expect are ones that are in demand for reasons other than the frog image per se. For example, the Hires Cough Cure card brings $30 because the product is both Hires and medicinal, not because frog collectors have driven the price up. Stock cards with frog images rarely sell for over $8. Watch for the frog die-cut issued by Soapine, the Kerr's "Ox and Frog" fable card, and the Coats Thread card with marching frogs, as these three cards have appreciated due to demand by soap and thread collectors. Also keep an eye open for the Pond's Extract cards with frog images, as these are popular with patent medicine collectors.

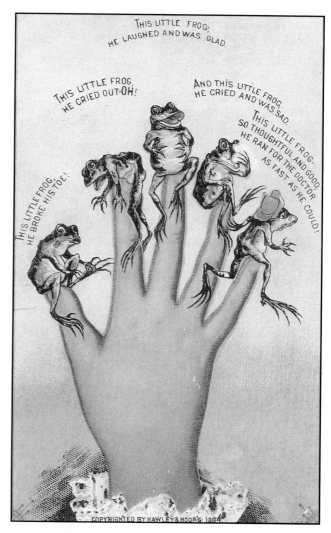

Stock card, $12.00.

Carter's Little Nerve Pills
"Don't be nervous," huge frog stands, comforts infant $10.00

Celluloid Collars & Cuffs
red imp in celluloid on cattail directs croaking frog singer $8.00

Hires Cough Cure
"They must be very hoarse,." girl spoons Hires to 3 frogs $20.00

Household Sewing Machine — stock card
frog hunting with gun eyes a flying duck at pond $5.00

Hoyt's German Cologne
frog on mushroom pours cologne from bottle to flowers $8.00

J & P Coats Thread
many military frogs march in line, leader has cattail hat $10.00

J & P Coats Thread
big pond frog beside box of 12 colorful spools of thread $10.00

Kendall's French Laundry Soap
die-cut frog on rock, "Clean Up" written on throat $20.00

Kerr's Thread
"Ox & Frog" from Aesop's Fables series, large ox, 2 frogs $20.00

Larkin's "Elite" Toilet Soap
fishing frog gets a bite, basket $10.00

Larkin's "Elite" Toilet Soap
sensitive frog plays flute in moonlight by pond's edge $10.00

Muzzy's Starch
3 imps with flower hats hunt a fly, frog in shorts as horse $10.00

Pollywogs Cigars — stock card
"Flirtation" from frog set developing marriage themes $12.00

Stock Card — clothing imprint
"Chicago Church Choir Pinafore," Gilbert & Sullivan frogs $15.00

Stock Card — clothing imprint
big frog in fancy hat with business card in mouth $4.00

Stock Card — stationer imprint
circus frogs perform stunts, cattail, mother with polywog $8.00

Stock Card — stove imprint
4 frogs smoke pipes and hang from rope $12.00

Stock Cards — grocery imprint
big frog shoots fat canon, 3 little frogs jump $5.00

Glass shades, stock card, $6.00.

Trix Breath Perfume, stock card, $15.00.

Pond's Extract "People's Remedy," $30.00.

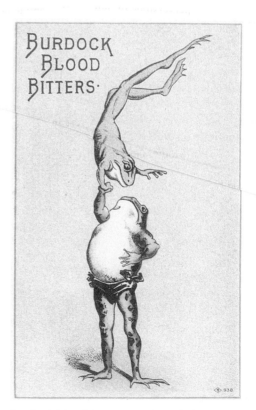

Burdock Blood Bitters, stock card, $12.00.

Furniture & Home Improvement

(See also: Kitchen; Pianos & Organs; Stoves.)

Furniture & Home Improvement Images

Trade cards with images of Victorian furniture and home improvement products offer a wonderful window into the homes of a century ago. Cards in this category include advertisements for everything from exterior paint and yard fences to chandelier lamps and linoleum. Many of these cards were produced by national manufacturers as stock cards to be imprinted by the local retailers who carried their goods. Of special interest to historians and restorationists are cards depicting original patterns of wall paper, floor coverings, and tapestries. The fresh, brilliant colors on these cards are helpful in cases where original articles have faded and shifted in unknown directions because of age and contact with other objects. Cards with images from around the home are also popular with home owners and bed and breakfast proprietors who are looking for ways to create an authentic Victorian balance of ferns, carpets, furniture, bric-a-brac, and tapestries.

Historical Notes

When we attempt to "recapture the charm" of a Victorian parlor, it is for us an exercise in nostalgia. Or when builders today custom order fancy Victorian-style wooden porch brackets and stair balusters, it is often done as a short-cut to make a new home feel established, lived in, and credible. Victorians garnished the exteriors of their eclectic Queen Ann's with elaborately scrolled embellishments, and they shaped the legs and arms of their parlor furniture with curious swells and tapers for a different reason. Those flamboyant flourishes were for them a celebration of technology and economic prosperity that many of us today will never quite understand.

Prior to the Civil War, most citizens lived in extremely modest homes. The front porch was a small, un-roofed but practical stoop. The fireplace was functional, but coarse and simple. Furniture, clothing, and decorative accents throughout the home were mostly homemade and relatively plain. Tastes were simple out of necessity, not choice. The finest designs of the era belonged to the wealthy elite, while the majority lived with what they could get.

The changes in life style that occurred for most Americans between the Civil War and WWI can hardly be overstated. This was the era in which the American middle class finally emerged in force and the culture of consumption established itself as the basis of modern industry. This was also the era of fancy advertising trade cards, which played no small part in the changes that ensued. The craftsmen and carpenters of previous generations were replaced in the 1870s to 1890s by a steam-powered woodworking technology that made earlier approaches and spartan economy of design obsolete. The novelty of intricately milled woodwork swept the nation. In instances where the desired effect was too involved for production-line milling, plaster casting and paint were an economical substitute. Even the smallest of homes were built with front porch embellishments and parlors, tiny as these porches and parlors were sometimes forced to be. (When necessary, the parlor doubled as a master bedroom served by one of the many folding beds found advertised in trade card ads.)

As the popularity of ornate woodwork and exotic interior furnishings increased, those who had the money to "outdo" their neighbors often did so by installing increasingly fancy fences, porch flourishes, staircases, parlor furniture, etc. Americans began importing curiosities for their parlor collections, and the growing demand for Oriental vases and fans inspired new looks in screens, drapes, and carpets. The inevitable reaction against the complexities and accesses of Victorian taste gathered force around the turn-of-the-century, when "progressive" voices urged Americans to adopt more simple, practical, and "scientifically ordered" living environments. The classic Victorian look of domestic clutter came to be viewed as old fashioned, and the era of eclectic flamboyance in American design came to an end.

Pricing Tips & Cards to Watch For

Trade cards with images of furniture and well-furnished rooms command strong prices. Simple stock cards with ads for furniture and home improvement items generally sell in the $10 to $30 range. Color stock cards of good quality, and cards privately issued, run more in the $30 to $75 range. Watch for ads with strong colors and realistic details, as these features command the greatest interest and effect prices dramatically.

Green Room, President's Mansion, $50.00.

Campbell's Varnish Stain, $25.00.

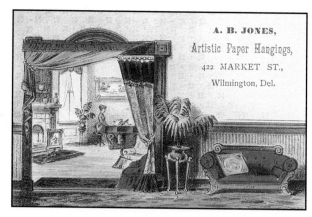

Jones Paper Hangings, stock card, $20.00.

Jones, McDuffee & Stratton, $15.00.

Burger & Co. Fine Furniture, $50.00.

Latimer Carpets & Rugs, stock card, $75.00.

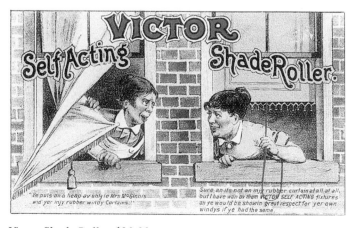

Victor Shade Roller, $20.00.

Carpets, stock card, $25.00.

Mark's Adjustable Chair, $15.00.

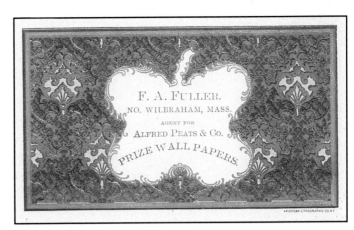

Alfred Peats & Co. Wall Paper, $30.00.

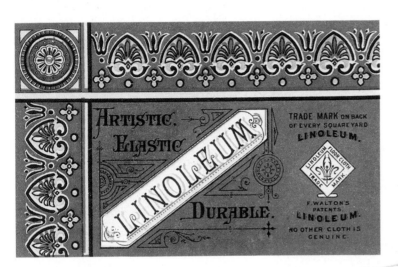

Walton's Linoleum, $20.00.

Hyde Wick Adjuster, $20.00.

Goodman & Bro's, stock card, $20.00.

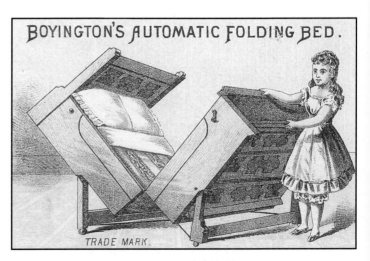

Boyington's Automatic Folding Bed, $30.00.

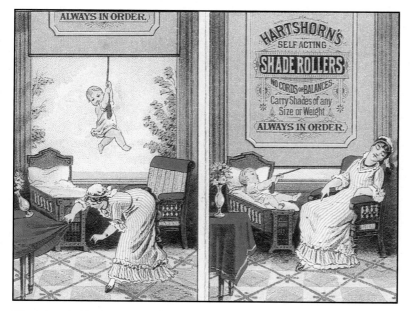

Hartshorn's Shade Rollers, $20.00.

Lustro Silver Polish, $15.00.

L & M Paint, $30.00.

Mauro & Wilson, stock card, $30.00.

National Lead Company House Paint, $30.00.

Bedette Portable Bed, $35.00.

Aromatic Pino-Palmine Mattress, $20.00.

Sanitas Enameled Tiles, $25.00.

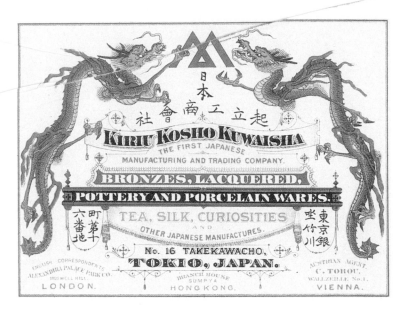

Kiriu Kosho Kuwaisha, $150.00.

Abram French Pottery & fine Art
man works in shop, rev: Wedgwood, Derby, Copeland, etc. **$25.00**

Bay State Carpet Co.
interior view of carpet rolls, store shown on back with ad **$25.00**

Bisel's Revolving Book-Case
2 views, "Lawyers, Physicians, Clergymen," rev. stock card **$10.00**

Brooks Furniture • Carpets • Etc.
Boston, bedroom set, tapestries **$20.00**

Burger & Hand Furniture
circle inset of birds in sky, fine furniture pictured **$20.00**

Fairfield Automatic Lawn Swing
"For Private Lawns, etc.," mother & daughter sit facing **$20.00**

Haida Lamps & Chandeliers
Haida stock card, shows chandelier, Gillmor's imprint **$30.00**

Hale & Kilburn Furniture
"Whoa Charlie," Chariot Chair, 4 other items, rev. stock card **$15.00**

Larkin Soap — Chautauqua Desk
die-cut folder of desk, rev. "Tale: Turks, dark disgrace" **$25.00**

Lueders Reclining & Invalid Chair
"Crown" chair shown on back of stock card "Agents Wanted" **$15.00**

New Home Sewing Machine
"New Home in the Old Home," family, fire in old hearth, dog **$8.00**

Paine's Furniture
child shows folding bed, furnished room, rev. view of bldg. **$30.00**

Rattan Furniture, Wakefield
wicker rocking chair shown in detail **$20.00**

Rob't Johns Portraits & Frames
front signed portrait of Johns; rev. details on frames **$15.00**

Sing Chong Company
dragons on front, rev.: Chinatown, lists imports, wholesale **$10.00**

Stewart Iron Works Fence
die-cut metamorphic, open: big house, new iron fence, 1902 . . . .**$75.00**

Stock Card — furniture imprint
man pulls drape for woman sitting, fireplace, tapestries **$20.00**

Stock Card — Marks Chair
ice fishing & ice boating scene, inset drawing of chair **$10.00**

Stock Card — portrait studio imprint
mother pulls tapestry aside to show dad sleeping girl, dog **$25.00**

Union Web Hammock
woman in hammock outside, book, butterfly, Good Luck shoe **$20.00**

White Sewing Machines
"Decorate your home with...," machine as furniture, fireplace **$10.00**

Kilborn's Health Bath, $40.00.

McArthur, stock card, $35.00.

Hair Products

(See also: Cosmetics & Perfumes; Patent Medicines; Soaps; Women.)

Hair Product Images

Many collectors are fascinated by images of hair and hair products in trade card advertising. As one becomes familiar with the hair fashions and fads of the Victorian period, the way a woman's hair is worn in an ad can even help date the time of the card's issue. Many ads for hair products picture a beautiful woman or girl reclining in a chair and enjoying a good brushing of her long tresses. Men appear less frequently in hair cards, but they do show up in whisker dye ads, and they are alluded to in many of the ads that discuss cures for baldness. The quality of trade cards for hair products tends to be very high, with most of these cards appearing as lovely private issues with a full range of colors and good attention to design. The stock cards that occasionally surface with hair-related advertising are typically imprinted for local "Hair Dressing Rooms" offering baths, haircutting, wavelets, and "Hair Goods of all Kinds."

Historical Notes

Women have long suffered a tension between what is practical and what is fashionable when it comes to hair. During the Victorian period, long hair was still viewed by many as a part of a woman's "glory," and very few men or women could sit comfortably with the thought of a woman cropping her hair. On the other hand, families were often large and demanding, and kitchens were often hot and steamy from washing and cooking chores.

Queen Victoria, the actress Lillian Russell, and nearly all of the wives of the late-Victorian presidents offered by example the chignon solution to the challenge of managing long hair. These women braided their hair and rolled it into a large knot pinned at the back of their heads. The look became fashionable, and the act of "letting down" one's hair at the end of the day became a savored Victorian ritual. The ritual was often completed, in some cases by a maid, through a luxurious 100-stroke brushing and the application of some form of "hair renewer" or "scalp invigorator." President Cleveland's young wife, Frances Folsom (the Lady Di of 1880s), was bold enough to sport a well-trained bang that curled down just above one eyebrow. The look caught on and helped contribute to the growing popularity of curling irons and experimentation in ringlets and Marcel waves throughout the 1890s. Buns continued to work their way up the back of the head until they arrived at the top just in time for the classic pompadour look of the 1900 Gibson Girl.

Pricing Tips & Cards to Watch For

The exceptional quality of so many hair product cards contributes to their popularity and strong prices among collectors. Several companies issued numerous hair cards, all of which are collected with enthusiasm. Watch for cards with ads for Hall's Vegetable Sicilian Hair Renewer, Ayer's Hair Vigor, and Barry's Tricopherous, as these are among the most beautiful, plentiful, and popular. These cards generally run $15 to $30 each. Also keep an eye open for the many Buckingham's Whisker Dye cards, some of which are metamorphics showing a white beard turning black, and others of which are quite scarce and highly collectible. The common whisker dye cards can be found for $15 to $20, but the scarce and rare ones have brought $50 or more in auctions.

Thompson Wave, $20.00.

Ayer's Hair Vigor, $10.00.

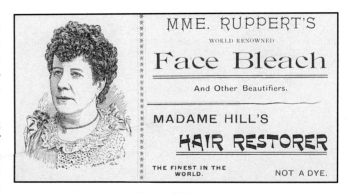

Mme. Ruppert's Face Bleach, $20.00.

Hall's Vegetable Sicilian Hair Renewer, $12.00.

Ayer's Hair Vigor "For the Toilet"
    lovely girl looking to her right and up, pink bow on shoulder **$8.00**

Barry's Tricopherous
    3 women in classical robes, servant offer bottle to mistress **$15.00**

Barry's Tricopherous
    lady reclines in red chair brushing long hair, toilet, bottles **$20.00**

Bell's Buffalo Soap
    "barber looks happy" doing customer, shaving mug, bottles **$8.00**

Buckingham's Whisker Dye
    3 views of bearded man, "Before — after inferior — Finally" **$25.00**

Buckingham's Whisker Dye
    metamorphic — beard changes, white "Before" — dark "After" **$15.00**

Hall's Vegetable Sicilian Hair Renewer
    "My old photograph before..." lady, long hair, mirror, bottle **$12.00**

Hall's Vegetable Sicilian Hair Renewer
    lady in white, butterfly, field, trees, distant water, fence **$12.00**

Hall's Vegetable Sicilian Hair Renewer
    5 "attractive faces" from around world in ethnic garb **$25.00**

Hall's Vegetable Sicilian Hair Renewer
    girl with big bottle, "Saved Papa's Hair from turning gray..." **$20.00**

Henry Loftie — Fine Human Hair
    portrait of Mrs. Grover Cleveland, bangs, rev. wig prices **$20.00**

Hill's Hair & Whisker Dye
    man comb's formula into beard in front of mirror, bottle **$35.00**

Lyon's Kathairon for the Hair
    2 views: lady combs, bottle/bald man pours bottle into hand **$25.00**

Mansfield's Capillaris — stock card
    girl, fancy hat, "a positive cure" for baldness, dandruff, etc. **$6.00**

Murray & Lanman's Florida Water
    maid combs woman's long hair, bottle on table, fountain **$20.00**

Packer's All-Healing Tar Soap
    "What will he do?," back of bald head, "shampoo with..." **$20.00**

Parker's Hair Balsam
    blonde young woman, blue bow, "Restores youthful color" **$8.00**

Parker's Hair Balsam
    2 bald men, 2 bald women, begging "queen" for product **$15.00**

Carboline, $25.00.

Ayer's Hair Vigor, $20.00.

Magnetic Hair Pins, $60.00.

Barry's Tricopherous, $15.00.

Holidays & Santa Claus

(See also: Brownies & Elves; Cupids & Cherubs; Patriotic; Toys.)

Holiday Images

Scenes of Santa Claus and Christmas are extremely popular in trade cards, but other delightful holiday symbols and images are also highly prized. Easter is second to Christmas in frequency of appearance, followed by numerous images and references to the Fourth of July and New Year's. Other holidays that make appearances, but far less often, include Washington's Birthday, Valentine's Day, Decoration Day, April Fool's Day, May Day, Thanksgiving, and possibly Halloween. Christmas and Easter account for perhaps 80% of the holiday images found in trade cards.

Santa Claus is depicted in most of the Christmas images, but his wardrobe varies from blues and browns to reds and greens. Numerous cards combine holidays in "Season's Greetings" themes, some of which include depictions of Father Time as a symbol of the New Year. Easter images usually feature colored eggs and bunnies, but scenes of crosses, angels, and church choirs can be found. Direct references to Halloween are almost unheard of in trade cards, but several cards were issued with depictions of witches that look and feel a lot like the Halloween images that later emerged in turn-of-the-century post cards. The quality of the holiday coffee sets distributed by Woolson Spice and McLaughlin's is high; beyond those, holiday cards vary widely in quality. Most non-coffee holiday illustrations were produced as stock cards that were imprinted by local stores for seasonal promotions.

Historical Notes

When the *New York Sun* ran its famous "Yes, Virginia, there is a Santa Claus" editorial in 1897, merchants throughout the city undoubtedly smiled in relief, knowing that the old man had just squeaked through an important test. Santa had become for Americans more than a symbol of the joy and mystery of things "which neither children nor men can see," as Francis P. Church had so eloquently put it in his response to Virginia O'Hanlon's letter. Santa had also become a symbol for lavish spending and the harbinger of the holiday jingle of ringing cash registers.

Advertising trade cards with holiday-related themes document the commercialization of the American calendar. Partly through the prodding and hype of these cards, religious and national holidays evolved during the trade card era from days of special family and community observances to protracted seasons of extravagant spending. Christmas trade cards with images of Jesus in a lowly manger do not exist; cards with images of a jovial St. Nick loaded with store-bought goodies are legion. Images of an Easter cross are rare; illustrations of fat bunnies and huge eggs imprinted for Easter sales abound. American flags and patriotic symbols are sprinkled through many of these images, lest there be any confusion about the legitimacy of good citizens preparing for their holidays by hunting down fashionable gloves, sweet candies, fringed cards, imported coffees, and wrought-iron doll carriages. Holiday spending had become, after all, a national tradition.

The evolution of Santa Claus himself is also recorded in advertising trade cards. In cards from the 1870s and 1880s, Santa is shown in green or blue suits more often than in red ones. He sometimes wears a blue coat with a red hat, or other times a red coat with green pants. Sometimes he wears a long stocking cap with a tassel at the end, other times he's in a brown cap or hood. Generally speaking, the more familiar the Santa looks, the newer the card.

Pricing Tips & Cards to Watch For

Stock cards with imprints for holiday goods and sales, but with non-holiday images, experience little special demand and typically sell in the $5 to $10 range. Stock cards with illustrations that clearly relate to specific holidays bring more, depending upon the holiday and the quality of the image. Christmas stock cards, especially with Santa scenes, bring the highest prices. Stock cards with Santas often sell for $15 to $25, or occasionally more for exceptional or rare examples. Privately issued cards with Santas run more in the $20 to $50 range. Over-sized holiday cards distributed in sets by the coffee companies typically sell for around $15, but they can bring more if the image is particularly compelling. Holiday stock cards with patriotic images are growing in popularity, and many of them now bring $15 or more. As always, watch for cards with a full range of bright colors and well-developed designs, as these are the quickest to sell. Keep an eye open for the rare "Child's Dream" metamorphic card that opens to a Santa, as it is now selling in the $150 range.

Goshen Sweeper, Grand Rapids, $30.00.

C. P. Forbes Jeweler, stock card, $8.00.

J & P Coats Thread, $8.00.

Union Pacific Tea, $6.00.

Leader Flour, stock card, $8.00.

The "Fair," stock card, $8.00.

Goshen Sweeper, Grand Rapids, $20.00.

Woolson Spice Co., $12.00.

Bismarck Range, stock card, $20.00.

Compliments of the Season, stock card, $15.00.

Independence Day, stock card, $10.00.

Joseph Forgette, stock card, $10.00.

Paas Egg Dyes, $15.00.

Clarence Brooks Varnishes, $20.00.

Easter Gloves, stock card, $4.00.

Atmore's Mince Meat
Santa in brown suit stuffs food from basket down chimney **$15.00**

Birthday stock card — coffee store
"Happy May Thy Birthday Be" boy, snow, dog, old man, fire **$5.00**

Christmas Day stock card — #2 of 5
"9 o'clock" family at tree, piano, toys "Union Pacific Tea" **$10.00**

Fearless Cook Stove
"Merry Christmas" over doorway, Black cook with turkey **$40.00**

Mandel Bro's — Holiday Gifts
girl, bonnet, purse with "MB" monogram "Happy New Year" **$8.00**

Santa stock card — "Ticket Agent"
"The Arrival," blue Santa, arm down chimney, bag, toys **$10.00**

Santa stock card — "Zinn stores"
blue Santa, sled, dropping gifts down chimney, church steeple **$8.00**

Santa — "A Christmas Box" stock card
metamorphic "Where's Santa Claus?" opens to Santa, toys **$75.00**

Santa — Ehrics' Scrap Book
metamorphic "Child's Dream" girl in bed: Santa, toys 1882 . . . .**$150.00**

Valentines stock card — card store
"Valentines, Wholesale & Retail" large feather, 1878 . . . .**$5.00**

Washington's Birthday — stock card
"Doing the patriotic," monkey reads Declaration, 2 kids sleep **$8.00**

Woolson Spice Co. — Lion Coffee
"The Christmas Party" boy takes girl's hand, tree, 1893 . . . .**$12.00**

Woolson Spice Co. — Lion Coffee
barefoot boy, glasses, instructs bunnies, eggs in hat 1893 . . . .**$12.00**

Dilworth's Coffee, $6.00.

Children's Valentines, stock card, $8.00.

Santa Claus Soap, $60.00.

Kerr's Thread, $20.00.

Paper Hangings, stock card, $8.00.

Horses

(See also: Animals; Cows; Farm; Transportation.)

Horse Images

Delightful images of horses are popular and plentiful in trade card advertising. Some collectors search for cards with champion race horses that are named (with the horse's record time often listed below). Other collectors focus on Currier & Ives trade cards with identified champions or with scenes from the Currier & Ives "Horse Comics" series. Farm and agricultural collectors often show a preference for illustrations of horses pulling implements. Patent medicine collectors hunt for horse cards with medicinal advertising, while animal lovers frequently enjoy quiet scenes of healthy horses in the pampered company of adoring children. Because horses can show up incidentally in ads for every product imaginable, the color and quality of horse images varies widely.

Historical Notes

Few people today can imagine how important horses once were in the everyday lives of Americans. The role of horses as draft animals is recorded in farm-related trade cards depicting proud, strong horses pulling equipment and wagons in fields and on roads. Horses were also important for commercial and private transportation. There was a great deal of pride and pleasure to be found in hitching up a good horse for trot down a beautiful riverside path or a high-stepping promenade down main street. Trade card advertisements indicate that those who did not own their own roadsters could rent a horse and buggy from local liveries for around $2 an afternoon.

Horses also provided a major form of Victorian entertainment. Steeple chases came naturally to those who lived in wooded farm lands, but harness racing was even more popular in America. Competitive trotting has its roots in "brushing matches." Brushes occurred when drivers encountered each other in wagons or carriages, then cracked their whips to see who could reach a specified intersection or landmark the fastest. Young men were known on occasion to "lay back for a brush" (slow down) along favorite stretches of roads, hoping for suckers against which to test their spirited horses. Assisted by the mass-produced prints of Currier & Ives, harness racing grew into one of Victorian America's most powerful and romantic symbols of prosperity and good times.

Thoroughbred racing evolved in America from the days of Indian horses and cowponies, which were once saddled up to run against farm horses and quarter horses in flat-out dashes for prize money. Thoroughbreds eventually became more common, and the breed improved, until they dominated all such competitions. Driven largely by gambling interests, thoroughbred races were shortened so more heats could be run in an afternoon. To level the field for competitive betting, races were broken down by age groups, number of previous wins, best times, etc.

The entertainment and excitement of horse racing, as well as the chance races afforded to get out, dress up, show off, and smoke expensive cigars in public, all insured the popularity and profitability of race tracks. By the turn of the century, horse racing had become so popular that fairground races became regular features at nearly every county seat in the country. It is small wonder that so many trade cards with racing images were produced.

Pricing Tips & Cards to Watch For

Privately issued trade cards with horse images tend to be a little on the expensive side, partially because these cards are often of above average quality, and partially because they often advertise products that experience above average demand. Cheaply made stock cards, soap cards, and thread cards with illustrations of horses rarely bring over $10, but the best of these cards can sometimes run much more. Watch for the stock cards that feature named champions, as these will run $15 to $25, and occasionally more. The Currier & Ives "Horse Comic" stock cards typically bring $35 to $75, while their champion racer cards bring more like $50 to $100. Cards advertising horse remedies usually sell for $15 to $30, but keep an eye open for the Dr. Haas' cards, which can bring $75 and up.

Prof. Bristol's 30 Educated Horses, $50.00.

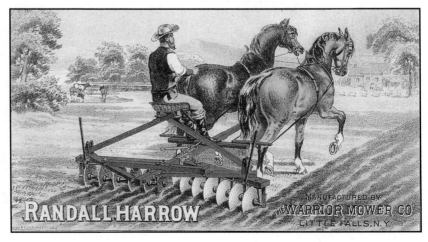

Randall Harrow, $30.00.

Ayers Hair Vigor
2 dogs, girl with long hair down feeds apple to horse $10.00

B.T. Babbitt's Soap
"First in the Race," girl sits sidesaddle on pony, soap box $20.00

Central City Road Cart
brown horse in blinders stands in front of cart & driver $50.00

Currier & Ives stock card
"Blood Will Tell," horse races against a train, 1879 ....$50.00

Currier & Ives stock card
"A Crack Trotter Between Heats," trainer forces gin, 1880 ....$50.00

Derby Smoking Tobacco
spectators at the Derby, horses getting ready to race $75.00

Dr. Haas' Horse & Cattle Remedies
"To the rescue," sick horses on left, 5 healthy on right, 1883 ....$80.00

Eclipse Halter
"Happy Medium Sire," stallion stands, halter, yellow blanket $35.00

Eureka Harness Oil
"Robert J., 2:01½, The World's Champion Pacer" horse $20.00

Gombault's Caustic Balsam
"The Monk," trotter going left, small pneumatic tires on sulky $20.00

Mellin's Food for Infants
"The Country Doctor," 2 people in sleigh, horse, moon, 1900 ....$15.00

Merchant's Gargling Oil
Arabian scene, white horse, 2 men apply medicine, tents $15.00

Pierces's Coach Colors
4-horse loaded stage coach stops for mule & wagon $15.00

Pond's Extract
child on Shetland pony, St. Bernard dog, basket, medicine $20.00

Stock Card — "Putnam Nail"
"Buffalo Girl" trotting right, big wheels on sulky, 1883 ....$20.00

Stock Card — clothing imprint
"A Brush on the Brighton Road," teams race in sleighs $5.00

Stock Card — harness imprint
"Maud S. and Jay Eye See," trotters racing $20.00

William Deering Draft Binder
broken-down horse talks to farmer about Deering binder $15.00

Prof. D. M. Bristol's Horses, $50.00.

Spooner Patent Horse Collars, $50.00.

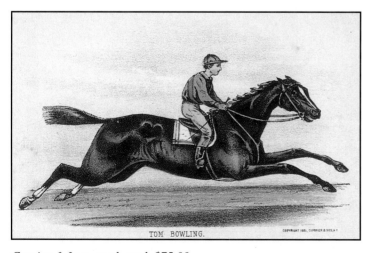

Currier & Ives, stock card, $75.00.

Arbuckle Coffe, #65 of 100, $20.00.

Hotels, Resorts & Seashore

(See also: Exploration & Travel; Transportation.)

Hotel, Resorts & Seashore Images

Trade cards with images and advertising relating to hotels, resorts, and the seashore vary widely in terms of quality and historical significance. On one end are the numerous stock cards with cute or comical beach scenes. Many of these cards capture the spirit of a day excursion from the city or of an extended stay at one of the popular Victorian seashore or lake-side resorts. Some of these images include an illustration of an identifiable pier, boardwalk, or hotel. The best of these cards have good images and are imprinted for specific resort services like boat rentals, excursion transportation, or resort-area dinning. As usual, the quality of these stock cards ranges from very poor to very nice.

On the other end are the scarce and highly-prized private issue cards with detailed (although sometimes exaggerated) illustrations of specific hotels, resorts, or famous retreats. These cards are in a unique class because so many of them were produced as "line drawings," and often copper- or steel-plate engravings. Engraved cards were almost always produced on white stock with black printing, so some collectors show less interest in them, holding that these black and white cards are "bland" compared to the best full-color cards produced by the chromolithographic process. Other collectors cherish engraved cards, noting the special craftsmanship involved in producing beautiful images using only one color and working with metal plates. However judged, engraved hotel cards are in high demand, and they typically bring very strong prices.

Historical Notes

The middle-class Victorian vacation often included travel and extended stays at hotels and resorts. During the closing decades of the Victorian era, an estimated 200,000 Americans vacationed in Europe each year, with Mark Twain's *The Innocents Abroad* serving as a humorous travel guide for those who could not visit, gawk, and embarrass themselves in other people's lands first hand. For those who yearned for invigorating mountain air, the Rocky Mountains provided an affordable alternative to the Alps. Several hotels in the Colorado Springs area offered European-style resort luxury, Pullman railroad car access, and "curative" mineral waters that could be bathed in or consumed. Older "watering holes" like Saratoga Springs also prospered during this period, especially through the addition of new attractions like horse racing, bicycle paths, arcades, and zoos.

Seashore resorts, however, remained the most popular choice for those eager for a break from the city. Coney Island and Atlantic City were the favorites of New York and New Jersey residents planning day excursions, while destinations like Cape May and Ocean Grove were often preferred by those who had the time and money to relax for longer retreats. Other regions offered their own water-side resorts. Cedar Point was a favorite day-excursion destination for residents of Toledo, Akron, and Cleveland, and Michigan's Grand Hotel on Mackinac Island offered the wealthy elite of Chicago and Detroit a hotel resort that was ranked as one of the finest in the world. The Coronado Hotel in San Diego and the Seal Rocks area of Northern California helped service the West Coast in style, and Henry Morrison Flagler's chain of resorts from St. Augustine to Palm Beach offered service in the South.

Pricing Tips & Cards to Watch For

Stock cards with generic beach scenes seldom bring over $5 unless the imprint is of special interest or the image is of exceptional quality. Many of the cards with beach scenes were issued in delightful sets that are fun and affordable to complete. Stock cards with good imprints for resort services or attractions typically bring $5 to $15. Cards with named hotels and resorts bring $20 and up, depending upon the card's scarcity, the history of the hotel, and collector interest in the specific region. As a general rule, $30 to $50 is the average range for the engraved hotel cards. Cards for European hotels are not necessarily more or less valuable than ones for American hotels, even when the imprint is in a foreign language.

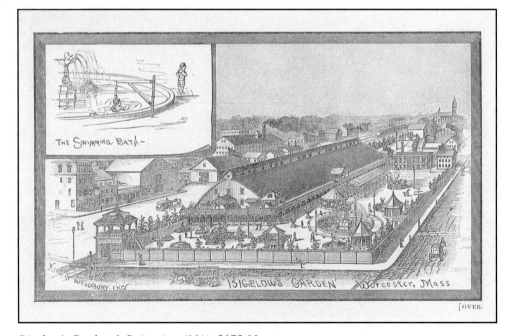

Bigelow's Garden & Swimming (MA), $175.00.

Clark's Thread
"Moonlight Coney Island," large card, quiet beach, moon $10.00

Clark's Thread
"Seal Rocks — near San Francisco" large card, resort on bluff $10.00

Fort Lee Park Hotel & Pavilion (NY)
looking at hotel over water, rev.: resort attractions listed $75.00

Grand Union Hotel (NY City)
"Opposite Grand Central Depot," red buildings, flags, bridge $30.00

Hôtel Schwanen Lucerne (Switz.)
busy lake scene, tall hotel, busy street, mountains $20.00

Maizena — National Starch Co. of NY
Atlantic City, NJ, boardwalk view, beach, hotels, 1901 . . . .$150.00

Manhattan Beach, Coney Isl. Steamers
"Bathing by Electric Light," night swimmers crowd beach $50.00

Melville Garden, Downer Landing (MA)
sky view of beach, boats, resort, rev.: list of attractions $30.00

Mont Alto Park Picnic Ground (PA.)
"Fiddlers Green can be engaged... through R.R. Agents." $25.00

Pabst Whitefish Bay Resort (Wis.)
lake Mich. resort photo, steps down to shore, tel. "Toll 1." $30.00

Palmer House (Chicago)
engraving of huge hotel, flag, busy street, rates on rev. $30.00

Rob Roy Hotel, Queenstown (Ireland)
engraving of large hotel, rev.: "Water Baths... tel. No. 27" $30.00

Rockaway Beach Excursions — steamers
"Children who stay," sick child/"who go...," healthy, in water $40.00

Saratoga Spgs — Grand Union Hotel (NY)
detailed engraving of hotel, horses, "largest Hotel in world" $50.00

Starin's Glen Island, Long Island (NY)
"A Day Summer Resort," women, child swimming $30.00

Stock Card — "Atlantic City Excursions"
man runs to catch train, dog, "Off to the Sea-Shore" $8.00

Stock Card — "Boats to let by..." (MA)
couple on beach, ship, lobster, birds "Near the Warf." $5.00

Stock Card — "Chosen Friends" (NJ)
4 kids in waves, "3rd Annual Excursion" $1.00, 1883 . . . .$10.00

Stock Card — "Robinson House" (Pitts.)
"Terms Reasonable — In sight of Exposition Building," bird $5.00

Stock Card — "Sea Foam House" (MA)
girl spills clam chowder on couple's head, "Dinners — fish etc." $8.00

West Brighton Beach Hotel (Coney Isl.)
crowded beach scene, busy hotel, many flags $60.00

Windsor Hotel — Bush & Tabor (Colo.)
engraving of large Denver hotel, busy street, 3 flags $40.00

Arrowhead Hot Springs (CA), die-cut, $50.00.

White's Rockaway Beach Excursions, $30.00.

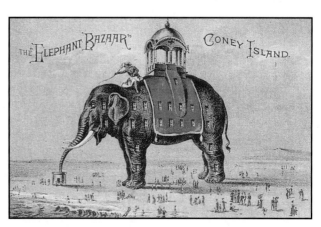

Ryan & Devaney Tin Roofers (NY), $60.00.

Humor

(See also: Metamorphics; Vegetable People & Whimsical.)

Humor Images

A good many Victorian trade cards used an element of humor as part of their design. Trade card humor typically relied upon such conventions as:

•Slapstick (e.g. a man slipping on a bar of soap),

•Satirical substitution (e.g. a spider using Merrick Thread for a web),

•Ethnic bashing (e.g. a Black man caught stealing chickens),

•Puns and riddles (e.g. a man hugs his moonshine apparatus and sighs, "I love thee still"),

•Novelty surprises (e.g. a flap opens and turns a sexy lady into a man),

•Exaggeration (e.g. a melon so big that it takes eight people to lift it),

•Literary satire (e.g. a pig misquoting Shakespeare),

•Whimsy (e.g. elves unloading gifts from a Montgomery Ward catalog),

•Innocent antics (e.g. a child accidentally spilling a sack of flour),

•Mischievous antics (e.g. naughty boys tying firecrackers to a cat's tail),

•Anthropomorphic antics (e.g. an elephant imitating Oscar Wilde), and

•Product complications (e.g. a man caught loitering because his pants became stuck in spilled glue).

The quality of these images varies, but it is often true that the more obvious the humor is in the ad, the lower the quality of the card's color and design. Thousands of stock cards were produced by local printers who worked up humorous images using limited resources, hoping that what their cards lacked in artistic sophistication was compensated for by the chuckles their humor evoked.

Historical Notes

If beauty is in the eyes of the beholder, trade card humor definitely is. Although some trade cards appear as funny today as they seemed to consumers a century ago, other cards are confusing to modern collectors, if not downright distasteful. Humor is a matter of both personal taste and cultural perspective, both of which come into play when examining humor in nineteenth century advertising. This is especially true of trade cards with negative stereotypes of ethnic groups, as these cards were once enthusiastically received but are now so embarrassing that some collectors are ashamed to even own them.

Fortunately, most of the humor in trade cards is not tied to ethnic put-downs. One also finds some very clever work done in trade cards with puns, riddles, satire, sight gags, exaggeration, the battle of the sexes, childhood mischief, and the like. The cards that used puns, riddles, and satire are probably the hardest to understand today, as many of these jokes rely on Victorian "inside information" that few of us today have had access to. It is not uncommon to see collectors gather around a given card at a show, pointing and speculating as to what the card could possibly mean.

For example, there are at least a dozen different stock cards with the gag where someone jumps up from a seat a says, "I never saw that Pin-afore." For modern collectors who have never heard of Gilbert & Sullivan's operetta, *HMS Pinafore*, these cards are completely baffling. Or for those who are unfamiliar with Oscar Wilde's American tour, the aesthetic craze, and Gilbert & Sullivan's satirical response in *Patience*, the dozens of cards with sunflower images, crooning men, swooning women, and sappy philosophical lines make no sense at all.

Pricing Tips & Cards to Watch For

Trade card humor is not collected widely as a genre in and of itself, so there has yet to develop any special demand for comical cards. Cheaply done stock cards with black and white illustrations rarely bring over $5, regardless of how funny the joke is. The cards to watch for are those with references to political, historical, and theatrical events. Cards that spoof historical figures like Vanderbilt and Gould are rapidly growing in popularity, as are cards with links to Gilbert & Sullivan productions. These cards can sometimes bring $15 or more based upon such references. The Arbuckle Coffee "Illustrated Jokes" series of 100 cards is also gaining favor, with many of these cards now bringing $10 to $20 from those who are trying to complete the set.

Le Page's Glue, $15.00.

Alden Fruit Vinegar — stock card
    Black man teeters on top of ladder, dogs fighting, apples fall $40.00

Alvin Joslin & His Little Chestnut Bell
    theatrical: "How do you do?"/Alvin: "All alive...Ting-a-ling" $15.00

Atkinson's Comedy Co. Peck's Bad Boy
    "Bring Fourth the Royal Bumper," goat targets man's rump $10.00

Boss Watch Cases — Jeweler
    "He stooped to conquer," naughty boy to pull string on watch $8.00

Burdock Blood Bitters — stock card
    cute child in military garb, big sword, hat down to nose $8.00

Dalley's Magical Pain Extractor
    stock card — girl rides sidesaddle on dragonfly over reeds $5.00

Fairbank's Soaps
    soap on stairway/man steps on soap & slips, hat falls off $8.00

Le Page's Glue
    cops pull man glued to seat in train station, 2 kids watch $20.00

Mitchell's Plasters — stock card
    "Yes Hubby I recognize...," wife on phone/monkey other end $8.00

Pearline Soap
    "Golly! Ib'leve Pearline make dat chile white," mom scrubs $20.00

Prudential Insurance
    "Far Reachin, Comprehensive, Solid," skinny man, 2 fat men $8.00

Stock Card
    "Buzz Saw Has an Off-Hand Way," man's hand gets cut off $5.00

Stock Card — "Great American Tea Co."
    boy jumps up holding rump: "I never saw that Pin-afore." $5.00

Stock Card — "Leopold Strauss"
    "Ingenious Mother," cow rocks cradle by swishing tail, string $5.00

Western Humor — 10 Designs
    "Take care of that Sidewalk Mr.," boys on sled, man falls $5.00

Willimantic Thread
    "People's Favorite Hobby," jockey rides spool horse on track $8.00

Wilson's Reliable Yeast
    "sudden raising?," man flies up from chair, sat on yeast box $15.00

Wells' Rough on Corns Cure, $25.00.

Eagle Brand Liquid Fish Glue, $30.00.

Arbuckle Coffee, $15.00.

Insurance

(See also: Transportation.)

Insurance Images

Many of the insurance trade cards issued after 1890 were stock cards with wonderful color images of children, pets, and quiet landscapes. The biggest users of these cards were Metropolitan Life, John Hancock, Home Insurance of New York, and Prudential. Insurance cards from before the 1890s tend to be different than these later, mass-distributed cards. With the exception of some common, low-budget calendar cards distributed by the Home Insurance Company around 1879, most early insurance cards were privately issued. They were frequently produced as engraved cards, and they were apparently passed out more judiciously than the later cards, as many of them are quite scarce. The most common graphics found on pre-1890 cards are of the company's logo or home office building, scenes of fires or accidents, and views of ships and trains. Because the impression of integrity is critical in the insurance business, the quality of these graphics is usually quite high. Cards with comical illustrations are almost nonexistent in insurance cards.

Historical Notes

Insurance companies played a larger role in America's economic expansion than many people realize. John Copson established the first marine and fire insurance company in the colonies in 1721, and other companies offering a wider range of coverage followed. Monarchies could sponsor enormous projects and afford to lose a few ships along the way, but if a private citizen lost a ship, the disaster usually resulted in bankruptcy. Insurance companies spread the risks and losses of catastrophes so widely that some people who would never have had the courage to invest suddenly found that many projects were suddenly worth considering. Backed by insurance policies, shipping ventures and construction projects became realistic investments for more and more citizens, and in this way wealth grew and society reaped the benefits of increased imports, exports, and economic expansion at home. By the time of the trade card era, insurance had become so much a part of the investment equation that few businessmen would consider tackling any major project without first checking into coverage against losses.

As the American economy grew, the value of property and capital held by average citizens increased dramatically. Middle-class Victorians began to realize, partially through the careful instruction of trade-card-wielding insurance agents, that they, too, should own policies to protect their assets and provide for their families in case of accidents or death. Most people could not afford full insurance coverage for every area of their lives, but they were willing to take out special policies or enter into special group "relief fund" agreements.

The back of one Travelers Insurance Company trade card bragged that they offered "The Best Insurance Ticket for Visitors to the Columbian Exposition," and that this special 1893 policy would "cover not only the accidents of travel, but also the many dangers on the streets and in the Exposition Grounds." The Standard Accident Insurance Co. of Detroit issued a trade card listing competitive rates for "Injuries Received in Wreck of Railway Car," but the card's fine print qualified: "Women Insured Against Death Only." Injuries sustained by women were apparently viewed as only inconveniences. For members of the working class, local lodges, temples, clans, castles, or fraternal orders often provided the only coverage for sickness and death that they would ever have, and it was partially for such coverage that some men joined these groups. The back of a colorful trade card issued by "The Maccabees" stresses the death and accident benefits of membership and ads: "Cares for its helpless and destitute members through an ample Relief Fund."

Pricing Tips & Cards to Watch For

The many stock cards that were issued by insurance companies, while often lovely, experience very little special demand and can often be purchased for under $10. Privately issued insurance cards are in much greater demand, and usually sell for $15 and up. Watch for early engraved cards with good graphics or designs that include illustrations of home offices or fires, as these can sometimes bring $30 or more.

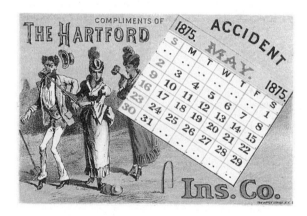

Hartford Accident Ins. Co., $75.00.

Jones Life, Fire, Accident Insurance, $125.00.

Fidelity & Casualty Co. of N.Y.
"Insures Against Accident," 3 views of wheelman, bike crash $30.00

Fidelity & Casualty Co. of N.Y.
19 tiny views of accidents, gun, fire, bike, train, ship, etc. $25.00

Insurance Co. of North America
black & white engraving of home office, 1883 ....$50.00

John Hancock — stock card
girl in snowflakes with hat & muff, rev. claims $6.00

Manufacturer's Fire & Marine Ins. Co.
2 sailing ships in dark stormy sea, Boston $40.00

Metropolitan Life Insurance
boy in red, white & blue, big hat, American flag $6.00

Phenix Insurance
die-cut of fireman coming over wall with hose, double sided $20.00

Prudential Insurance
boy doodling chalk art/ad on fence, girl, doll on grass $10.00

Prudential Insurance
hold-to-light, ship, logo rock, light: "Strength of Gibralter" $30.00

Prudential Insurance
salesman calls on woman at door, children, dog $8.00

Standard Accident Insurance, Detroit
"Send 1 Home," 2 views: train/family, women not covered $50.00

Sun Fire Office, New York Branch
folder, sun logo, complex design of circles, lines $25.00

Traveler's Insurance
"Columbian Exposition 1893," Columbus, Expo skyview, ship $35.00

United Sates Mutual Accident Assoc.
views of 9 types of ships: Brigantine, Bark, Schooner, etc. $20.00

Watertown Fire Insurance Company
complex design, view of huge burning house, 1881 ....$50.00

Travelers Insurance, $40.00.

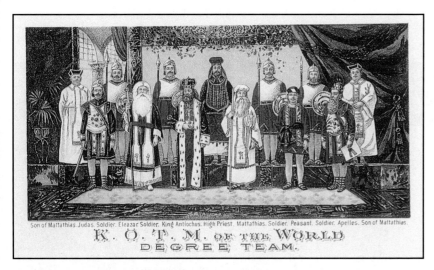

Maccabees — "K.O.T.M. of the World," $50.00.

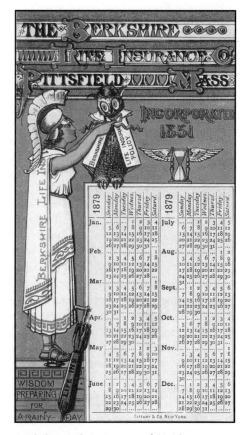

Berkshire Life Insurance, $40.00.

Jewelry, Clocks & Watches

(See also: Clothing & Dry Goods.)

Jewelry, Clock & Watch Images

There are a remarkable number of trade cards with images and advertising for jewelry stores, watches, and watch cases. Most of these cards are of two types. The first type includes the inexpensive stock cards that were typically purchased in quantities of 100 to 1,000 and then imprinted with local jewelry store advertising. In some cases these stock images fit the advertising, as with the common gilded cards showing people in front of enormous jewels, jewelry, or watches. But more often than not, the images on these cards are unrelated to the imprints. The second type of card common in this category was distributed by watch companies. The back of one Waterbury trade card outlines the basic program: "These Cards will be sent free of cost in lots of 525, to any Recognized Retail Watch Dealer desiring the same.... There will be no printed matter upon the backs — the entire space being left for each dealer to utilize as may be desired."

Besides the Waterbury sets, there were dozens of other cards issued by Keystone and Boss' Watch-Case. Because these cards were "private designs" commissioned by nationally recognized watch companies, yet were distributed specifically for local store imprinting, there is some debate as to whether they qualify as stock cards or private issues. Either way, finding them all offers a special challenge in collecting.

Historical Notes

The days of "rising with the sun and bedding with the moon" came to a hurried end as trains and factories worked their way into the American landscape. Prior to the inauguration of "Standard Railway Time" in 1883, communities were left to set their own clocks. The easiest approach was to wait for the sun to come directly overhead, and then to set the time at 12:00 noon. The entire community could check the local clock tower (or listen for factory whistles or military guns) to see how their time was going. Jewelers often displayed clocks in their front windows to assist those who might be checking their pocket pieces as they wandered by.

The trouble was that when it was noon in one town, it was only 11:48 AM in the next; and if one was traveling by train and had just set one's watch at the previous town, it was already 12:07 PM. There was some resistance to Standard Railway Time, especially in rural states where farming families lived closer to "God's Time" and continued to rise with the sun and work according to the demands of the season. In the end, states like Ohio and Georgia gave in after "Standard Time" became federal law.

Pricing Tips & Cards to Watch For

Collector demand for stock cards with local imprints for stores dealing in jewelry, clocks, and watches is limited mostly to collectors and historians searching for local and regional artifacts.

These cards seldom bring over $5 unless the card is extraordinary. Cards designed with watch images and distributed by national manufacturers like Waterbury, Keystone, Crown, and Boss generally sell for $8 to $20. Because so many different images were used by these companies, some of these cards happen to have topical appeal as well as their appeal as watch cards from interesting sets. Watch for cards like the ones issued by Boss dealing with "Base Ball Games" and "Pugilistic Tussle" (boxing), as these are becoming popular with sports collectors and can bring double the normal Boss price or more. Also keep an eye open for truly scarce jewelry, clock, and watch cards that were not issued in huge quantities for local imprinting. These cards are viewed by collectors quite differently than the cards discussed at length above, and they can rarely be found for under $20 when offered for sale.

Engle Clock, "8th Wonder," $15.00.

Ingersoll American Watches, Yankee, $50.00.

Acme Lever Collar & Cuff Button
  naked child picks through jewelry box, large cuff link $25.00

Aurora Watch Co.
  woman, straw hat, leans on fence, watch to ear "Tick! Tick!" $20.00

Birthstone stock card
  12 birthstone rings, baby in center circle, 1909 ....$15.00

Boss' Pat. Watch-Cases
  "Troubadour" courts woman, case as instrument, poem $8.00

Boss' Pat. Watch-Cases
  "Our Special Artist," man paints ad on easel, poem $8.00

Boss' Pat. Watch-Cases
  "Pugilistic Tussle," boxer uses case as punching bag, poem $12.00

Crown Filled Watch Case
  balloon lifts man riding in watch-case basket $8.00

Illinois Watch Factories
  2-sided card, looks like envelope ripped open, watch parts $10.00

Non-Pull-Out Ring (Keystone)
  "airground," pickpocket caught trying to steal watch, fight $30.00

Non-Pull-Out Ring (Keystone)
  woman snags watch on branches, case holds $25.00

Peep O' Day Alarm Clock (Ansonia)
  metamorphic, man happy with new alarm clock, sunrise $25.00

Seth Thomas Watch
  "On Time" person holds glowing watch in dark, train arrives $25.00

Stock Card — jeweler imprint
  boy in hat looks at huge jewels $5.00

The Dueber Watch Case
  train leaves man on track as train pulls out, watch blamed $30.00

Waterbury Watches
  "I'm all right...," man with beard, "Ma" leans on his shoulder $12.00

Waterbury Watches
  "Three little maids from school" — Mikado, Gilbert & Sullivan $12.00

Waterbury Watches
  old man, 2 young ladies, Ladies watch only $4, "off easy" $15.00

Waterbury Watches
  2 men, lady, paper, "J for Jack; L for Laura; E for Eddie" $20.00

Waterbury Watches, $25.00.

Boss Pat. Watch Cases, $8.00.

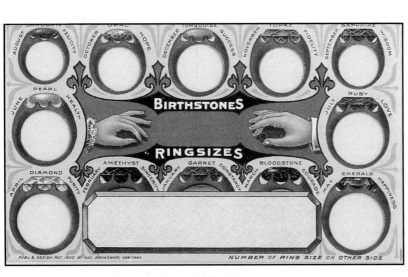

Birthstones & Ring Sizes, stock card, $12.00.

Waterbury Watches, $25.00.

Kitchen

(See also: Enterprise; Food; Soaps; Stoves.)

Kitchen Images

Interest in trade cards with kitchen-related advertising and images is strong. The "Country Living" and "Victoriana" movements have fueled demand for authentic items capturing the nostalgic charm of nineteenth century living, and few artifacts capture that charm like images from early kitchens. Trade cards in this category include all cards with advertisements for kitchen products and others promoting products that are shown in kitchen settings. The cards in the highest demand tend to be those with illustrations of granite ware and those advertising meat choppers, jelly presses, coffee mills, and similar food processing equipment. Some of the best images of kitchen scenes are found in ads for soaps, cooking ranges, and food. Trade cards with ads for china, silverware, tea sets, icebox refrigerators, water coolers, ice cream freezers, etc. can also be included in this grouping. Stock cards are relatively scarce in this category, and the quality of the privately issued cards tends to be slightly above average.

Historical Notes

The enormous kitchen hearths of colonial days, with their many trammels, pot crooks, lugpoles, pots, and kettles, gave way during the industrial revolution to heavy iron ovens and cooking ranges. The new coal-burning ovens and ranges did a better job of containing heat and directing energy to specific tasks like boiling water, warming sad irons, and heating canned meat. Such efficiency was especially important in the densely-populated urban centers that emerged during the late-Victorian period, as residents of these regions could never hope to procure enough wood to keep the old style of kitchens in service. Victorian kitchens moved into smaller quarters at the back of the house and were separated from living spaces once heating stoves and furnaces had been improved and the cooking hearth was no longer needed for warmth in the winter season.

In the post-Civil War boom of the late 1860s and early 1870s, Harriet Beecher Stowe (author of *Uncle Tom's Cabin*) and Catherine E. Beecher elevated Victorian kitchen engineering to a new plateau. They together launched *The American Women's Home*, which espoused a new view of kitchens that included better lighting, efficient storage space, and new arrangements of cooking ranges and equipment. New models of ovens and ranges evolved simultaneously with increasingly practical designs in pots, pans, and granite ware vessels. Ice box "refrigerators" and ice delivery to special chutes located near the back porch became commonplace during the trade card era in most major cities, further accelerating the evolution of traditional kitchen floor plans and procedures. Trade cards from the 1880s and 1890s record all of this and more, making them some of the most exciting of all cards to collect.

Pricing Tips & Cards to Watch For

Few kitchen-related cards are available for under $10. Watch for soap, food, and stove cards with good kitchen

Riessner's Milk-Overboiling Preventer, $40.00.

THE COMFORT ENJOYED IN THE HOUSEHOLD WHERE RIESSNER'S MILK OVERBOILING PREVENTER IS USED.

THE CONSEQUENCE & RESULT IN THE HOUSEHOLD WITHOUT RIESSNER'S MILK OVERBOILING PREVENTER.

scenes to find the best bargains. Nationally issued granite ware cards have moved into the $12 and up range, with the best of these cards (the "Ironclad" Enameled Iron Ware cards) drawing takers even into the $75 vicinity. See the "Enterprise" article for more information on the increasingly popular Enterprise meat grinders, mills, choppers etc., but be alert for trade cards issued for these products by other manufacturers as well. Also keep an eye open for icebox/refrigerator cards, particularly those issued by the Challenge Company of Grand Haven, Michigan, as these are now bringing $50 and up.

Agate Iron Ware, $20.00.

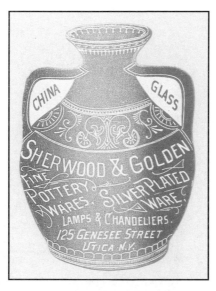

Sherwood & Golden, die-cut, $20.00.

Granite Iron Ware, $12.00.

Meriden Britannia Silver Plated Ware, $40.00.

Granite Iron Ware, $20.00.

Morning Light Range, $25.00.

Florence Oil Stoves, $20.00.

Grand Rapids Regrigerator Co., $20.00.

Little Giant Meat Cutter, $20.00.

American Machine Ice Cream Freezers, $25.00.

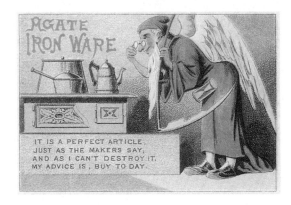

Agate Iron Ware, $20.00.

Ironclad Enameled Iron Ware, $50.00.

Great Atlantic & Pacific Tea Co., die-cut, $12.00.

Armour's Beef Extract
kitchen, woman pours broth into fancy server, vegetables $20.00

Chase & Sanborn's Coffee
die-cut folder of tea cup, Columbian Expo 1893 . . . .$20.00

Granite Iron Ware
"The Attack," boy after food, granite plate, cup, pitcher, etc. $15.00

Granite Iron Ware
boy & girl as clowns, big pot on wheelbarrow $12.00

Granite Iron Ware
"For Kitchen & Table," milk maid with granite bucket, cow $12.00

Granite Iron Ware
girl lifts lid to let boy fall off high-wheeler bike into pot $12.00

Granite Iron Ware
girl dries pot in kitchen at table, spoon $15.00

Hartford Wine & Water Cooler
folder, combination refrigerator, water spigot, door open $30.00

Jones, McDuffee & Stratton
fancy Oriental serving bowl, "Crockery, China, Lamps" 1882 . . . .$15.00

Kedzie Water Filter
"Good Health," mother toasts son with water from filter $35.00

Safety Oil Can
folder, well-dressed lady, girl, filling lamps from red oil can $30.00

Sherwood's Broiler
"The Cook happy after using...," chef sits, hat, holds broiler $15.00

Sterling Chopper
woman with hair in bun grinds meat, laughing girl points $30.00

White Mountain Ice Cream Freezer
boy in red hat with hands on chin $15.00

Stickney & Poors Spices, $20.00.

Ivorine Soap, $10.00.

Granite Iron Ware, $20.00.

Dr. Price's Cream Baking Powder, $15.00.

Labor & Industry

(See also: Chinese; Farm Related.)

Labor & Industry Images

Images of working men and women and views of industry and industrial products are popular with many collectors. The kinds of jobs found in trade card illustrations range from images of domestic servants interviewing for household positions to scenes of doctors and lawyers with clients in their offices. Depictions of manual laborers at work are far less common than scenes of middle-class consumers shopping or strolling about at leisure. Some of the most commonly featured occupations in trade cards include: store clerks and salespeople, maids and butlers, painters and construction workers, miners and blacksmiths, policemen and mailmen, firemen, teachers, clergymen, and farmers. For all of their contributions to the rise of industrial America, women and children rarely are shown working outside of the home in positions other than as domestic servants, newspaper peddlers, and shoeshine boys. Images of industry and industrial products are somewhat scarce, but cards can be found for such things as specialized tools and hardware items, engines, leather belting, pumps, oils, and construction materials like tin, lumber, and plaster.

Historical Notes

The emergence of industrial America during the late-Victorian period can be summed up in one word: change. The minor shifts and major adjustments that industrialization entailed impacted virtually every aspect of American life, from how society dressed, ate, and traveled, to the ways people organized themselves, voted, and worked. The responses to the most dramatic of these changes varied. Some people organized themselves in conservative political and religious organizations and fought change, while others embraced change and formed "progressive" alliances that promoted every new fad and idea in some kind of naive frenzy to lead their generation to a future utopia.

Advertising trade cards fueled many of the changes of this period. This is especially obvious in the areas of fashion and diet, where trade cards presented new styles of dress and tastes in food in rapid-fire succession. But trade cards also quietly recorded many of the deeper, more fundamental changes that were afoot. Cards with images relating to labor and industry offer incidental glimpses into America's transition from an agrarian-based culture (with intimate family and community connections) to an industrial society (with commuting workers, unattached families, and disjointed communities). A few cards are direct in their critique and response to the issues. This is particularly true with cards that carry union and labor messages, but it also shows up in cards imprinted by everything from local churches and temperance unions to hundreds of stock cards "humorously" exposing the breakdown of families, the challenges of poverty, and the growing alienation within multi-cultural neighborhoods.

Pricing Tips & Cards to Watch For

As the importance and popularity of "social history" has grown, so has the interest in trade cards with labor and industry themes. Stock cards with historically significant images and imprints can be found in the inventories of dealers who are unaware of the demand for these cards for around $5. (Some of these same cards bring $30 or more when offered in auctions where collectors who recognize the material must compete to get them.) Privately issued cards with good occupational images, or cards advertising special tools or industrial equipment, usually run $20 or more. Interior factory views are scarce. Arbuckle Coffee issued a series of 50 state map cards with illustrations of "the peculiar industries and scenery of the States and Territories" that includes some great cards in the $5 to $15 range. Watch for cards advertising items like fire-fighting equipment, industrial oils, commercial scales, and railroad supplies, as scarce examples of these cards frequently bring $100 or more.

Smith/Snyder Iron Roofing, $50.00.

National Laundry Journal, $40.00.

Arbuckle Coffee "State Map" series
"Connecticut" map, women working pivot lathes, steel, etc. **$8.00**

Arbuckle Coffee "Illustrated Jokes"
homely Irish woman interviews, domestic job, from *Judge* **$15.00**

B & S Mechanical Machinists' Tools
Clamp Ring for Micrometer Calipers, "Something Else New" **$20.00**

Buffalo Forge Co.
men working forges & hand blowers in shop, anvils, etc. **$40.00**

Central Trades & Labor Union Picnic
"Chinese Must Go," stock card, Chinese running race, 1880 . . . .**$25.00**

Fitzgerald Patent Plaster — stock card
"Exterior Covering of World's Fair Buildings is...," 1893 . . . .**$20.00**

Mayer's Shoes
6 men dance in street arm & arm, all different occupations **$15.00**

Morse, Eddy & Co. Machinery
Tripp's Counter Skiver shown, makers of boot machines, etc. **$20.00**

Newcastle Iron Stove — Peckham
miner with pick in mine, lamp flame on hat, red shirt, stove **$25.00**

People's Cyclopedia of... Knowledge
standing salesman sells copy of book to man sitting in office **$20.00**

Plumber — "Steam & Gas Fittings"
ad over early stool, "Copper, Tin & Sheet Iron Worker" **$8.00**

Sackett's Plaster Boards
2 men install 32"x36" boards, stud frames, apply mud over **$20.00**

Union "Strike!" card — stock image
Journeymen Bakers' & Confectioners' Union, "Buy only..." **$10.00**

Valley Smelting Works, Golden, Colo.
engraving of gold/silver smelting plant, smokestacks, mts. **$75.00**

Walker Porcelain Lined Pumps
3 views of plant in Goshen, IN, "Hand Carts, Barrows, etc." **$125.00**

Wentworth Noiseless Saw Vise
carpenter with saw in vise, dog howling, visitor plugs ears **$30.00**

Western Electric Co. — stock card
"Sunrise" Swiss Alps, from Columbian Expo, "Chicago, 1893" **$25.00**

Whitman & Barnes Mfg. Co.
Brownies, Ferris Wheel, Columbian Expo., engines, belts, etc. **$35.00**

Comstock's Dead Shot Pellets for Worms, $10.00.

Doig's Box Nailing Machines, die-cut, $50.00.

Dusky Diamond Soap, Kirk & Co., $15.00.

Lawn Mowers & Landscaping

(See also: Farm Related.)

Lawn Images

Quaint images of Victorian women in fancy hats and dresses pushing heavy iron lawn mowers are very popular with collectors. A wide variety of lawn mower designs can be found in trade card images, but the formula for showcasing these mowers is fairly predictable. In most instances, the mower is shown in bright colors plowing through thick grass and leaving behind a perfectly manicured lawn (with no clippings). A distant house, usually an eclectic mansion, nearly always appears in these ads, as do stately trees, fountains, garden urns, and distant lakes or rivers. To demonstrate the ease of operation, the mower is invariably shown being pushed by a remarkably overdressed girl, boy, or young woman. Besides these delightful mower images, one also finds in this category scenes of water pumps, sprinklers, and yard tools, as well as advertisements for hammocks, lawn furniture, and seeds for ornamental gardens. Because these products were designed for creating an Eden of one's yard, trade cards for these products appeal to a consumer's sense of beauty and pride, hence the colors and quality of lawn-related cards tends to be very high.

Historical Notes

Prior to the Civil War, well-groomed lawns were seldom found other than on the grounds of the biggest mansions and country estates. Municipal parks were almost nonexistent, and the culture of the Victorian porch had yet to evolve. People did not pay much attention to yards. The yards of many homes were intentionally small, because maintaining neat grass required back-breaking work with a sickle or the controlled grazing of a goat, cow, or horse. British estates had begun using lawn mowers on a limited scale as early as the 1830s, but the first American lawn mower patent was not issued until 1858. Mass production of lawn mowers did not occur in America until the 1870s, when increases in middle-class wealth and changes in aesthetic fashion brought mowers into favor.

Through the wide-spread exposure that lawn mowers received at the 1876 Centennial Exposition, the middle class began to re-examine their yards. As prospering families began building larger and more ornate homes, they began incorporating into their designs bigger yards and increasingly large porches with commanding views of their new middle class "estates." The market for mowers expanded, and new designs followed in quick succession. Lawns, like porches, became stages for Victorian shows of fashion and prosperity. Lawn games like croquet and tennis were played in stylish clothes and conducted as outdoor parties for all to watch.

Sections of large lawns were plotted as ornamental gardens, complete with fountains, arbors, floral carpet bedding, trellises, and gazebos whenever possible. Garden clubs emerged and nurtured their own growth through neighborhood competitions with prizes in numerous classes and divisions. Newspapers began run-ning garden sections, and periodicals like *House and Garden* and *Better Homes and Gardens* seized the imaginations of housewives eager for tips on what to try next. Those who lacked the resources for full-scale yard engineering participated in the movement as best they could, often planting a few wild flowers beside the front step, setting up an urn, or cultivating a handful of geraniums in a homemade flower box.

Pricing Tips & Cards to Watch For

Stock cards and black and white private issues are not common in lawn-related advertising. When such cards are found, they rarely bring over $10 unless they are engraved and of exceptional design or significance. A couple Enterprise sprinkler cards and a few common mower cards can sometimes be found for under $20, but most privately issued lawn-related cards sell for $20 and up. Watch for cards advertising eccentric-looking lawn mowers, as these cards tend to be early and scarce. Cards advertising hammocks and lawn furniture usually bring $20 to $50, depending on the rarity and the appeal of the design. Cards for flower seeds are also popular, and when colorful and well designed, they can often bring $15 to $35.

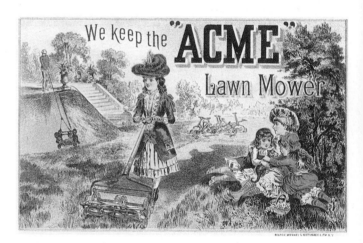

Acme Lawn Mower, $20.00.

Charter Oak Lawn Mower, $30.00.

Buckeye Force Pumps
    girl pumps, hose watering yard, distant mower, house, etc. **$25.00**

Buckeye Lawn Mower
    "Child's Play To Use It," boy pulls like horse, girl drives **$20.00**

Buckeye Lawn Mower
    "Buckeye Boy" portrait, boy mows, distant windmill, etc. **$25.00**

Buckeye Senior Mower
    boy mows in straw hat, big red house **$25.00**

D.M. Ferry & Co Flower Seeds
    lovely bunch of "Nasturtium" flowers "Painted from actual..." **$15.00**

Darling's Lawn Dresser — stock card
    "Nothing better for Lawns," blossoms, flowers, lake scene **$4.00**

Enterprise Lawn Sprinklers
    Horace Greely, farmers, sprinkler/Horticultural Bldg., 1893 .... **$15.00**

Excelsior Side Wheel Mower
    lady mows in dress, hat, man reads paper, dog, big house **$20.00**

New Model Mower
    simple mower stands idle, no people, distant mansion **$20.00**

Pennsylvania Lawn Mower
    metamorphic: Black man & Irish push together/girl gets new **$75.00**

Philadelphia Lawn Mowers
    "At Horticultural Hall — Fairmount Park," boy mows, 1887 .... **$30.00**

President Lawn Mower
    metamorphic: Black man cuts grass, sickle/new lawn mower **$75.00**

Reid's Flower Seeds
    2 panels: "I bought" lady, great flowers/"I didn't" bad crop **$15.00**

Smith's Sprinkler & Force Pump
    1 girl pumps from bucket to flowers, 1 to wash window, etc. **$50.00**

Vick's Floral Guide for 1891
    James Vick, Seedsman, rev: *Vick's Illustrated Monthly* Mag. **$20.00**

Waters' Tree Pruner
    man in derby snips high branch, woman prunes shrub, house **$40.00**

Mexican Hammock, $20.00.

Clipper Mower, $25.00.

Enterprise Lawn Mower, $150.00.

Meats & Seafood

(See also: Cowboys; Cows & Dairy; Farm Related; Food; Pigs.)

Meat Images

The variety of images found on trade cards advertising meat products is almost overwhelming, especially if one includes the many hundreds of cards issued in sets by the Liebig Company of Europe. Discounting the hundreds of foreign Liebig cards that were printed in other languages, there are an estimated 500 hundred or more different American Liebig cards dating from the 1872 – 1890 period. Many of these cards are extremely scarce and highly sought after, both in America and in Europe, where Liebig collecting is very well established.

Libby, McNeill & Libby produced many of America's most popular meat cards. The Libby cards include some forty outstanding color images produced by one Chicago lithographer (Shober & Carqueville). Libby also issued three sets of cards with scenes from Shakespeare's plays. A good many meat cards employ images that have topical appeal with collectors today (e.g. cowboys & Indians, ethnic, patriotic, etc.), so that competition for certain cards is heating up and completing sets is rapidly becoming difficult. Cards with images and advertising for oysters are also very popular. Outside of several sets of ham cards and most of the sets issued for Fairbanks Lard, trade cards advertising meat-related products are mostly in color and of about average quality.

Historical Notes

Shelves of books have been written about cowboys, cattle drives, and the emergence of the meat-packing industry in Chicago. The one area that historians have tended to short shrift is the role played by meat-related advertising propaganda in maneuvering American consumers into new eating habits and altered perspectives about what constituted a legitimate meal. In this area, Victorian trade cards offer unique insights that have yet to be fully explored.

The trade card advertising that proved critical in the growth of the meat-packing industry focused on several things. First, they tried to grab attention through often bright, and frequently humorous, images. Cards were designed to catch people's eyes, to entertain, and to create favorable sentiments that would spill over into the feelings of consumers about these meat products that were new to the shelf. Among such cards are numerous sets with clever word plays and alterations of Shakespearean lines, as well as hundreds of cards with sight gags and satirical substitutions of meat products for everyday objects and portions of the human anatomy.

The more subtle agenda of these cards was to mold consumer attitudes about diet and the convenience of processed and pre-cooked foods. Consumers were re-educated in their thinking through such lines as these, each quoted directly from a different Libby, McNeill & Libby's card:

"Lightens the Burdens of the Farmer's Wife • Picnic & Excursion parties Cannot do without • tho' she... on pleasure bent... had frugal mind... bought... • Used by all... • We have had Company come and I did not know what I should give them to eat. • Used by all armies of the world • Economical • So handy to have in the House • Receive the Highest Award Everywhere • keeps the Children quiet • it made him feel so good • God Bless... • The Farmer Recommends..."

Consumers were conditioned to view these products as convenient, economical, and healthy. Meat packers must have believed that their advertising was effective in helping to shift America's eating habits toward their products, or they never would have issued so many cards over a twenty-year period.

Pricing Tips & Cards to Watch For

Recent efforts at organizing and cataloging meat cards has stirred considerable attention, and meat card prices have begun to move up. The most popular cards tend to be the colorful sets issued by Magnolia Hams, Counselman Hams, Atmore's Mince Meat, American Liebigs, Wilson, and Libby, McNeill & Libby. All of these cards are running $10 and up, with many of the earliest and best designed examples bringing several times that amount. Watch for cards with patriotic, ethnic, and historically significant themes, as they bring $30 to $75 in some circles. Armour and Swift each issued a few nice cards that run $15 to $30, but nothing in the sorts of sets that draw special attention from collectors.

Interest in the two and three color Fairbank Lard cards with pigs remains spotty, with prices running anywhere from $8 to $20. Oyster cards were the early leaders in meat prices, but prices for most of these cards appear to be flattening out. Stock cards with oyster ads usually sell for around $10. Privately issued oyster cards bring more like $25 to $50, or more for rare and early examples. Keep an eye open for the oyster die-cut cards with Jumbo (the elephant) images, as these run $300 and up.

Armour's Extract of Beef, $35.00.

Atmore's Mince Meat & Pudding, $15.00.

Atmore's Mince Meat & Pudding, $15.00.

Minced Codfish, Henry Mayo, $25.00.

Norfolk Oyster Company, $50.00.

Liebig Extract of Beef, $25.00.

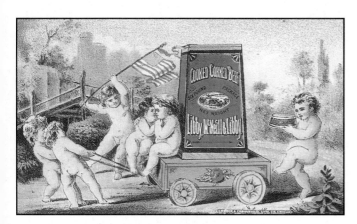

Libby, McNeill & Libby Corned Beef, $35.00.

Libby, McNeill & Libby Corned Beef, $25.00.

– 153 –

Johnston's Fluid Beef, $20.00.

Libby, McNeill & Libby Corned Beef, $25.00.

Paragon Dried Beef, Henry Mayo, $35.00.

Libby, McNeill & Libby Corned Beef, $25.00.

Chas. Counselman Royal Hams, $30.00.

Liebig Extract of Beef, $25.00.

Atmore's Mince Meat & Pudding
  2 women in kitchen, one with 2 pies, Christmas tree behind $15.00

Chas. Counselman Royal Hams
  "Now is the winter of our Discontent made...," family at table $20.00

Chicago Packing & Prov. Co
  clown in blue stripes, hat, holds box with ad on stick $25.00

Fairbank Corned Beef — Lion Brand
  lion in derby, branding iron, cattle run into processing plant $40.00

Libby, McNeill & Libby Canned Meat
  King Henry the Fourth, "Falstaff at the Inn" grabs Francis $12.00

Libby, McNeill & Libby Corned Beef
  "Hamlet, Act 5th, Sc. 2d," 2 men, "Sweet lord..." $15.00

Libby, McNeill & Libby — Tripe & Beef
  "Comedy of Errors," Act III, Scene 1, 4 males, merry feast $12.00

McFerran Shalleross Magnolia Hams
  "Children Cry For...," child, doll, in bed, ham, 1878 . . . .$40.00

Ocean Gem Mackerel
  fishing boat, nets out, inset of dock processing crew $20.00

Platt & Co. Baltimore Oysters
  woman in cap, apron, leans on counter, card in hand $35.00

Rex Extract of Beef — Cudahy's
  die-cut folder of bottle, white card, Black, gold, red label $20.00

Royal Brand Lobster, Mackerel, etc.
  lakeside picnic scene under tree, 3 females, 1 man, products $25.00

St. Louis Beef Canning Co.
  "Merry Maiden and the Tar," she feeds, he tickles her chin $30.00

Swift's "Winchester" Hams & Bacon
  "A Tempting Breakfast," girl at table, ham & eggs $40.00

Wilson's Cooked Corned Beef
  2 big men, "We were fattened on it!," sun smiles, banner $15.00

Wilson's Corned Beef
  2 men, European restaurant, "some of that,-what you call-" $20.00

Libby, McNeill & Libby Corned Beef, $25.00.

Libby, McNeill & Libby Corned Beef, $25.00.

Mechanical & Toy Banks

(See also: Toys.)

Toy Bank Images

Trade cards with images of toy banks are scarce and highly prized. The quality of these cards tends to be exceptionally good, and their images invariably feature detailed color illustrations of the banks advertised. With the exception of the Speaking Dog and Tick Pony cards, the graphic appeal of the twenty or so trade cards commissioned by toy bank companies depends almost entirely upon fancy lettering and the presentation of the banks themselves. Several stock cards were produced with images of generic "still" banks, but the quality and appeal of these cards is quite low. A few collectors also include mechanical bank "flyers" in this category, which would be the big exception to the rule of quality. The twenty-five or so known mechanical bank flyers were all printed on thin paper stock and in only one color of ink, thus making them of inferior quality if judged by normal trade card standards.

Historical Notes

Victorian toys are popular with many collectors today, and trade cards for these toys are very valuable and rare. Among the most cherished of all Victorian toys are "mechanical banks," which were made of iron and included moving parts. Many of these banks are now being reproduced, but original mechanical banks in good condition sell for hundreds, thousands, and even tens of thousands of dollars each. The value of the toy banks themselves helps explain why mechanical bank trade cards are so expensive. A quick study of the relevant trade cards indicates that these banks were promoted as "made wholly of iron highly finished in brilliant colors." The illustrations of the banks depicted on these trade cards were "finished" themselves in the corresponding "brilliant colors" to reinforce the point.

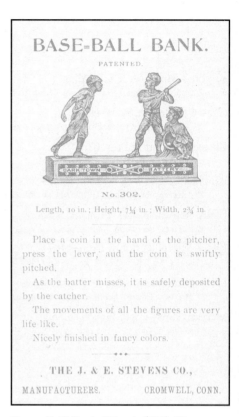

Base=Ball Bank (Flyer), $170.00.

Of even greater interest are the routines that these mechanical devises were engineered to perform. From the Base Ball Bank card (a.k.a. "Dark Town Battery"): "Place a coin in the hand of the Pitcher, press the lever, and the coin is swiftly pitched. As the batter misses, it is safely deposited by the catcher." Or, from the Mason Toy Savings Bank card: "The Comical appearing Hod Carrier receives the Coin in Hod, and throws it forward, depositing it in the Bank. The Mason raises & lowers trowel, also brick, while the Hod is moving forward & back." Children could apparently get a lot of action back then for the 50¢ to $1.00 for which these banks sold. Toy "still" banks are also valuable, as are the two known trade cards advertising them. Stock cards with imprints for stores that handled toys sometimes advertise that they sell banks, which confirms that these toys were more popular than the scarcity of trade cards for them suggests.

Pricing Tips & Cards to Watch For

Trade cards advertising toy banks are among the most expensive in the hobby. Any full-color mechanical bank card in fine condition is worth a minimum of $400. Watch out for American Eagle cards that have been trimmed. For some reason, most of the examples that have turned up have had the advertising space at the bottom cut off, and this makes a difference of hundreds of dollars. The Base Ball Bank card is one of the most prized of all trade cards, with one having fetched a record $7,700 in a 1994 Victorian Images trade card auction. Also keep an eye open for the Watch Dog Safe card, as one of those brought close to $6,000 in an auction back in 1991.

Money Bank (stock card?), $25.00

Singer Sewing, $15.00.

American Eagle — bottom trimmed
J. & E. Stevens Co. — mother eagle, 2 eaglets, nest $450.00

Bad Accident
J. & E. Stevens Co. — Black man, watermelon, mule cart $4,000.00

Circus
Shepard Hardware Co. — clown on pony cart, circular track $6,000.00

French's Automatic
J. Barton & Smith Co. — 2 views: up/down boy on trapeze $1,500.00

Humpty Dumpty
Shepard Hardware Co. — clown bust, white-powdered face $900.00

Jolly Nigger (5" x 6¾" — trimmed)
Shepard Hardware Co. — looks straight ahead, only 1 known . . .$1,100.00

Punch and Judy
Shepard Hardware Co. — designed as mini-stage, club $1,300.00

Safe Deposit ("still" bank)
toy safe bank "With Silver Plated Combination Lock" $2,500.00

Speaking Dog
Shepard Hardware Co. — girl & dog bank, shown in room, table . .$500.00

Stock Card — shows generic "still" bank
"Busting the Bank," #2 of 4: "Playing Bank President" $10.00

Stump Speaker
Shepard Hardware Co. — Black man, big head, carpet bag $1,500.00

Trick Dog
Shepard Hardware Co. — clown holds hoop, barrel, dog $6,000.00

Trick Pony
Shepard Hardware Co. — pony bank shown on table, vase, wall . .$500.00

Uncle Sam
Shepard Hardware Co. — Uncle Sam, umbrella, "U.S." bag $1,000.00

Watchdog Safe
J. & E. Stevens Co. — safe, dog pictured on door, "Barks" $6,000.00

Meachanical Bank Flyers . . . .$35.00 (common) **to $250.00**

American Eagle, full margins, $1,500.00.

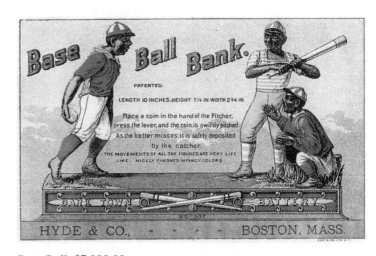

Base Ball, $7,000.00.

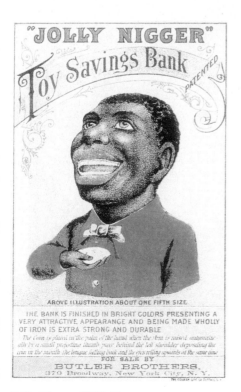

Jolly Nigger, $700.00.   *Mason, $2,000.00.*   *Picture Gallery, $7,000.00.*

Metamorphic & Novelty Cards

(See also: Humor; Puzzles; Risque.)

Novelty Cards

Trade card lithographers sometimes went to extremes in their efforts to engage consumer attention. In addition to the creativity found in trade card graphics and illustrations, there are hundreds of clever cards that were constructed in ingenious ways that went beyond the limitations of the standard two-sided rectangular card.

Many of these novelty cards attempted to create an entertaining experience for consumers that would make the card and the product advertised stand out from the crowd. Whether the card was produced in the die-cut shape of a boot or designed as a hold-to-light that brightened the colors of a woman's dress, the goal was the same: to maneuver potential customers into seeing a product in a memorable way. A good portion of all novelty cards were designed with "before and after" principles in mind, allowing consumers to manipulate and interact with cards to consider the "outcomes" of using or not using the products advertised. Whether or not the claims found in these ads were credible, most novelty cards delivered messages in forms that were unforgettable.

Metamorphic Cards

Metamorphic cards were designed with one or more flaps that folded open and shut to alter the card's illustration. Most metamorphics were vertically oriented with a short bottom flap that folded up to show a "before" scene and down to reveal an "after" improvement. In most cases, the hair, forehead, and eyes of a character in a metamorphic illustration stayed the same, with smiles, frowns, and clothing changing as the flap was opened and closed. Flaps that hinged from the top or side of a card are less common, and cards with multiple flaps are scarce. Metamorphic cards are often found with missing flaps or worn hinges that testify to the use that these cards drew from fascinated consumers.

Donaldson Brothers of New York produced far more metamorphics than any other lithographer. The majority of their cards date from the 1880s and were commissioned by patent medicine, tobacco, and clothing manufacturers. As a general rule, men grew fatter in their improved "after" states, and women changed from conservatively buttoned-up dresses to daringly low-necked bodices. Humor was used in nearly all of these cards, and in most cases the before and after story was told in satirical verse.

Mechanical Cards

Mechanical cards were designed with one or more specially hinged, rotating, or sliding parts. These cards were typically engineered so that when one portion of the card was manipulated, another part of the card responded in some intriguing way. The most common style of mechanical card featured a cut-out window and a cardboard wheel that rotated behind it bringing different images into view. Other mechanicals had tabs that pulled, "pop out" three-dimensional effects, or arms and legs that moved when the card was opened. One bizarre type of mechanical card used loose sand inside the card beneath a clear plastic window. When the card was turned, the sand flowed down, creating the effect of a bottle or pot being emptied or filled, depending upon the image into which the widow was integrated. As with metamorphics, many of these cards were used repeatedly until the cards were worn out or damaged severely.

Hold-To-Light Cards

Hold-to-light cards were designed so that printing on the back of a card would show through and merge with the front image when the cards was held in front of a light. The most common effect was for eyes to "open" when a bright light caused black pupils printed on the back of a card to show through the closed pale eyelids of a sleeping consumer depicted on the card's front. Another common effect was for an image of a product to magically appear as a vision or dream near the main character's head. Diamond Dyes was one of the few companies to use bright colors instead of black ink on the backs of their H-T-L cards. Splashes of color on the backs of their cards were lined up with images of faded clothing on the fronts, so that when held to light the color of the clothing appeared brighter, as though freshly soaked in dye. Because hold-to-lights were printed on thin paper stock, many of these cards turn up with creases, tears, and stains that show through the card.

Die-Cut Cards

Die-cut trade cards were popular both as stock cards and as private issues. The most common stock die-cuts are

Dolly Madison Cigar, stock card, $100.00.

in the shapes of fans, painter palettes, hats, and boots. Other cards that were mechanically cut during production can be found in the shapes of dogs, cats, boxes with lids that open and shut, and tea cups. Privately issued die-cuts can be found in the shapes of products like pickles and corsets or in the shapes of trade marks like the "Light Running" dog and the "Keystone" keystone. Another type of die-cut is a basically rectangular card that has been slightly altered, as when a window has been cut out or an outside edge has been sculpted to the shape of a tree branch. Some collectors include with die-cuts the many toy and doll advertising cards that came pre-cut, ready to be cut, or perforated to be punched out without scissors. Such advertising cards were often lovely, and they frequently included folding parts or stands that would make playing with them easier.

Other Novelties

Other novel approaches in trade card construction and design are relatively scarce. A few cards were designed as puzzles with strings or moving parts that needed to be manipulated to solve the puzzle or remove a linked piece. Another type of card, the hold-to-heat, appears normal until the card is placed near "a lamp or a red hot stove for one minute." These cards employed a heat sensitive ink that only became visible when the card grew hot. Optical illusion cards were typically printed on rectangular cards, and were novel in that they required to viewer to stare at them or turn them around in special ways to create unusual visual effects.

A few novelty cards were printed on materials other than cardboard or paper. Celluloid, an ivory-colored nineteenth century plastic, was used for a few trade cards, and one tin box manufacturer printed "cards" on tin. Several firms in the wood and veneer business printed advertising cards on thin slices of maple or elm. The DeLong Hook and Eye company sealed sample hooks inside of their embossed "hump" cards. Slightly more common are cards with actual samples of varnishes, paints, or fabrics glued or attached to the outsides of cards that are otherwise normal. Variations of this include cards with pieces of "barometric cloth" attached for predicting weather,

Colgate Ribbon Dental Cream, $40.00.

or ones with pieces of luminous sandpaper glued on for striking matches in the dark.

Pricing Tips & Cards to Watch For

Demand for novelty cards is strong, but uneven. Many die-cuts bring only slightly more than a similar rectangular card, while other die-cuts bring breathtaking prices. Generally speaking, the common stock die-cuts sell for $5 to $15, with scarce or beautiful examples bringing perhaps double those prices. The privately issued die-cuts usually go for $10 to $25, but watch for Heinz pickle or Hires Root Beer die-cuts, which can bring $25 to $100. Metamorphics, mechanicals, and hold-to-lights are the most popular novelty cards, with competition for certain examples sometimes driving prices into hundreds of dollars. Even the most common of these cards will bring $15 or more when found in great condition. Metamorphics with unusual folds, and mechanical cards with particularly interesting movements, start at $30. Watch for any novelty cards with patriotic images or advertising for tobacco, patent medicine, or farm-related products, as these tend to draw the greatest interest. Be leery of cards with damaged or missing parts, or of cards that appear to be die-cuts but were actually cut from normal cards, as alterations and damage reduces the value of these cards dramatically.

Spurr Patent Papered Wood Hangings, $25.00.

Scovill's Blood and Liver Syrup, $20.00

Union Club Coffee, $35.00.

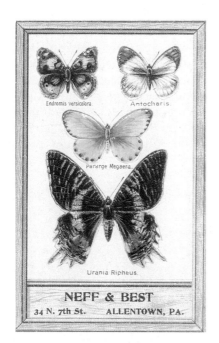

Neff & Best, stock card, $12.00.

DeLong Hook and Eye, $20.00.

Hecker's Self Raising Buckwheat, $15.00.

Diamond Dyes, $15.00.

Wanamaker & Brown Clothing, $50.00.

Kerr's Thread, $25.00.

Buckeye Binder, $40.00.

Keystone Agricultural Implements, $75.00.

Hood's Vegetable Pills, $15.00.

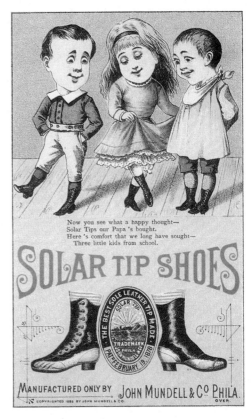

Solar Tip Shoes, $25.00.

Universal Clothes Wringer Puzzle, $15.00.

Walker, Stratman: Bone Fertilizers, $140.00.

Dingman's Soap, $20.00.

Arrowhead Hosiery
 die-cut of Indian arrowhead, rev. ad for socks $20.00

Bassett's Horehound Troches
 die-cut of bottle, "Sore Throat" tablets inside $15.00

Bortree Duplex Corset
 "Secret Out — Mrs. Brown," 2 ladies at keyhole/lady in corset $20.00

Buckeye Works Harvesting Machines
 die-cut metamorphic: barn, doors open/factory, shop work $25.00

Cascarets Candy Cathartic
 2-sided sand mechanical: sad child on pot/pot fills, smiles $35.00

Columbus Buggy Co.
 mechanical: "Fortune Teller" gypsy, card, turn wheel, 1888 . . . .$125.00

Die-Cut Standing Dog — stock card
 legs bend to stand, ad hangs by chin, "Sterling Playerpianos" $20.00

Hall's Balsam for the Lungs
 metamorphic: sick, thin man by window/fat, happy family $20.00

Heinz 57 Pure Food Products
 spinner toy card, 2 holes, string: Heinz Pier, Atlantic City $75.00

Henry's Carbolic Salve
 metamorphic: Alphonso's face bad/Imogene will marry him $20.00

Hood's Sarsaparilla
 metamorphic: side flap, "maid"/white horse crashes window $25.00

Myers Pumps & Hay Tools
 die-cut folder: cowboy hat/farm girl squirts boy's hat off $25.00

Pears' Soap
 die-cut glasses to wear on nose, eyes, pupils punched out $20.00

Pearson Crackers
 die-cut & embossed in shape of cracker — seems real $20.00

Snyder's Catsup
 mechanical: man at table, steak, frown/smile & catsup 1891 . . . .$35.00

St. Jacobs Oil
 metamorphic: many combinations, double side flaps, man $40.00

Stock Mechanical — clothing imprint
 "She cannot keep away from him" pull tab, makes couple kiss $25.00

Sweet, Orr & Co. Pantaloon Overalls
 metamorphic: Longshoreman, "I'm not a tramp"/"ne'er rip" $40.00

Tarrant's Seltzer Aperient
 metamorphic: wife tells sick husband to take it/gets better $20.00

Town Talk Flour — Lawrenceburg Mills
 novelty barometer: cloth changes colors, boy in goat cart $40.00

Van Houten's Cocoa
 die-cut mechanical: spin windmill arms, holes, read ad $50.00

Warrior Mower Co.
 metamorphic: flap folds up, horses struggle/easy cutting $90.00

White Sewing Machine
 metamorphic: family struggles, dad cranks/easy sewing $30.00

Woolson Spice — Lion Coffee
 "Shadow Card" of Mrs. Langtree, flowers/silhouette, 1896 . . . .$15.00

Fancy Goods, stock card, $20.00:

Tarrant's Seltzer Aperient, $25.00.

Burdick & Son, Tin Boxes, Signs, etc., $100.00.

Patent Medicines
(See also: Beer, Whiskey & Wine; Cosmetics; Hair Products.)

Patent Medicine Images

The incredible variety of outstanding images found on trade cards issued by patent medicine firms is one of the reasons why these cards are among the most collected in the hobby. Images range from black and white stock card illustrations of boys playing, to privately issued color cards showing caring husbands and wives ministering to each other in times of illness. Humor was frequently used in medicinal advertising, as was fear. Images of children with pets or children getting into harmless trouble are also common. Some of the most interesting medicine trade cards feature "before and after" themes, where a sick or dying consumer in one image is depicted in a second image as robust and happy, thanks to the medicine taken. Many of these "before and after" ads were designed as novelty cards, typically metamorphics with folding flaps, but sometimes as hold-to-lights or mechanicals. As a general rule, medicinal trade cards that depict the product and a health "crisis" in a color illustration on the front are preferred by collectors over cards that carry all of the advertising on the back.

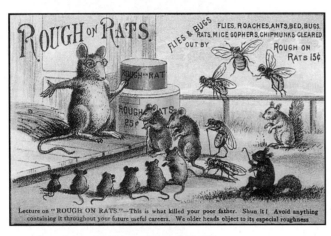

Rough on Rats, Wells' products, $30.00.

Historical Notes

The term "patent medicine" can be misleading, in that very few nineteenth century medicines were patented in the sense that we imagine today. In order to receive a patent, a medicine manufacturer would have had to disclose for public record the ingredients of his product, and, for a variety of reasons, few companies were interested in making their formulas public knowledge. Most of the medicine companies that commissioned trade cards did own patents, but their patents applied only to their trademarks and brand names, not the contents of their packages.

The patent medicine industry was competitive, but extremely lucrative for those who played the game well. Because the formulas of most medicines were not patented and were unavailable for public scrutiny, and because legislation regarding truthful labeling and advertising had not yet been passed, anyone who had the courage to buy empty bottles and dump herbs, alcohol, and nar-

cotics into them was free to go into the medicine business. Several whiskey distilleries had lucrative wholesale businesses built on bulk sales directly to bottlers of patent medicines. In addition to alcohol, other "secret" ingredients common in patent medicines included opium, morphine, and cannabis. It is doubtful that many consumers were "cured" by patent medicines, but these concoctions undoubtedly alleviated symptoms and kept folks coming back for more.

Thompson's Eye Water, $15.00.

The energy and air of legitimacy that was needed for the patent medicine industry to flourish was provided through various types of advertising. Medicinal advertising almanacs with weather information, folk insights, and humor were popular throughout the Victorian period, but it took a fairly established firm to come up with the money to issue an entire booklet. Small-time entrepreneurs working out of cellars and barns could buy official-looking stock cards and have them imprinted with medicinal ads locally for a total investment of less than $5 per thousand. As some of these small companies prospered, they reached the point where they could begin commissioning their own cards. Privately issued cards were usually designed with illustrations that fit the themes of specific brands, and they often included illustrations of packages so that consumers would recognize the product when they saw it on a shelf.

Other patent medicine promotions included large "store cards" that were used in retail displays, handbills and posters that were used in cities, barn signs for along roads and train routes, fence signs, and even graffiti on rocks and cliffs. One American explorer was so impressed by all of the "Plantation Bitters" advertising he had seen back in the states that he decided to leave that company's familiar logo carved on the face of a volcanic cliff at latitude 83° 24' N as proof that an American had set the "farthest north" record for the 1880s. Historians estimate that patent medicine companies accounted for over half of all the American firms that spent $50,000 or more in advertising in 1893.

Patent medicines were distributed in numerous ways. In some cases, agents were solicited to peddle bottles of "snake oil" door to door or as members of traveling medicine shows. Other agents were hired to recruit local drug and grocery stores into stocking specific brands. These "drummers" frequently traveled with cases of trade cards that could be left in packaged "decks" with retailers that decided to carry the line. Most of these cards were designed with blank spaces for local imprinting, and in some cases the manufacturer would even do the imprinting free of charge for their dealers. By the late 1890s, several national mail-order firms were advertising patent medicines in their catalogs right along with corsets, clocks, and apple peelers.

Pricing Tips & Cards to Watch For

Demand for patent medicine trade cards is very strong, but it is sometimes tricky to tell the difference between a card that will bring $15 and one that will bring $50. Generally speaking, stock cards stay in the $5 to $15 range, and privately issued cards run $10 to $30. As always, watch for cards of exceptionally intriguing design or quality, as these usually draw the greatest interest. The biggest problem in pricing medicinal cards is the rarity factor, which only experienced collectors and dealers will really have a handle on because there are so many thousands of patent medicine designs. Some of the best cards were issued by national firms in quantities that make them relatively common, while other cards that appear less appealing can be far more rare and valuable. The best tip for pricing medicine cards is to get as much exposure to them as possible, and then to be alert when something comes up that seems unfamiliar. Cards advertising "bitters" tend to draw slightly higher prices, as do cards that mention opium, morphine, or cannabis. Watch for Dr. Kilmer cards, as any of them can bring over $20, and the highly-prized "Standard Herbal Remedies" card showing a bottle with a man's anatomy sold for over $600 in a 1995 auction.

Scott's Emulsion of Cod Liver Oil, $20.00.

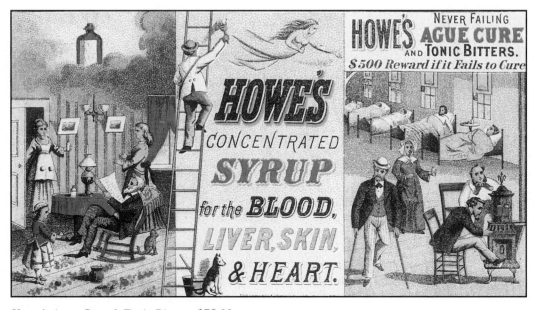

Howe's Ague Cure & Tonic Bitters, $75.00.

Packer's Cutaneous Charm, $40.00.

Perry Davis' Pain Killer, $15.00.

Emory's Family Pills, $15.00.

Humphrey's Witch Hazel Oil, $12.00.

Pond's Extract, $20.00.

Taylor's Cherokee Remedy, $25.00.

Kingsland's Chlorinated Tablets, $20.00.

Thompson's Eye Water, $15.00.

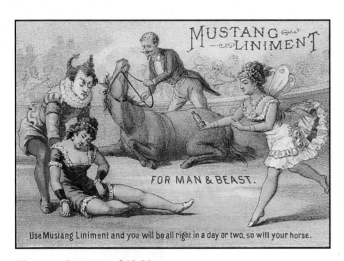

Mustang Liniment, $40.00.

Dr. Harter's Wild Cherry Bitters, $70.00.

Dr. Haas' Alterative for Horses & Cattle, $80.00.

Mennen's Corn Killer, $10.00.

Tarrant's Seltzer Aperient, $12.00.

Johann Hoff's Malt Extract, $30.00.

Wells' May Apple Pills, $25.00.

Ayer's Sarsaparilla, $15.00.

Ayer's Cherry Pectoral, $15.00.

Brown's Iron Bitters
"Mrs. Langtry, the Jersey Lily" sits with bucket, apron $15.00

Brown's Iron Bitters
lady in bonnet peeks around pillar $8.00

Brown's Vermifuge Comfits
girl hands mother flowers, baby in arms, bassinet, bottle $12.00

Burdock Blood Bitters
laughing boy on stool with bottle in hand $10.00

Carter's Backache Plasters
"Dran' Pa, O'o' ought to put on...," child, old man hold's back $15.00

Carter's Iron Pills
"Don't rise; I know how you feel...," 2 ladies, big chair $6.00

Dr. Kilmer's Standard Herbal Remedies
bottle, man's anatomy, drug store shelves $600.00

Dr. Pierce's Medicines & Surgical Inst.
2 views of buildings, portrait in center, book below $60.00

Hood's Vegetable Pills
girl, cap, hands on chin, elbows down $8.00

Jayne's Tonic Vermifuge
"Naughty Puss!," girl clawed by cat, ball, table, flower vase $10.00

Kilmer's Ocean-Weed Heart Remedy
drape pulled to show boats on water, heart on side $20.00

Knapp's Throat Cure
monkey feeds lozenges to giraffe from top of tree $60.00

Lydia Pinkham's Vegetable Compound
signed portrait card of Lydia Pinkham $12.00

Merchant's Garglin Oil
horse sticks head through lucky horseshoe $10.00

Mrs. Winslow's Soothing Syrup
mother, child on shoulder, bassinet, bottle on table, plants $25.00

Pond's Extract
"United States Army Uniforms-1890" — soldiers on steps $10.00

Prickly Ash Bitters
Roman lady sips glass, slave serves bottle on tray $35.00

St. Jacob's Oil
"Conquers Pain," monk, red robe, Statue of Liberty pose $20.00

Tarrant's Seltzer Aperient
lawyer at roll-top desk, "Keepwell" name on office door $10.00

Uncle Sam's Condition Powder
2 horses, 2 cows, sheep in pasture, distant barn $20.00

Wright's Indian Pills — stock card
girl on swing, bonnet, doll in lap, "Cure Dyspepsia" $6.00

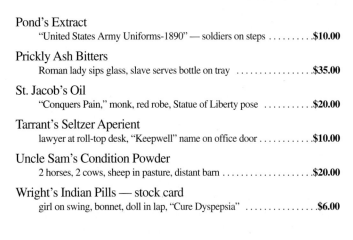

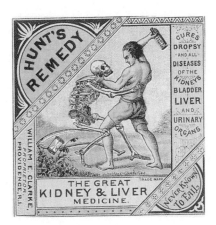

Hunt's Remedy, $100.00.

Hops & Malt Bitters, $25.00.

Santa Abie King of Consumption, $75.00.

Pianos & Organs
(See also: Furniture & Home Improvement.)

Piano & Organ Images

Trade cards with images of pianos and organs are among the most beautiful of all product cards. Manufactures often spared little expense when commissioning cards for these "big ticket" items, as it was crucial that consumers get the impression that they were dealing with a firm that could deliver a beautiful product of the highest quality. Not many piano cards were issued in black and white, but a few companies like Decker Bros., Chase, and Haines Bros. did commission intricate designs that were printed in only brown or blue ink. Stock cards were also used by a few manufacturers, but the cards that they selected were typically of good quality and tasteful designs. The biggest users of stock card were Ivers & Pond of Boston and Weaver Organs of York, Pennsylvania. The most desirable cards are usually the color ones issued by a manufacturer with detailed illustrations of the product in a church or parlor setting and imprinted with the name of a local retailer who carried the line.

Historical Notes

The appearance of proper training and cultural refinement was highly valued by most Victorians. Among such middle-class tests as wardrobe, porch and lawn presentation, and dinning etiquette, families that wished to be viewed with full social status had to pass the test of parlor recitals. Musical talent was cultivated in children in a variety of ways, and in cases where there was little evidence of natural talent, basic music recognition and reading skills, as well as the ability to fake it when necessary, was settled for. Concerts were attended and church choirs were joined. Marching bands were formed by men and musical receptions were arranged by women. And every family of any serious social standing was required to plant a fancy organ or piano in their front parlor for visitors to inspect, test, and admire.

In most cases, the parlor organ or piano was used for the musical training of children, for bonding and spiritual inspiration as the family gathered around to sing an evening or holiday hymn, and for social entertainment when an accomplished player performed and guests sang along. Well-trained and pleasant singing voices were as valued as keyboard skills, but it usually took a family piano or a parlor organ to get a voice in the kind of shape required to pull off an impressive performance.

For families with limited budgets, parlor organs (or "cottage organs" as they were sometimes called) were popular through the end of the 1890s. Surprisingly enough, organs were often only about a third of the price of pianos, even though organs were typically more ornate and attractive as parlor "furniture" than most pianos were. Additionally, organs typically took up less space than pianos, and they were more suited to the church hymns that were initially favored by most middle-class homes. Parlor organs began to slide from favor by 1900, however, for all the same reasons they had initially made sense. Pianos came to be viewed as a better show of wealth, and they were better suited for the popular sheet music that had finally won acceptance in even conservative homes.

Pricing Tips & Cards to Watch For

Very good values can still be found in trade cards with wonderful advertisements for pianos and organs. Stock cards with piano dealer imprints on the back are of little interest to most collectors outside of the region in which the card was issued, so these cards rarely sell for over $5. Stock cards used by manufacturers and imprinted with line-drawn illustrations of their pianos and organs on the reverse draw more attention, but still seldom bring over $5 to $15. Of greater interest are the color images of specific brands shown in parlors or churches. Cards of this type with good designs bring $10 to $40. Because few collectors are currently competing for piano cards, it is unusual for any of these cards to sell for over $40, regardless of the card's quality and scarcity. Watch for this situation to change in the near future, and keep an eye open for any impressive-looking cards priced under $15, as such cards will probably be going up substantially in price in the years to come.

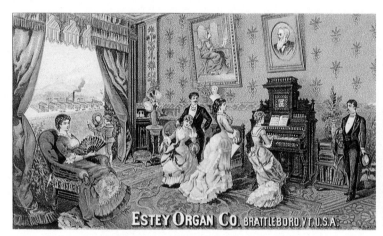

Estey Organ Co., $25.00.

Emerson Piano, $20.00.

B. Shoninger Organs
"The Young Musician (Mozart)," organ, stained glass, recital $20.00

Chase Organ Co.
2 couples, lady plays organ, factory in distance $25.00

Decker Bros. Grand Piano
concert, woman sitting at piano, orchestra ready to start $15.00

Estey Organ Co.
boy in Derby strums tennis racket, girl leans at window 1890 . . . . . .$6.00

Estey Piano Co.
lady stands by piano, factory picture over, stained glass $15.00

Estey Piano Co.
"First Music Lesson," mom pushes boy, piano, factory outside $15.00

Evertt Piano — John Church Co.
2 ladies in front, 1 leans, big recital behind, man plays 1893 . . . . .$15.00

Haines Bros. Upright Piano
2 couples, 1 couple sings, other lady plays piano, man leans $20.00

Ithica Organ & Piano
very fancy, large organ shown, no people $20.00

Malcom Love Piano
lady plays big upright, looks over left shoulder $25.00

Mason & Hamlin Organ
"Church, Chapel & Parlor," lady plays, man, mom, girl listen $20.00

Mason & Hamlin Organ & Piano
4 views of people playing, 1 in church, eagle, many awards $20.00

Story & Clark Organ
"The First Lesson," mom holds child on stool, dad watches $15.00

Waterloo Organs — Malcom Love & Co.
4 ladies, one playing organ, one in green chair with fan $15.00

Sohmer Pianos, $20.00.

Estey Piano & Organ, $15.00.

Sterling Organ, $15.00.

Estey Phonorium, $15.00.

Mason & Hamlin Organ & Piano, $20.00.

Pigs

(See also: Animals; Cows; Meats.)

Pig Images

There are many dozens of trade cards with great pig images. The term "pig" is used for all of these images, even though some of the cards themselves make reference to "hogs." Generally speaking, the term hog can apply to animals that are not domesticated pigs, whereas the term pig covers both the large domestic farm animals used by meat packers and the intelligent, smaller animals that were sometimes kept for family pets and used as household garbage disposals. Pigs appear in dozens of mostly humorous stock cards, but pig images are more widely collected as they appear in several sets of privately issued cards used by meat packers and the Dr. Haas' Remedy Company.

The makers of Fairbank's Lard were particularly prolific in producing anthropomorphic pig images, but most of their cards were printed using only two or three colors. The makers of the Haas Hog Remedy (sometimes called Dr. Haas' Hog and Poultry Remedy) used more colors than Fairbank's, but the quality of these comical cards from around 1882 – 83 is still quite low. The pig cards issued by the Chas. Counselman Royal Ham Company are better, and those issued by the Swift Company and Hammond's Meats are among the most attractive issued. Magnolia Hams issued a number of humorous ham images, but they shied away from depicting pigs as salesmen of their pig kin (only two examples known), perhaps judging that such images were in bad taste.

Historical Notes

Rural families often kept a few pigs out back for several reasons. Pigs could grow fat on kitchen "slop" that had to be dumped somewhere anyway, and most other animals would turn their noses or get sick eating what pigs enjoyed. Pigs required less living space than other livestock, and they were easier to butcher and preserve for those who lacked the equipment for handling and processing cows that weighed many hundreds of pounds. Additionally, because of their manageable size and high level of intelligence, many families actually enjoyed a pig or two as a sort of family pet or mascot. One of the reasons why pigs appear in so many children's stories, rhymes, and anthropomorphic illustrations is because those who spend time with pigs will often swear that each pig has an eccentric "personality" of its own.

Farmers feared a number of contagious livestock diseases, especially "hog cholera," which could sweep through livestock without warning and leave every pig dead. "Dr." Jos. Haas used a rather unique approach in peddling his hog remedy to worried farmers. The back of one of his many trade cards explains: "When the Remedy is used as a preventive, I will insure your hogs by the head for a year, and will make a deposit of the necessary money to make such insurance good. If any hogs die from disease I will pay for them at their market value."

The number of claims filed against Dr. Haas is unknown, but cards with such propositions disappeared by the mid-1880s.

Pricing Tips & Cards to Watch For

A sizable collection of cards with clever and delightful images of pigs can be assembled quite cheaply. Stock cards with pig images rarely cost more than $5. Recent auction exposure has begun to push prices up for the 60 or so known Fairbank's cards with pig images, but many of these cards can still be found in dealer inventories for $8 to $15. The 16 or so Counselman Ham cards with pig images typically run in the $10 to $30 range. Watch for high quality cards with unusual pig images, like the Blair Hog Ring cards or the Nelson Morris card showing pigs playing baseball, as these will often bring $25 or more. Also keep an eye open for Dr. Haas' cards, as they are currently selling for $75 and up when found in very fine condition.

Wild Indian Lung Balsam, stock card, $15.00.

Keystone Watch Cases, die-cut, $8.00.

Chas. Counselman Royal Hams
pig as king on throne, crown, sword, etc. $35.00

Chas. Counselman Royal Hams
2 pigs as horses, wagon loaded with hams, pig driver $35.00

Domestic Sewing Machine
"Prize Chester White Boar Kennett," white pig, bowl, fence $10.00

Dr. Haas' Hog and Poultry Remedy
"Relief Committee," 2 pigs, chicken, sailboat, cases: Dr. Haas $80.00

Dr. Haas' Hog Remedy
"At the Rink," pigs roller skating, one fallen, couple in hats $80.00

Fairbanks Lard
2 pigs as safe crackers in night theft, can't open, corncobs $20.00

Fairbanks Lard
"Boy stood on burning deck... found a keg of Lard," pig, deck $15.00

Fairbanks Lard
"This hog was fat..." verse, lady pig in dress feeds hog corn $25.00

Hammond's Meats & Lard
pig tied to small cart: "A Little Sulky" won't budge for boys $25.00

Nelson Morris Hams
die-cut folder, "See our Exhibit at World's Fair," views, 1893 . . . . . .$20.00

Oscar Wilde Stock Card — satire
"Begorra & I belave I am Oscar Himsilf," Irishman, pig, 1882 . . . . . .$20.00

Peckham Agricultural Boiler
white pig in apron puts other pig in boiler, brown pig, glasses $40.00

Pillsbury's Best Flour — stock card
"Pig-A-Rious Position," thief grabs piglet/pig grabs his pants $8.00

Stock Card — clothing imprint
pig runs, firecrackers exploding, tied to tail, 1881 . . . .$5.00

Stock Card — dry goods imprint
woman with small pig on leash tied to leg, stick, windmill $5.00

Swift Silver Leaf Lard
"Tally Ho!!!," 6 pigs as horses, tin pail as coach, pig riders $30.00

Swift Silver Leaf Lard
pig classroom, teacher sits, 5 students in a row, pig dunce $30.00

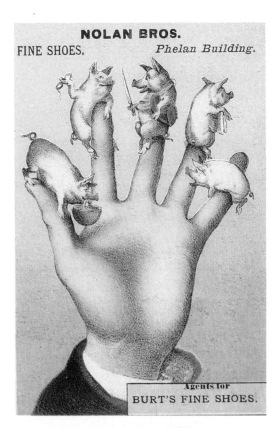

Five Little Piggies, stock card, $12.00.

Blair's Hog Ringers & Rings, $50.00.

Fairbanks Lard, $15.00.

Political & Patriotic

(See also: Columbia; Expositions; Statue of Liberty; Uncle Sam.)

Political & Patriotic Images

Many trade cards use images that subtly reflect social movements and the political temper of the late-Victorian period. For example, the Celluloid Collar & Cuff cards that present Chinese immigrants in an unfavorable light reflect the concerns of American laborers who feared losing their jobs to hard-working immigrants. Those concerns hardened into hostilities that found political expression through the formation of the Workingmen's Party in 1877 and the passage of the Chinese Exclusion Act of 1882. In-so-far as Celluloid Collar & Cuff cards promoted negative stereotypes of Chinese workers and perpetuated the "Chinese Must Go!" slogan, the images and themes of these cards are "political" in nature. Seen this way, trade cards with "patriotic" images are also political artifacts in that they reflect (and once fed) the rise of American nationalism, which was clearly one of the most significant political developments of the late-Victorian period.

I'll just wash up a little
with **Uncle Sam's Tar Soap,**

For I've been building a navy,
Fit with the world to cope.

Uncle Sam's Tar Soap, $75.00.

In practice, many collectors of political trade cards are less philosophical in their approach. Most collectors show a strong preference for cards making straightforward political statements and cards directly linked to specific presidential elections. Because there are so many hundreds of "patriotic" images in trade cards, many collectors specialize in patriotic images apart from other political cards, or even focus more narrowly on specific patriotic images of things like eagles, flags, American war ships, etc.

The quality and nature of political and patriotic images varies immensely. On the low end are hundreds of stock cards with line-drawn illustrations of early presidents and crudely-designed illustrations of children playing Bunker Hill fife and drum parade

games. In the middle range are stock cards with political cartoons poking fun at robber barons and business tycoons, as well as the rather generic "Take-Your-Pick" presidential campaign stock cards showing the leading candidates from the major parties. One also finds in the mid-range an assortment of patriotic cards with amateurish color images exploiting stock patriotic symbols for quick and easy consumer approval. At the top end in political and patriotic cards are the carefully designed private issue cards with unique graphics or combinations of patriotic symbols in ways that are cleverly integrated into the card's over-all advertising message.

Historical Notes

Yankee pride supplied much of the courage and energy America needed to outlast King George's resolve during our Revolutionary War. Political action and local democratic participation were cornerstones upon which the American system was built. But it was not until after the Civil War, during the upheaval and adjustments of America's transition from an agrarian society to an industrial world leader, that nationalism became a defining feature of the American character. Trade cards document the increase of America's international activity, and they were themselves contributors to the new way that Americans began viewing their place in the world community.

One of the keys to America's cohesion despite the diversity of her population was the solidarity that emerged through the rise of nationalism. Trade cards played an important role in establishing and reinforcing America's national symbols, legends, and rituals. Trade cards also helped establish national landmarks like the Statue of Liberty, the Brooklyn Bridge, and our Capital building, as well as several natural landmarks like Niagara Falls, the Rocky Mountains, and the Mississippi River. Patriotic rituals, especially expositions, national elections, and the observance of the Fourth of July, also played an important role in promoting a cohesive culture and shared vision of who and what Americans were. And all of these rituals were faithfully celebrated in trade cards.

Lucas Enamels
Tip Top for Gangways
and Cabins.

Off Santiago, July 3rd, 1898.
"When all the work was done so well, it is difficult to discriminate in praise."—SAMPSON.

U.S. CRUISER   NEW YORK

COPYRIGHT 1898 BY KOEHNER & HAYES

White Fleet Stock Card, Lucas Paints, $10.00.

The following list should help in dating many political trade cards.

Major Candidates in national elections during trade card era:

- 1876 **Rutherford Hayes & William Wheeler**
  Samuel Tilden & Thomas Hendricks
  Ulysses S. Grant (dropped from race)

- 1880 **James Garfield & Chester Arthur**
  W.S. Hancock & William English

- 1884 **Grover Cleveland & Thomas Hendricks**
  James Blaine & John Logan
  B. Butler/John St. John

- 1888 **Benjamin Harrison & Levi Morton**
  Grover Cleveland & Allen Thurman

- 1892 **Grover Cleveland & Adlai Stevenson**
  Benjamin Harrison & Whitelaw Reid

- 1896 **Wm. McKinley & Garret Hobart**
  Wm. J. Bryan & Arthur Sewall

- 1900 **Wm. McKinley & Theo. Roosevelt**
  Wm. J. Bryan & Adlai Stevenson

Pricing Tips & Cards to Watch For

One of the first things that collectors of political trade cards need to do is to memorize the faces of all the major presidential candidates between 1876 and 1900. Victorian advertisers assumed that consumers would recognize the portraits of these men without assistance, so in many cases political figures appear without identification. In some cases, the face pictured belongs to a political figure, but in other cases the depiction is of a theatrical star, the owner of a company, or the fictional creation of an imaginative artist. Because most general collectors and dealers are unable to identify many of these faces, a collector who does is at a significant advantage.

Prices and demand for trade cards with political themes is strong. Outside of the $2 to $3 stock cards with portraits of the first 17 presidents, most political and presidential cards fall in the $15 to $50 price range, even though relatively few of these cards were printed in full color. Cards with patriotic themes are far more likely to be found in full color. Patriotic stock cards generally sell in the $5 to $15 range, but certain images can bring far more than that. Watch for privately issued political and patriotic cards with strong messages and good images, as competition for such items can be fierce. Privately issued cards showing several presidential candidates in a single scene or that combine several popular images like Uncle Sam, an exposition, an eagle, and an American flag will often bring $50 or more. Keep an eye open for a rare Birdsell 3-panel folder that shows Uncle Sam and Columbia at a horse race with four candidates as jockeys, as this card has brought over $700 at auction.

St. Louis Beef Canning, $50.00.

Congress Bitters, $15.00.

Ludlow's Shoes, $15.00.

Blackwell's Durham Tobacco, $60.00.

Vanderbilt Political Cartoon Card, $20.00.

Merrick's American Thread, $20.00.

Clark's Thread, $6.00.

White's Business College, presidential stock card, $30.00.

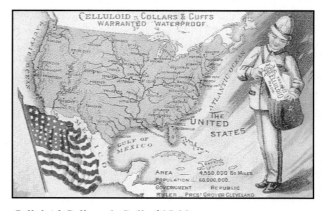

Edwin Burt Fine Shoes, $6.00.

Celluloid Collars & Cuffs, $15.00.

Atlantic & Great Western Railroad
floor map: "Hall for Republican National Convention — 1876" **$100.00**

Babbitt's 1776 Soap
boy as patriot, flags, canon balls, drum, uniform, soap box **$10.00**

Bunker Hill Flag Stock Card
shows flag, battle, "1775" **$8.00**

Bunker Hill Harness Oil
classic "fife & drum" march up hill, flag **$12.00**

Capadura Cigars
Grant, Hayes, Butler, all smoke same cigars, from *Puck* **$60.00**

Enterprise Beef Shaver
"Hatchet-can't-lie-man," Geo. Washington, Admin. Bldg. 1893 . . . . .**$15.00**

Estbrook's Steel Pens
red, white, blue beardless Uncle Sam, eagle, pen tips shown **$40.00**

Little Yankee Plow
Uncle Sam in white felt hat, "See the Victorious Little ..." **$50.00**

Merrick Thread
"Cradle of American Liberty," mother, baby, spool crib 1887 . . . .**$15.00**

Merrick's Thread
"Young America," 2 children, flags, eagle, drum, U.S. map **$12.00**

Pillsbury's Best Flour
"We Feed the Nations of Earth," folder, Uncle Sam, ethnics **$30.00**

President Series Stock Card
black & white portrait, Zachary Taylor, statistics **$4.00**

Presidential Stock Card — clothing
mechanical: "Your Choice," rotate, Garfield/Hancock, 1880 . . . .**$75.00**

Presidential Stock Card — clothing
flag, Cleveland & Harrison portraits, running mates **$20.00**

Presidential: — Wright's Indian Pills
"1892 Republican Nominees" Harrison/Reid, capital, eagle **$50.00**

Sollers Shoes
"Children are proud the Streets to Parade," 6 kids, flag, 1877 . . . .**$10.00**

Standard Sewing Machine
"The Nation's Pride," big parade, flag, "1848, 1812, 1776" **$12.00**

Stock Card — pharmacy imprint
"Protecting the Flag," girl in dress holds smoking gun, flag **$10.00**

Stock Card — Burdock Blood Bitters
"Tariff — Our party is right...," man, white beard, hand in coat **$10.00**

White Improved Sewing Machine
"For President," Cleveland & Blaine "Take Your Choice," 1884 . . . . .**$40.00**

Military Ships, stock card series, $10.00.

Merrick's Thread, $40.00.

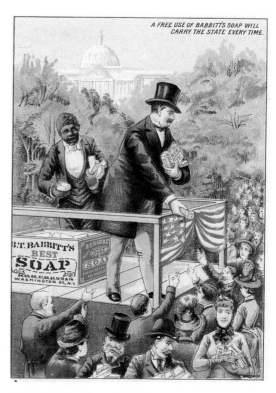

Babbitt's Best Soap, $30.00.

Puzzles, Brain Teasers & Optical Illusions

(See also: Novelty.)

Puzzle Cards

Advertising cards that used puzzles as a gimmick to capture and hold a consumer's interest form a unique class of novelty cards worthy of special discussion. Like all novelty cards, these cards attempted to engage potential customers in an "interactive" way that would leave an impression and hopefully result in increased business. Unlike other novelty cards, if puzzle cards were to be appreciated they usually required exerted effort and concentration on the part of consumers. Within this class of cards one finds a variety of styles and levels of difficulty.

Hidden Picture Cards

Hidden picture cards are the most plentiful of all puzzle cards. Most of these cards were printed around 1880 as black and white stock cards. Color images are relatively scarce in hidden picture cards. Several patent medicine companies made attempts to integrate hidden objects in their privately issued cards with themes relevant to their products, but most hidden picture cards show little connection between their images and the goods or services advertised. Animals are usually hidden in these cards, but occasionally one encounters such unusual hidden objects as: "Fat man on roller skates," "Nigger eating watermelon," or "Buffalo Bill breaking glass balls."

Optical Illusion Cards

Optical illusion cards typically asked a consumer to stare at an image and then to look away to experience an unusual visual effect. One popular version required a viewer to stand a card along a line, and then to move one's eyes close and to stare. The brain would merge the images on each side of the card, creating the effect of the undressed woman on the left wearing the corset drawn on the right.

Other optical illusion cards involved two pictures "hidden" within one image. The best known example of the "upside-down" variety of optical illusion card was issued by a tea company in 1889, but other examples exist. This A&P version depicts the sad faces of two women sipping tea. When the card is turned upside down, their frowns turn to smiles, their chins turn to noses, and a new image of happy women emerges from the same original illustration. The "young woman-old hag" variety of optical illusion was popularized by the Phenyo-Caffein Company, who issued a card with the caption, "My Girl & Her Mother. Do You See Both?" The image is still used one hundred years later in psychology classes to teach the principles of selective perception and perspective. Most people have a hard time finding both figures in the same image. (Hint: the chin of the girl looking away is the nose of the hag looking down.)

Rebus Cards

Rebus cards offered riddles in messages composed of tiny pictures strung together with syllables or words. In some cases, the rebus was short and obvious, as with a stock card that uses the cliche, "Strike the (picture of an iron) while it is hot." Most rebus puzzles were longer and much less obvious. In fact, many collectors own rebus cards that they have never been able to completely decipher. The challenge of these cards is twofold. First, some rebus puzzles use illustrations of objects from the nineteenth century that are difficult to identify today or are no longer called by their Victorian names. And secondly, some of the lines that were encoded in rebus cards were dependent upon familiarity with phrases from plays, poetry, and stories that no longer circulate in American culture.

Other Puzzle Cards and Brain Teasers

Other puzzle cards and brain teasers were less common. Star puzzles and cube puzzles with geometric problems to be solved by drawing lines or moving coins were used on some cards, as were mathematical puzzles, riddles, and cards with story problems. A few cards were issued in the style of jigsaw puzzles that had to be cut into pieces and put together in a new way for the message to emerge. Sliding block puzzles were a big fad around 1880, and two versions of a "hold-to-heat" political stock card depict one of these puzzles with the faces of presidential candidates on each of the blocks. Disentanglement cards were typically composed of die-cut pieces linked together in ways that made unhooking them a challenge.

Pricing Tips & Cards to Watch For

Hidden picture stock cards usually sell in the $4 to $10 range, with privately issued examples sometimes bringing double that amount. Other types of puzzle cards tend to be more scarce and in higher demand, with most examples selling in the $15 to $40 range. Watch for good disentanglement puzzles, as these can draw interest and higher prices from toy collectors. Puzzle cards that catch the attention of topical or product collectors can also bring much higher prices, as with rebus cards with political themes that have sold at auction for over $200. Also watch for puzzles that must be solved by rotating disks and aligning images, especially "Around the World" ones signed by Sam Loyd, as these can bring $100 or more.

Clark's Thread, $6.00.

Amos H. Van Horn Furniture
$75 Parlor Suit Prize (to be awarded in 1886) $12.00

Boston & Meriden Clothing
cube puzzle: cash prizes by 1885 . . . .$8.00

C. B. Castle Jeweler
rebus $15.00

Disentanglement Puzzle
unhook the linked pieces $30.00

Dr. Seth Arnold's Balsam
hidden pict: scene — 2 old ladies, bottle, table, cat: find kitten $12.00

Dr. Thomas' Eclectric Oil
rebus (1882) $40.00

Great American Tea Company
opt. illusion: stare at star/look away/see General Grant $25.00

Great Atlantic & Pacific Tea Co.
opt. illusion: upside-down images, 2 ladies, happy/sad 1889 . . . .$20.00

Handy Box French Shoe Blacking
rebus $20.00

Hidden Picture — stock card
"Sing a Song of Sixpence," find 10 birds, king, pie $10.00

Hidden Picture — stock card
hidden pict: stream & home scene, find: mouse, lizard, etc. $4.00

Hidden Picture — stock card
hidden pict: ox head, "Find the Drover" $4.00

Hood's Sarsaparilla
"Star Puzzle" $10.00

Hunnewell's Cough Remedy
hidden pict: "Puzzle Card" open cage "Find the Canary" $40.00

James Pyle's Pearline
opt. illusion: find the "Maid in the Moon" star message, 1896 . . . .$20.00

Newcomb Loom Co. — Davenport, Iowa
"Cracker Jack Puzzle" $30.00

One Woman's Life at the Theater — play
rebus $40.00

Puzzle Card — stock card
hidden pict: Washington, Buffalo Bill, "Nigger," Fat Man, etc. $4.00

Sanford's Ginger
opt. illusion: "Test for Color Blindness," stare at star $20.00

Sapolio Soap
follow the lines, "Is Marriage a Failure!," 5 portraits ea. side $10.00

SSS — Swift Specific Medicines
hidden pict: Indian camp scene, bottle, find: cow, whale, etc. $30.00

Standard Sewing Machine — stock card
rebus symbols: key, iron, musical note $12.00

Tollgate N° 2 for Sexual Diseases
hidden pict: queen, clown, gorilla, elephant, etc. 1879 . . . .$8.00

Presidential Election Stock Card, $35.00.

Kamo Baking Powder, $15.00.

Durham Smoking Tobacco, $30.00.

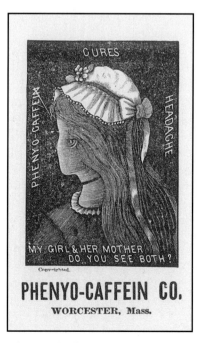

Phenyo-Caffein Headache Cure,
$15.00.

Risque

(See also: Corsets; Humor; Metamorphics; Women.)

Risque Images

Victorian trade cards with risque images and themes can be found in three basic styles. The most common style employs images and lines of text that have double meanings, with the second level of interpretation sometimes being remarkably brazen. Malydor, "The Gentlemen's Friend," produced a good example. The card shows a parrot in front of a hotel with four cats dancing behind the sick bird and other cats peeking from hotel windows. The card carries the caption, "I wish I had let those cats alone." In this case, the risque interpretation is targeted at the "gentleman" of indiscretion who has picked up a venereal disease from a "cathouse."

The second type of risque card also employs double meanings. With these cards the initial meaning appears to be boldly sexual, but further inspection proves those conclusions to be rash. These cards are usually designed as metamorphics with folding flaps. When opened, they often reveal that what had appeared to be a portion of unclothed female anatomy is actually a pair of bald heads, the backside of a farmer's pig, or the legs of another man.

The third type of risque card delivers a degree of nudity or provocative action, but usually presents the image as if it were a reproduction of classical art, a whimsical wood nymph illustration, or an innocent private moment captured by an artist but devoid of any impropriety. Within this group one finds the many cards with scenes of "allegorical" women draped in billowing robes that don't quite cover everything, images of half-naked Indian maidens, and the highly suggestive images of Victorian women "caught" by artists as they kiss their boyfriends, sleep, change their clothes, or bathe. Trade cards that are straightforward in their delivery of nudity or sex are almost, but not quite, nonexistent.

Historical Notes

As with all cultures, Victorian society was riddled with paradoxes. Among such ironies as robber barons who donated libraries and immigrants who pushed for the Chinese Exclusion Act, one finds perhaps the most intriguing paradox of the nineteenth century: the Victorian sex ethic. While some groups within the culture were reasonably consistent in the practice of their religious and philosophical positions concerning sex, as a whole, the Victorian age presented incredibly conflicting messages concerning sex and sexuality. For example, some of the same women who blushed over an exposed ankle wore dresses with necklines provocatively open, and some of the husbands who dared not speak of their own wives' corsets kept mistresses or saw prostitutes throughout their entire marriage.

Paradoxes in the Victorian sex ethic are evident in hundreds trade cards. When Congress passed the 1873 Comstock Act prohibiting the transportation of obscene material through the mail, Anthony Comstock was given authority to judge what material was and wasn't obscene. Through the support of the federal government, Comstock institutionalized a Victorian ethic that defined obscenity as virtually any work mentioning sex in anything other than evasive and indirect language. One man, Dr. Edward Foote, was nearly jailed under the provisions of the Comstock Act for mailing copies of his bestselling Plain Home Talk medical adviser because it included a chapter on contraception. Given the temper of the U.S. postal service, it is not surprising that so many trade cards veil their sexual themes in double meanings that would be embarrassing and difficult to attack in court.

Pricing Tips & Cards to Watch For

Interest in cards with risque themes is strong. Most of these cards are well designed and colorful, but even the cheaply done stock cards with risque undertones can draw prices around the $10 range. Risque stock cards designed as metamorphics or mechanicals run $20 to $50, but when designs are particularly compelling or imprints are exceptionally significant, prices can go higher. Privately issued cards vary according to the interest generated by the type of product advertised. Risque cards issued by alcohol and tobacco companies will often price in the $30 to $100 range, while risque cards issued by cosmetic companies tend to bring half that amount. As always, watch for cards that will catch the attention of collectors from as many topical areas as possible, as with the risque metamorphic that includes a golf image and an alcohol-related imprint.

Golf Metamorphic, stock card, $250.00.

Allen's for weak "Generative Organs"
    "Apollo — Ideal of Manly Beauty," naked statue in only fig leaf $30.00

Beach Metamorphic — stock card
    legs of couple below umbrella/2 men, "Manhattan Cafe" $30.00

Bon Ami Cleanser
    maid with box sees couple kissing in reflections from pans $15.00

Capadura 5¢ Cigar
    table, woman in sheer nightgown holds card, cigar box 1883 . . . .$40.00

Day & Night Tobacco
    H-T-L, "Everybody likes it Day & Night," sexy lady appears $50.00

Garland Stoves & Ranges
    H-T-L, "Happy Home," naked woman barely covered by sheet $40.00

I.W. Harper Whiskey
    couple kissing on whiskey cases, men "Wish They Had Some" $50.00

I.W. Harper Whiskey
    mechanical, slides out: pretty lady: "Pull off my gown," 1900 . . . .$100.00

Kent's Corn Planter
    lady snags skirt up on pumpkin, farmer watches, spills milk $50.00

Lash's Kidney & Liver Bitters
    rain, lady hem up "like to see it clear up" boy: "so would we" $25.00

Malydor "The Gentlemen's Friend"
    parrot: "Wish I'd let cats alone" & "cathouse," sex diseases $150.00

New Home Sewing Machine
    folder, 4 scenes, "Machine or French Sewing Girl" Act 3, kiss $30.00

Parker's Hair Balsam
    naked woman in hammock, long hair, moonlight $20.00

Stock Card
    beach scene, women changing in bath house, boy peaks $8.00

Stock Card: "The Palace" imprint
    2 prostitutes, smoking "Dem Golden Slippers I'm going for..." $15.00

Wool Soap
    die-cut oval, 2 kids in white nightshirts, no pants, 1896 . . . .$10.00

Brotherhood Wine Co., $100.00.

Murray & Lanman's Florida Water, $25.00.

Red Raven Splits, $100.00.

Root Beer, Sodas & Waters

(See also: Beer, Whiskey & Wine; Patent Medicines.)

Root Beer, Soda, & Mineral Water Images

Many wonderful images can be found on trade cards that were designed to promote root beer, soda, and mineral waters. Because these products were often presented to the public as non-alcoholic alternatives to intoxicating beverages, most of these cards were designed with bright wholesome images of subjects like children and family pets. Hires Root Beer issued approximately 30 trade cards prior to the 1904 St. Louis World's Fair, and many of their cards are among the most attractive and popular in the hobby. The first eight Hires cards date from around 1880, and they appear to be the only stock cards Hires used. Hires began commissioning their own cards in 1888. Williams Root Beer and Knapp's Root Beer also issued a number of delightful cards. Good color cards advertising soda and mineral waters are more scarce than those advertising root beer, but several nice images can be found including a few very rare cards issued by Coca-Cola.

Historical Notes

The development of America's soft drink industry is closely related to the rise of the temperance movement throughout the nineteenth century. Concerns about the physical, social, and economic problems associated with drunkenness pre-date the organization of the first American temperance societies in the 1800s, but it was not until these societies were chartered that the alcohol and saloon industries faced any serious political challenge. By the time of the Civil War, numerous communities throughout the East and Midwest had experimented with prohibitionist legislation and movements against alcohol had gained national attention. Once the Civil War was over, hundreds of abolitionists turned their crusading energies and organizations over to the cause of prohibition, and by the mid-1870s the Women's Christian Temperance Union was hitting full stride.

The effects of the temperance crusade rippled through society in a number of directions. President Hayes bent to pressure from his crusading wife, "Lemonade" Lucy, and in 1881 he outlawed the sale of all intoxicating beverages at military posts. Paralleling this rise in prohibitionists pressure was a growing epidemic among men, including those at military posts, of chronic backache trouble that could only be treated through stiff doses of "bitters" laced with whiskey at 40 proof or better. Women also developed their share of chronic troubles during this time, with Lydia Pinkham's Vegetable Compound generously offering some of the best solace that an herb and alcohol elixir could provide. Among the many alcohol and narcotic concoctions that emerged in communities where the temperance movement flourished was "Doc" Pemberton's brain tonic called "Coca-Cola," named so from the coca leaves (cocaine) and kola nuts (caffeine) that gave it kick and flavor.

The temperance movement also helped spur the development of legitimate non-intoxicating beverage alternatives. Soda fountains evolved as wholesome options for those who missed saloons or wanted to sit in the company of "respectable" women, and bot-

tled waters from famous mineral spring resorts grew in popularity. Charles Hires saw an amber opportunity and began marketing his root beer as "a most Delicious, Sparkling Temperance Beverage."

Pricing Tips & Cards to Watch For

Interest in soft drink trade cards is strong, and most cards in this category are a bit tough to come by. Stock cards with imprints for local bottlers of root beer, ginger ale, mineral waters, etc. usually sell for under $10, but if the image or company imprinted is exceptional, prices can go much higher. The early Hires stock cards sell for $100 and up. The later Hires cards were produced in such large quantities that prices remain in the $12 to $30 range for most of them, despite their beauty and popularity. Other privately issued root beer cards tend to fall in the $10 to $30 range. Keep an eye open for Coca-Cola cards, as they can bring $1,000 or more.

Tufts' Arctic Soda, $75.00.

Hires Root Beer, $15.00.

Allens Root Beer Extract
small square card, woman's head, flowered bonnet, pink bow **$10.00**

Bryant's Root Beer
little boy raises box like weight lifter, red stage, 1896 . . . . **$25.00**

Hemingway & Bradley Soda & Mineral
stock card, winter scene, "Manf'gs & Bottlers of..." **$10.00**

Hires' Root Beer
girl sits on pillar, white garland & slip, box of Hires, 1889 . . . . **$25.00**

Hires' Root Beer
"What! Never tasted...," girl, apron, Hire's box, glass, 1890 . . . . **$15.00**

Hires' Root Beer
girls smiles, "Ledger" paper hat, white dress **$12.00**

Hires' Root Beer
"all gone," boy, sombrero, hand in pocket, empty glass, 1894 . . . . **$15.00**

Hires' Root Beer
"His First Suspenders," brown pants rolled to knees, 1896 . . . . **$15.00**

Hires' Root Beer
painting: Parting of Ruth & Naomi, 2 women, man, Mideast **$12.00**

Knapp's Root Beer
"Guess what...," 2-sided, girl pokes box out back, 1893 . . . . **$20.00**

Poland Water, Poland Spring
folder, views: spring house & bottling works/old lady & girl **$50.00**

Rieger's Lemon Sugar
Uncle Sam on big lemon, ethnic types, "Boss Lemonade" **$45.00**

Stock Card — confectionery imprint
2 boys, lady, huge seltzer bottle squirting into glass **$12.00**

Stock Card — piano imprint
2 dogs as boys, torpedo-shaped "Lemon" bottle, empty glass **$8.00**

Walsh's Old Time Birch & Root Beer
rev. of stock card: father time, clock, "Dealers... SELL it" **$15.00**

William's Root Beer
3 kids play train, case of extract, bottle "whistles," 1892 . . . . **$15.00**

William's Root Beer
boy with glass and girl framed in pink flowers, ad on right **$12.00**

Hires' Root Beer, die-cut, $30.00.

Knapp's Root Beer, $25.00.

Williams' Root Beer Extract, $30.00.

Sewing Machines

(See also: Clothing & Dry Goods; Sewing Threads.)

Sewing Machine Images

Images of sewing machines probably appear more often in Victorian trade cards than any other type of mechanized devise. Hundreds of stock cards with imprinted ads and sketches of various machines were issued by large and small manufacturers alike. Of greater interest are the many color cards privately commissioned by the major machine manufacturers. Some of these images are rather straightforward in their approach, offering a crisp illustration of the machine and a minimal amount of explanatory text. Others are far more creative, offering romantic visions of homes that are magically transformed by new machines or of marriages lifted from chaos to bliss on account of one well-planned purchase. A number of these cards also emphasize the "furniture" aspect of sewing machines. This is especially true of some of the New Home Sewing Machine Company cards that depict their machine prominently displayed in the public spaces of home for the admiration of all who visit.

Although numerous sets of stock cards with sewing machine imprints were distributed, sets of privately commissioned machine cards are almost nonexistent. Singer provides the notable exception. They issued several large sets, the first of which was copyrighted in 1892 in anticipation of the Columbian Exposition, and the last of which was released shortly after the turn-of-the-century. These popular "Singer in Foreign Lands" cards were apparently distributed as complete sets in envelopes and boxes, but were also handed out individually by local retailers who imprinted their names on the lower portion of the cards' backs.

Historical Notes

England was experimenting with mechanical devices for sewing as early as the 1790s, but it wasn't until the 1830s that France and America began closing in on a practical design that could revolutionize they way families kept themselves clothed.

The labor-saving potential of these machines was readily apparent, but sewing machines were not embraced without some thought as to their potentially negative consequences. In fact, Walter Hunt withdrew his own American patent request for an improved sewing machine in 1838 based upon his concerns about the potential of the machine to disrupt the established capital and labor balance. Hunt was far from alone in this concern. In France, an early sewing machine factory was destroyed by a mob of workers, and when Elias Howe developed a breakthrough in machine design in 1843, he had to go to England for financial aid because so many Americans were worried about thousands of workers who could be displaced.

Isaac Singer followed Howe into the industry with a patent of his own in 1851, and by the time of the 1876 Centennial Exposition, Wheeler and Wilson, Domestic, New Home, and White were all setting up exhibits and peddling machines by the thousands. But escape from the drudgery of home sewing did not come cheaply; Singer pioneered the marketing technique in the 1850s of dividing regions into exclusive "territories" on the condition that agents would agree to sell their machines at the set price of $125 each, which was an incredible amount of money at that time. Hundreds of small manufacturers entered and left the sewing machine industry during the trade card era. The most significant player to leave the field was Albert Pope, who in 1878 switched from manufacturing sewing machine gears to bicycles, and who through his "Columbia" highwheeler almost single-handedly launched the Victorian bicycle craze that swept the nation.

Pricing Tips & Cards to Watch For

Many beautiful and historically significant sewing machine trade cards can still be purchases for under $15. Stock cards with sewing machine imprints sell in the $5 vicinity, with most privately issued cards bringing $8 to $15. For a sewing machine trade card to bring over $20 in the present market, the card must be very early and scarce or exceptionally well-designed and of special topical interest.

New Home Sewing Maching, $15.00.

Domestic Sewing Machine, $10.00.

Davis Sewing Machine
woman on bench, 4 pigeons, distant man lays on sign **$10.00**

Domestic
3 ladies making dress from pattern, maid serves **$10.00**

Domestic Sewing Machine
2 girls making dress for doll, machine **$12.00**

Household Sewing Machine
woman in chair, doll in lap, daughter on floor, machine **$12.00**

Howe Machine Co.
3 views of "How(e) it happens to be the best," man holds sign . . .**$15.00**

Leader Sewing Machine
rose, woman at machine, fairy sits on covered top, 1884 . . . .**$30.00**

New Home
"Monkey & the Cat's Paw," lady, son, monkey hurts cat **$6.00**

New Home Sewing Machine
"New Home in the Far West," wife sews on porch, man, 1881 . . .**$8.00**

New Home Sewing Machine
bright flowers, new house (eclectic style), machine **$8.00**

New Home Sewing Machine
"Painful Alternative," wife says: Machine or Divorce **$15.00**

Royal St. John Sewing Machine
girl on platform demonstrates machine, amazed crowd **$20.00**

Wanzer Sewing Machines
Oriental-looking husband, wife, child, man uses machine **$25.00**

Weed Sewing Machine Company
"A Weed that cannot be Weeded out," machines, parts, weeds . .**$40.00**

Wheeler & Wilson, $8.00.

Singer Sewing Machine, $4.00.

New Home Sewing Machine, $12.00.

Wheeler & Wilson, $8.00.

Wheeler & Wilson, $8.00.

Sewing Threads

(See also: Clothing & Dry Goods; Sewing Machines.)

Thread Images

Trade cards produced for thread advertising probably include the widest range of imagery found in any product category. Sets of stock cards were imprinted by most of the major thread companies, and a few of these sets were produced only in one or two colors. Beyond those few black and white sets, most thread cards employ a good assortment of colors, stock cards or not. To facilitate product recognition, the majority of all privately issued thread cards somehow depict a spool of thread with their logo showing somewhere on the card's face. The back's of many cards carry additional advertising, as well as the imprint of a local retailer. Children, pets, birds, and nature scenes together account for perhaps three quarters of all the images found on thread cards, but given the many hundreds of cards issued, that still leaves a lot of room for other subjects that can appear. Some of the more interesting topics found in thread images include things like ships and trains, activities like fishing and exploration, popular icons like Santa Claus and Uncle Sam, cultural trends like aestheticism and racism, and people like presidents and kings.

Historical Notes

The emergence of America's cotton and textile industries was one of the most defining developments in American history. The cotton industry of the South fostered a paternalistic, agrarian-based culture powered by African-American slaves, while the textile industry of the North cultivated a capitalistic, manufacturing-based culture reliant upon the exploitation of child labor. The two parallel cultures were both intolerant and interdependent upon each other, and despite the criticism both cultures received from outside observers, the steady and increasing demand for the products of these industries guaranteed that little would change without catastrophic intervention. In the South, the intervention came in the form of the Civil War, which, according to some interpretations, was partially drummed up by Northern industrialists lusting for more control over cotton. In the North, the intervention eventually came in the form of labor riots, unions, and Progressive Era legislation.

America's first textile factory was established in Rowley, Massachusetts, in 1643, but the industry remained relatively inconsequential until after the American Revolution. In 1790 Samuel Slater emigrated from England with stolen technology and established state-of-the-art cotton mills in Rhode Island. Slater's first mill was powered by water and featured 250 spindles "manned" mostly by children aged four to ten. Captains of industry quickly emerged throughout New England as the principals of water-powered mills were realized and applied in every type of manufacturing possible. America's industrial revolution was on the verge of picking up steam as dozens of farming communities evolved into mill and manufacturing towns in a single generation.

The textile industry stayed near the heart of New England's industrial base, even though that industry itself remained in many ways essentially unchanged from when Slater recruited his first crew of children as operators. When America suffered its first major industrial disaster, the accident occurred at a Massachusetts textile factory after a roof collapsed on nearly 700 workers. A good share of the 77 employees who were killed were children under 13. And when labor leader "Mother Jones" marched into New York in 1903 to disrupt President Roosevelt's vacation on Long Island, she led a band of youngsters representing some 1.5 million children working in textile mills, often for less than $2.00 a week. Changes in the industry were hard and long in coming. Among the many ironies of the Victorian trade card era are the images of carefree youngsters that were used in the promotion of threads that were spun and braided by exploited children.

Pricing Tips & Cards to Watch For

Thread cards offer some of the best collecting opportunities in trade cards. There are enough $5 cards with delightful images to keep a collector happily adding to a collection for many years, but there are also enough scarce and rare gems to keep it interesting for a lifetime. The J. & P. Coats cards are often the most inexpensive privately issued cards in a dealer's inventory, with most of their 400 plus images running in the $3 to $6 range, and very few of them selling for over $15. But some of the Coats cards are challengingly elusive, as collectors soon realize once they begin trying to complete sets. The Clark's O.N.T. Spool Cotton cards are similar in their abundance and affordability, except for the oversized Clark's cards, which tend to run in the $10 to $25 range. Calendar cards by either of these companies also run in a bit more expensive, as do their best and rarest images when dealers happen to be alert enough to catch them.

Every thread company issued at least a few cards that are in the $25 to $50 range, but the card companies to especially watch for are Chadwick's, Kerr's, Belding, and California Silk, as most of the cards issued by these companies sell for well above normal thread card prices. In fact, most of the larger Belding and California Silk cards start at $50 and go up quickly from there. Watch for the Belding cards with Indians, a cable car, or a battleship made out of white spools, as these cards easily bring $100 or more.

Kerr's Thread, $25.00.

J & P Coats Thread, $15.00.

John D. Cutter Silk Threads, $15.00.

Barbour's Irish Flax Thread, $20.00.

Eureka Silk Thread, $10.00.

J. R. Leeson Spool Linen, $25.00.

Corticelli Spool Silk, $15.00.

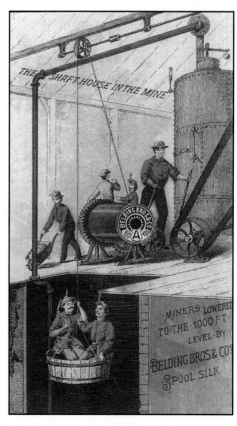

Belding Bros. Spool Silk, $50.00.

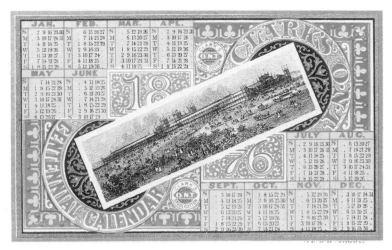

Clark's Thread, $60.00.

J & P Coats Thread, $20.00.

Eureka Spool Silk, $75.00.

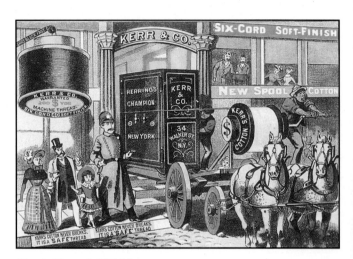

Kerr's Thread, $25.00.

Clark's Thread, $6.00.

Merrick's Thread, $8.00.

Clark's Thread, die-cut, $8.00.

Brook's Thread
2 sailors, one sits on deck, other stands threading needle **$8.00**

Chadwick's Thread
boy uses thread to fly kite, girl helps, ready to let go **$8.00**

Clark's Thread
metamorphic: sad Mr. & Mrs. Jones/happy, fixed clothes **$15.00**

Clark's Thread
boy leap-frogs over 3 spools, 2 other boys watch **$4.00**

Clark's Thread
lighthouse scene, thread spool as light, 4 people observe **$12.00**

Clark's Thread
folder: girl fishing/parlor scene,1880 calendar on back **$15.00**

Clark's Thread
Uncle Sam, woman, eagle & lion, Cupid, Prang: Paris, 1878 . . . . **$20.00**

Clark's Thread
Christmas tree, toys, girl holds 2 dolls, sits on spool **$6.00**

Corticelli Spool Silk
cherubs use thread & pulley to raise obelisk in Egypt **$15.00**

J. & P. Coats Thread
boy & girl pull wagon, huge spools as wheels, 2nd boy drives **$6.00**

J. & P. Coats Thread
"We Beat Them All," boy rides train, spool engine, waves hat **$6.00**

J. & P. Coats Thread
Black lady pulls mule, man scratches head "Ef dis don't fetch" **$12.00**

J. & P. Coats Thread
boy in blue suit, hat, near sea, chases butterfly with net **$6.00**

J. & P. Coats Thread
2 boys in caps pull big turtle from pond using thread **$8.00**

Kerr's Thread
"Never Played Out," girl plays violin, boy on spool listens **$8.00**

Kerr's Thread
"Takes the Cake," 3 whites watch Black cake-walk, boy spins **$20.00**

Merrick's Thread
"Sure now Jimmy," girl uses thread to pull boy's tooth **$8.00**

Merrick's Thread
"A Friend in Need," girl sews boys pants, watering pail **$5.00**

Willimantic Thread
3 children in meadow pull butterfly from net **$8.00**

Willimantic Thread
"Home Treasures," blonde girl, cat pulls thread from parrot **$8.00**

Willimantic Thread
"The Favorite for 1885," big spool on girl's sled, doll, dog **$10.00**

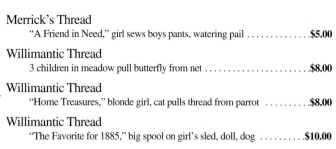

J & P Coats Thread, $6.00.

J & P Coats Thread, $6.00.

Clark's Thread, die-cut, $15.00.

Eureka Spool Silk, $10.00.

J & P Coats Thread, $6.00.

Shoe & Shoe Polish

(See also: Clothing & Dry Goods.)

Shoe & Shoe Polish Images

Trade cards advertising shoes, boots, and shoe care products are plentiful and popular with a growing number of collectors. Shoe cards as a group offer a better sampling of clever and whimsical images than most other product groups, but the range of subjects treated in shoe cards tends to be somewhat narrow. For example, there is a wonderful selection of great shoe cards with humorous "satirical substitution" images of children riding enormous shoes as if the shoes were sleds, wagons, or boats, but there are very few shoe cards with images relating to political leaders, holidays, sports, or other subjects of topical interest.

Advertisements for leather polishes, blackings, "dressings," and preservative oils were often printed on low-quality stock cards, but not always. A number of companies issued some great shoe care cards, with Bixby and Frank Miller providing some of the most interesting cards in the industry. Advertisements for shoes, boots, rubbers, and shoe parts like soles, screws, and nails were rarely printed on stock cards, and were usually privately commissioned. As with most other important product groups, many of the most colorful shoe cards were privately designed by manufacturers and then freely distributed to retailers who had their own names imprinted in the spaces provided. Cards issued by A.S.T.Cº were often printed in oversized formats on thin paper stock. The many Henderson "Red School House" shoe cards with scenes from the classroom form an interesting mosaic of images that together offer some unusual insights on Victorian education. The earliest shoe cards were issued mostly by Reynolds Brothers and the Sollers Co. during the 1870s.

Historical Notes

William Young created a bit of stir in Philadelphia in 1800 when he started producing shoes that were right and left foot specific, but most shoemakers held steadfast for another few decades to the thinking and methods that had been passed down from the days of sandalmaking in Egypt. Significant changes in America's shoemaking trade began in the mid-1840s when a machine was finally perfected to replace the traditional hammer and lapstone that had been used by many generations of shoemakers for the conditioning of leather.

By the time of the Civil War, another machine had come into use for driving pegs into the soles of shoes. As with several other important American industries, the Civil War gave a kick start to several fledgling shoe operations and turned them into big-time enterprizes. By the end of the war, factories were cranking out thousands of standard-sized "left" and "right" foot boots that soldiers came to appreciate and insist upon after the war when they went to order their next pair of shoes. Thousands of local shoemakers became increasingly irrelevant as the responsibility of shoe production was turned over to higher technologies and assembly-line production.

Pricing Tips & Cards to Watch For

Collector interest in shoe-related trade cards has lagged behind many of the other product areas, so prices for great shoe cards still remain quite reasonable. The greatest interest so far has been shown for Frank Miller Blacking cards, the most expensive of which depict display boxes of the product and are currently selling for over $100 in auctions. Most other shoe-related cards fall into the $5 to $15 range. Watch for the Wales Goodyear card with a winter carnival scene or the Goodyear Welted Shoes card with a mountain hiker rubbing his blisters, as these two cards are bringing over $50 each. Also keep an eye open for the handful of shoe cards with illustrations of subjects like Indians and Uncle Sam, as these cards draw the attention of topical collectors and can pull prices that spike considerably above normal shoe card values.

Bixby's Royal Polish, $15.00.

Shoe Stock Mechanical Card, $75.00.

American Shoe Tip Co. (A.S.T.Cº)
girl paints logo on easel, boy points, shoe picture on wall $8.00

Die-cut Boot Stock Card
woman's high-top shoe shape, imprinted by local store $15.00

Dieterichs' Leather Preserving Oil
4 chicks nesting in a shoe that floats at sea $15.00

Harris' Standard Tip Shoes
boy hammers shoe on anvil, blacksmith, 2 boys watch $20.00

Harris' Standard Tip Shoes
4 kids, dog, fife & drum parade, ad banner & drum, 1884 . . . .$20.00

Harris' Standard Tip Shoes
boy charges top of hill, holds up banner and shoe $15.00

Hatch Flexible Shoe
dancing man with shoes, 6 watch, Black man bare feet, dog $10.00

Henderson's "Red School House" Shoes
school scene "Billy so glad, he blew his gun at master's head" $15.00

Iron Wire Clinching Nails
cobblers line up buying shoe nail/"Old Way" inset, man works $25.00

John Kelly's Fine Shoes
girls stands on butterfly in sky, holds shoe on tray $10.00

Mundell Solar Tip Shoes
boy in hat, girl, baby, big black dog, "Baby's Shoes" $10.00

Mundell Solar Tip Shoes
Foolish Man/Wise Man: sad family, bills/happy family $12.00

Mundell Solar Tip Shoes
man with yellow hair & beard like sun, 6 kids get shoes $12.00

Queen's Dressing
Black woman holds bottle, shoes: "remarks on de' oder side" $25.00

Silver Tips
barnyard scene, 5 kids, huge boot, dog chases rat out toe $15.00

Sollers Shoes
"Sollers Floral Soiree," young couples dance, band, 1877 . . . .$20.00

Sollers Shoes
"These beautiful shoes...," girl, framed picture of shoes, 1874 . . . .$30.00

Stock Card
"A Glove Fit," salesman offers shoebox, man, big foot, 1880 . . . .$8.00

Wales Goodyear Shoe Co.
die-cut rubber, "Best Rubbers in the World are Branded..." $20.00

Candee Rubbers, $12.00.

Mundell Solar Tip Shoes, $10.00.

Harris' Standard Tip Shoes, $15.00.

Soaps

(See also: Arctic.)

Soap Images

Victorian trade cards with advertisements for various types of soaps are so plentiful that many collectors have refused to take them seriously. Hundreds of soap ads were imprinted on dull stock cards with generic illustrations, and many of the privately issued soap cards look so much alike in their styles and images that they easily create a blur as one flips through the stacks of a dealer's inventory. Only recently have more collectors begun to pick through soap cards with a thoughtful eye and to discover the collecting potential found in the seemingly endless parade of soap card ads and images. A few collectors have been quietly assembling wonderful assortments of the ethnic images found in Fairbank's Soap cards, the highly elusive bear images used by Van Haagen Soap, or the delightful elephant images favored by Ivorine. Other collectors are waking up just a little late, because certain soap cards have now become difficult and expensive to find.

The stock cards that were used by soap companies range in quality from very low to quite high. Most of the stock images selected for imprinting by small soap manufacturers feature predictable scenes of children, pets, and nature. Here or there one finds a local soapmaker who took a risk with a lone stock card that used a political or off-color image, but for the most part, soap companies distributed unremarkable sets of cards more suitable for the scrap books of Victorian children than the albums of collectors today. Most of the best soap cards were produced as private issues by successful companies with widespread product distribution. Some of these companies produced dozens of cards with images covering a wide range of topics. Kendall Manufacturing issued over 100 custom-designed cards for "Soapine" alone, plus they put out another 150 or more stock cards with Soapine advertisements that can easily pass as private issues because of the quality of the imprinting. Curtis, Davis & Co, Lautz Bros., Jas. Kirk, B.T. Babbitt's, and James Pyle's are a few of the other manufacturers that issued large numbers of soap cards.

Historical Notes

Soapmaking is a simple, but distasteful procedure. For those who made their own soap at home, there were several "recipes," none of which required expensive materials or fancy techniques. Families that could not afford to buy pre-packaged lye made their own by pouring water into a barrel filled with ashes saved from a stove or fireplace. The water that sifted its way through ashes would come out as lye on the other end, but folks had to be careful how they handled it, because a splash of lye could burn skin or take out an eye. On soapmaking day, families would stir their lye into all of the stored up grease and lard they had on hand, and then let the lye do its work. When the mixture got thick, they could pour it into simple molds and let it harden into cakes. If they wanted to get fancy, they could stick with only pure lard, which kept the soap white, and they could pour in sassafras oil, lilacs, or rosebuds to give their soap a pleasant scent. Later, those who cared to bother could cut their cakes into bath bars and shave bricks into thin flakes for laundry use.

Handling the lye and storing the old grease and lard were among the biggest deterrents in home soapmaking. On the other hand, with such low costs in materials and equipment, soapmaking was an ideal enterprise for many entrepreneurs looking for a quick way into the business world. Butchers, slaughterhouses, and meat packers were more than willing to work out deals with contractors who could haul off their waste, and every business and home in the city had ashes piling up that needed to be hauled away.

As Victorian middle-class consumers got used to buying soap instead of making it, there got to be so many local soap manufacturers that dreaming up new names to print on paper wrappers became a real challenge. Besides the obvious cop-out names like Tip Top Soap, Denver's Best Soap, and Acme Best Bar Soap, there are a number of intriguing brand names to be found. Some soaps were named after the scents that were added, like Tulip Soap, Oak Leaf Soap, or Magnolia Soap. Other soap makers tried to exploit pop culture fads, as with Telephone Soap or Koko Soap, which was a rip-off from Gilbert and Sullivan's hit, *The Mikado*. Among the most puzzling choices for soap names are Oat Meal Toilet Soaps (for bad complexions?), Nine O'Clock Tea Soap (for recycling dishwater?), and Good-Will Laundry Soap (love tokens from husbands who had been out all night?). For those who think that Procter and Gamble's "Ivory Soap" is a rather uninspired brand name, take heart from the fact that the original brand name did not stick. The soap was first introduced in 1878 as "P & G's White Soap," a Pulitzer Prize winner if ever there was one.

Pricing Tips & Cards to Watch For

The majority of all soap cards are imprinted stock issues that are still selling in the $3 to $8 range, making soaps one of the most affordable of all products to collect. Privately issued cards tend to sell for $8 to $15, with only a small number of exceptions. The exceptions to watch for are the now-popular Soapine cards (which sell mostly for $15 to $35), Ivorine elephant cards (which start at $35), Fairbank's ethnic cards (some of which bring $100 or more), and Van Haagen bear images (which can sell for $50 and up). Keep an eye open for the large Soapine card that pictures a whale breaking through waves with a box of soap on his back and the normal-sized Soapine that shows a beached whale with the name Soapine in an arch over the image, as these cards can bring $100 or more.

Soapine, $40.00.

Fisk & Co. Japanese Soap, $20.00.

Glenn's Sulpher Soap, $15.00.

Maple City Self Washing Soap, $15.00.

Soapine, $15.00.

Welcome Soap, $6.00.

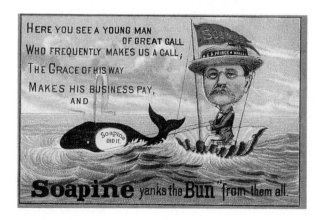

Soapine, $20.00.

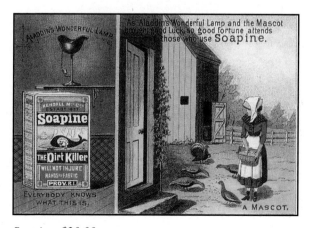

Soapine, $20.00.

Maypole Soap, $15.00.

Scourene, $8.00.

James Pyle's Pearline, $5.00.

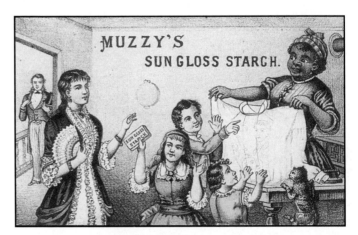

Muzzy's Sun Gloss Starch, $15.00.

Star Soap, $20.00.

David's Prize Soap, die-cut, $50.00.

Clairette Soap — Fairbank's
    die-cut of woman in hat on soap box, her face as trademark **$25.00**

David's Prize Soap
    wash lady in kitchen/2 ladies at "Prize" piano in other room **$10.00**

Father's Best Toilet Soap — stock card
    "Set of cards with every cake," camel loaded in desert **$5.00**

Gilbert Graves' Mirror Gloss Starch
    naked child sees self in large mirror, fancy pillow **$12.00**

Higgin's Laundry Soap
    "Afternoon in Central Park," 2-horse carriage, ad on side **$8.00**

Higgins' German Laundry Soap
    "On the road to Coney Island," man courts coy lady on train **$10.00**

Ivorine Soap
    girl works in yard, washtub & washboard, box of soap **$8.00**

Ivorine Soap
    "Sounding the Praises of...," 3 kids play pots like band **$5.00**

James Pyle's Pearline
    "My Busy Day," blonde girl in dress, bucket, soap, brush, pan **$10.00**

James Pyle's Pearline
    young girl plays soap box as a drum **$5.00**

James Pyle's Pearline
    young boy rides soap box like a horse, blocks **$5.00**

Jas/Kirk "Mottled German" Soap
    man, woman, dance with flags, gilded cards **$4.00**

Lautz Bros. Pure & Healthy Soaps
    girl with basket & soap box on steps at seashore **$6.00**

Lavine Soap
    boy bring wagon "City Express" with soap to 3 washing girls **$10.00**

Lavine Soap
    woman shows ankle, holds up lace, box of soap on table **$6.00**

Maple City Self Washing Soap
    happy girl washes doll clothes outside in washtub, box table **$15.00**

New Process Starch
    2 panels: Chinaman "Old Process"/mother, son, New Process **$15.00**

Sapolio — For All Cleaning
    9 fingernails in 3 rows, interpretations on reverse, 1890 ....**$15.00**

Swift's Washing Powder
    girl scrubs doll on washboard, stands on soap box **$15.00**

Thomson's Soap Foam
    woman using washboard & washtub, powder product on table **$25.00**

Welcome Soap — Curtis, Davis & Co.
    father welcomes suitor to big feast, mother, daughter watch **$6.00**

Wool Soap — Swift & Co.
    pretty woman in "Wintry winds" & snow, umbrella, basket **$10.00**

New Process Soap, $10.00.

Scourene, $8.00.

Master Soap, $6.00.

Sports & Recreation

(See also: Baseball; Bicycles; Toys.)

Sports & Recreation Images

Advertising trade cards with images of sports and recreational activities are rapidly gaining new fans as sports card collectors become increasingly aware of the intrigue and historical significance of these items. Several of the most popular sports in America today were "invented" during the trade card era, and even those sports that pre-date the Victorian era went through significant changes during that period as rules were officially drawn up and the first inter-collegiate and professional teams were organized. Trade card images from the 1870s to 1900 offer some of the earliest illustrations of sports like ice hockey, football, and tennis, as well as some of the most interesting color images from the nineteenth century of popular recreational activities like hunting and fishing. The quality of these images varies considerably. Many of these activities were captured in cheap stock cards printed in only one or two colors of ink. Others of these cards were commissioned by specific manufacturers who spared no expense in coming up with wonderful color images.

Some of the sports and recreational activities that appear in trade card images include: archery, badminton, baseball, bicycling, billiards, boating, bowling, boxing, bull fighting, camping, cards, cricket, croquet, curling, dog sledding, fencing, fishing, football, foot racing, golf, gymnastics, horse racing, ice fishing, ice hockey, ice sailing, ice skating, ping-pong, pole vaulting, polo, rodeo riding, roller skating, rowing, skiing, "sporting" (gambling activities), swimming, target shooting, tennis, tobogganing, weight lifting, and yacht racing.

Historical Notes

To understand the late-Victorian period, it is important to remember that nearly half of the "golden years" in advertising

Hunt's Remedy, $125.00.

trade cards once deservedly earned the nickname of the "Gay Nineties." Despite the staid stereotype of England's Queen Victoria in her high collars, black-veiled hats, and disapproving frown, America's Victorian young people loved to play and have a good time. Outdoor sports, indoor games, and backyard recreation were all important parts of the late-nineteenth century middle-class lifestyle.

Prior to the trade card era, leisure time had been primarily the privilege of the wealthy elite. But with America's post-Civil War growth in manufacturing, consumerism, and middle-class prosperity, there came a burgeoning of opportunities for leisure-time activities for an increasingly robust number of young people and energetic adults. Americans tended to acclimate themselves to their new leisure time possibilities through fads that swept the nation in waves.

The first fad to hit was baseball, which technically pre-dated the Civil War by several decades but never really established itself commercially until the 1870s, when stores started handling professional quality equipment and teams started putting players on salaries. From the 1870s on, a significant number of fans were paying money to see baseball games, and they were spending more money to buy equipment so they could themselves imitate their heroes at picnics and on weekends. Local amateur teams were formed complete with uniforms, groomed playing fields, and loyal fans. The language of baseball found its way into American vernacular, and the sport began to significantly impact culture.

The emerging Victorian lawn culture combined with the fad of physical fitness in three extremely popular yard games, each of which swept the country in waves from east to west. Croquet arrived from France via England around 1870, and within three years had worked its way out to homesteads in Kansas and Nebraska. The game was praised by adults for its "civilizing effects" on young people, who probably embraced the game mostly as an opportunity for flirting and courting

Tennis stock card, tea imprint, $25.00.

with the opposite sex. Since the game was played in the yards of respectable families, it was one of the few activities that young people of both sexes could enjoy without the ball-and-chain of a chaperone. At the height of its popularity in the 1880s, croquet sets were sold with candle sockets soldered to wickets to facilitate matches at lawn parties that trailed into dark hours. As with croquet, archery and lawn tennis each had their day in the sun of the lawns of the Victorian middle class.

The roller skating fad moved from New York to the west more slowly than the three big lawn fads because of the need for skating rinks. In communities that were unwilling to wait for the installation of hard maple floors at new facilities, chairs were sometimes moved aside at local theaters or halls, which often proved disastrous if the floor was made of pine or some other soft wood. Roller skating had established itself with the Newport crowd by the mid-1860s, but it took another fifteen years for the sport to settle in west of the Mississippi. However, once a town had built a rink, roller skating became part of the local culture. Parties of all sorts were held at rinks, including costume events, birthday celebrations, and holiday extravaganzas. Most rinks had galleries from which spectators could watch. Trade cards can be found imprinted for special events like exhibition skating, polo matches on skates (hockey), masquerade skating, skate races, and skate dances.

Pricing Tips & Cards to Watch For

Prices for trade cards with sports and recreation images are very volatile. Certain sports are hardly collected at all, while other sports are so competitively pursued that even stock cards with images of some sports can sell for $100 or more. The sports that currently draw the highest prices are baseball, hockey, tennis, cricket, and golf. Because there are fewer than a dozen known hockey images in American trade cards, and because several of these images date from the very first years of the sport, hockey card prices start at $50 and go up rapidly. Watch for the Atlantic & Pacific Tea card with a hockey scene, and the Bufford stock card titled, "Hockey on the ice," as these cards can bring $200 or more. Golf cards generally bring $30 and up, while tennis and cricket cards run mostly in the $15 to $40 range.

In pricing most other sports cards, one needs to pay close attention to the quality of the image, its apparent historical significance, and the nature of the card's advertising. No hard and fast rules apply, but in many cases stock cards in black and white will only bring $5 to $15, while better stock cards in full color will run $10 to $40. Privately issued cards with sports images will usually run anywhere from $10 to $50. Prices for cards with good hunting and fishing images can run slightly higher, especially if the advertising is for companies directly related to these activities.

Union Hardware Co. Roller Skates, $35.00.

Clarence Brooks Varnishes, $150.00.

Heckers Perfect Baking Powder, $15.00.

Dr. Jackson's Root & Herb Cordial, $40.00.

Spaulding's Football Player, die-cut,
$140.00.

Merrick's Thread, $10.00.

J & P Coats Thread, $10.00.

Rice & Hayward Biscuit & Crackers,
$8.00.

Parker Gun, $200.00.

Arbuckle Coffee Sports & Pastimes
#6 of 50: France — fencing, tennis, billiards 1893 . . . . **$15.00**

Belding Bros. Thread
"The Champion," girl in hat on thread spools as roller skates **$20.00**

Bowling Stock Card — paint imprint
pin boy struck by ball and pins, 2 other boys laugh **$20.00**

Boxing Stock Card
"Sullivan: Ye Jolly Miller," bloody nose, bare knuckle boxing **$75.00**

Carpenter's Automatic Back Brace
5 scenes around lady's portrait in center: bikes, gymnastics, etc. **$75.00**

Chest Shield Undershirt — stock card
"Arctic Sport," 3 men shooting walrus on ice flow, 1882 . . . . **$10.00**

Clark's Thread
Simple Simon "went to shoot a wild duck," gun, ducks fly over **$8.00**

Corticelli Silk Thread
woman ice skating, letting thread off spool, men follow **$25.00**

Currier & Ives Stock Card — 1879
"A Bad Point, on a Good Pointer," man shoots his hunting dog **$50.00**

Dr. Hunter's Expectorant
hunter in buckskins shoot wolf attacking winter sleigh **$30.00**

Enameline die-cut doll
"Wellesley College Girl" plays croquet in blue outfit **$25.00**

Enameline die-cut doll
Yale Boy in uniform, football **$40.00**

Ferndell
cats of "Tabby Town" play Ping Pong on kitchen table **$15.00**

Football Stock Card — rev. imprint
ball in air, 4 men charge man from other team, goal posts **$20.00**

Football Stock Card — "Estey Piano"
blonde youngster, blue eyes, red uniform, runs with football **$20.00**

German Yeast Co. — Omaha NE
"Sportingman," Black man, top hat, fighting cock & dog 1887 . . . . . . **$35.00**

Great Atlantic & Pacific Tea Co.
ice fishing scene, 4 holes open in ice, big fish, many men **$25.00**

Gun & Lock Smith, Sporting Material
stock card: "Bear-ly an Escape," bear chases man & hounds **$10.00**

Humphrey's Witch Hazel Oil
fencing — lady poses with sword, heart on chest, 1901 . . . . **$20.00**

Keystone Watch Cases
"Glass Ball Spring Trap Shooting," man shoots target ball **$15.00**

Keystone Watch Cases
"Artist on the Keystone Flying Rings," gymnast hangs on rings **$15.00**

Polo Stock Card — clothing imprint
3 men, 1 fallen, 2 small polo ponies, violent scene **$6.00**

Pond's Bitters
2 men, 1 on phone: "late to-night," other shoots billiards **$20.00**

Rowing Stock Card — "Honey Balsam"
man in uniform rows through ducks toward 2 fishing men **$6.00**

St. Louis Beef Canning
"so nice to camp out...," hunter, small tent, dog, gun, beef **$35.00**

Syracuse Chilled Plow
wading man catches fish at small waterfall, lady with net **$20.00**

Tennis Stock Card — "Asthma Cure"
woman in dress, feathered hat, poses with ball and racket **$15.00**

Vigoral — Armour & Co.
"Drink... A Foe to Fatigue," muscular arm lifts bar bell **$30.00**

Wheeler & Wilson Sewing Machine
yacht racing — Puritan beats out Genesta **$15.00**

Solar Tip Shoes, John Mundell, $20.00.

Canoe stock card, hardware imprint, $5.00.

Great Atlantic & Pacific Tea Co., $250.00.

Statue of Liberty
(See also: Columbia; Patriotic.)

Statue of Liberty Images

The dozens of trade cards with images of the Statue of Liberty are very popular with collectors. Generally speaking, the quality of these cards is above average, and in many cases the designs are clever and have been completed in striking colors. Even the stock cards upon which the statue appears usually are of good quality and of better designs than most stock cards. The statue is usually depicted in New York Harbor with the Brooklyn Bridge in the distance, but she can sometimes appear by herself in a different context or can be satirized by other figures who stand in corn fields or other settings.

Historical Notes

"Give me your tired, your poor, your huddled masses yearning to breathe free... Send these, the homeless, tempest-tost to me, I lift my lamp beside the golden door!"

Emma Lazarus penned these words in 1883 for a pedestal fundraiser for the Statue of Liberty. Her sonnet, "The New Colossus," reflected the dream of millions of nineteenth century immigrants from around the world who made their way to America in search of freedom, dignity, and economic prosperity. At the 1886 dedication of the statue, one uninvited woman shouted an ironic quip across the water from the deck of a ship chartered by the New York Suffrage Association: "Is it not despicable that if Liberty had life, she could vote neither in the United States nor in France?" While not every dream of every person could be realized in the turbulent realities of the day, at least from Miss Liberty's very first day she could stand as a symbol for the freedom people had in America to speak their minds.

Frenchman Auguste Bartholdi first began planning the statue in 1865. The statue was originally scheduled for an 1876 Centennial unveiling, but only the arm and torch arrived in time to be exhibited. The earliest trade card depictions of the statue pre-date its completion and reflect the variety of odd pedestal designs that were considered and rejected as the project dragged on. At one point, a patent medicine company volunteered to kick in a small fortune to help pay for the statue's pedestal, but only on the condition that they be allowed to hang an ad on the statue for one year. The media had already seen how Miss Liberty had been humorously exploited in trade card images showing her hoisting up threads and dumping laundry detergent into the harbor, so they knew the offer was for real. One cartoonist responded with a cartoon depicting the statue pasted from hair to toe with ads for everything from "Silker the Hatter" to "Dr. Lugs' Corn Frightener." When the statue finally arrived, Miss Liberty's copper skin was secured to an iron framework engineered by Gustave Eiffel, who shored up his reputation through the project enough to land a contract for the tower that carries his name from the 1889 Paris Exposition.

Pricing Tips & Cards to Watch For

Because of the historical and sentimental importance of the Statue of Liberty, and because souvenir items related to the statue have been popular for over 100 years, hundreds of collectors are interested in Statue of Liberty trade cards. As more collectors from outside of the traditional trade card marketplace begin to compete for good Statue of Liberty cards, prices are expected to rise. At present, most Statue of Liberty stock cards are still available in the $10 to $20 range, and most privately issued examples run $20 to $75.

Eagle Pencil Company, die-cut, $75.00.

Soapine, $25.00.

American Institute — 51st Grand Nat'l
    1882 Exposition card, Liberty inside red circle, ferns on left **$40.00**

Arbuckle Coffee (#48 of 50 views)
    New York (from "trip around the world"), Liberty, bridge, etc. **$8.00**

Bartholdi Central Draft Burner
    Liberty holds lantern, family reads at table, fireplace burns **$75.00**

Clark's Thread (one of 3 cards)
    New York harbor scene, "Naval Review," Santa Maria, 1892 . . . . . .**$15.00**

Eaton's Parlor Matches
    Liberty on left holds box of matches **$30.00**

Eldorado Engine Oil
    "The Great Bartholdi Statue," statistics below image **$20.00**

Merrick Thread
    skyview: Liberty holds 2 spools, harbor, bridge, gold letters **$15.00**

Merrick Thread
    skyview: Liberty holds 2 spools, harbor, bridge, red letters **$15.00**

Moline Plow
    "The Flying Dutchman" stands on stump, 3 horse teams plow **$40.00**

Pratts Astral oil
    "Copyright by Root & Tinker 1883," night scene, moon **$15.00**

Sangster Umbrellas & Parasols
    distant Liberty in rain, couple under umbrella, Amer. eagle **$30.00**

Singer Sewing Machine
    "Officially Authorized Edition," realistic Liberty, 1883 . . . .**$20.00**

St. Nicholas Hotel — stock card
    horseshoe with Liberty inside, 4 barracks on island **$15.00**

Stock Card — engraved
    bridge directly behind big Liberty, ships "Bufford 43" **$15.00**

St. Jacob's Oil, $20.00.

Brainerd and Armstrong Thread, $30.00.

Statue of Liberty, stock card, $15.00.

New Easy Lawn Mower, $35.00.

Stock Cards, Calling Cards & Rewards of Merit

(See also: Clothing & Dry Goods; Jewelry.)

Stock Images

Cards with "stock" images probably account for over 95% of all the cards that were produced during the Victorian period. In most cases, these stock images were generic enough that the same card could be purchased in bulk and imprinted by firms from a wide variety of industries. Stock cards with images tailored for use by companies within a single industry are less common, as it would not make sense for competing firms to distribute identical cards. The major exception is found with the stock cards that were designed for local retail stores, particularly in the fields of jewelry, clothing, dry goods, and groceries. Many hundreds of delightful stock images were designed with these industries in mind, presumably under the assumption that the use of these cards would be localized enough that competing firms would seldom overlap in their distribution. Additionally, many manufacturers distributed trade cards that were a cross between stock issues and private designs. These cards advertised brand name products like Keystone Watch Cases or Waterloo Organs, but they were designed in the spirit of stock cards with boxes left blank for local imprinting.

Stock cards are easy to spot when the image includes a blank white box that was designed for later imprinting, but not all stock cards are so obvious. Collectors occasionally compare notes and debate at length trying to determine if certain cards were privately commissioned with generic images or were designed as stock cards that were only ever used by a single firm. One of the most notorious of these on-going debates centers around dozens of Soapine soap cards that exhibit the characteristics of both stock cards and privately issued cards.

Stock cards, calling cards, and rewards of merit range in quality from very low to very high, but the reputation of these cards with collectors has been severely compromised by the abundance of thousands of poorly designed examples and amateurish black and white cards that rely on base humor for their appeal. Stock cards can sometimes be found as metamorphics, mechanicals, and puzzles. While stock trade cards were issued in nearly every size, shape, and style, calling cards were almost always designed in a horizontal orientation in sizes under 3½" x 2". Reward of merit cards were printed in both horizontal and vertical formats, but nearly all of these cards employ conservative designs. One reason to treat stock cards, calling cards, and rewards of merit together is that examples of the same card can occasionally be found imprinted for each of the three applications.

Historical Notes

Printers have relied upon stock images and reusable typographical characters since the development of the printing industry in the fifteenth century. As printing presses and the publishing industry evolved, primitive woodcuts gave way to durable engraved images produced on blocks in standard sizes that could be shuffled around as easily as movable type. Many of the letterheads and business cards used by merchants throughout the past few centuries employ these sorts of stock images.

During the 1870s, Louis Prang popularized a style of stock trade card that was different than most previous cards in its bold use of color and its less-than-subtle white boxes left blank for local imprinting. Steam-powered presses added another dimension to stock printing by enabling lithographers to produce color cards in such enormous quantities that prices dropped to a fraction of a penny per card. As the Victorian card culture developed, inexpensive portable card presses for imprinting local messages appeared in nearly every town. By the early 1880s, stock cards issued by lithographers like Bufford and Ketterlinus were being sold in bulk to entrepreneuring wholesalers who resold and imprinted them in communities everywhere. Local card dealers fueled the popularity of calling cards and rewards of merit by distributing free samples and offering delightful inventories at affordable prices.

Pricing Tips & Cards to Watch For

Stock cards, calling cards, and rewards of merit offer some of the best buys found in any area of Victorian antiques. For the most part, even the most charming examples of these cards typically sell for $5 or less. Dealers will often have shoeboxes of such cards for $1 each, and with a little rummaging one can sometimes find examples with imprints from one's hometown or with compelling images of anything from family pets to Asian landscapes. Keep an eye open for stock cards with special historical references, important company imprints, or images that have popular topical appeal. Early black and white Hire's Root Beer stock cards sell for over $100, as does the rare Shaker Extract of Roots stock card picturing a girl in a cap and shawl. Also keep an eye open for attractive stock cards with images of Uncle Sam, the Statue of Liberty, Blacks, and other topical images mentioned in this book, as these will frequently bring $10 or more.

Star Job Printing Press, $15.00.

American Tract Society — stock card
rev: "Sunday School Cards: Floral Texts, 24 for 25¢ etc." **$5.00**

Barnum — Manuf's of Gilt etc. Cards
"Card Collectors, by your Collections... over 5,000 styles" **$5.00**

Brown — Advertising Cards
"For Scrap & Card Albums put up in 10¢ etc. assortments..." **$5.00**

Calling Card — Sample No. 951
"20 cards assorted 20 cts. Without name concealed etc." **$1.00**

Champion Peach
"Cards Supplied... Name & Address Printed...$1 per 1000" **$10.00**

Clothing stock card — girl, seashore
"STOP & Think a Minute Before You Drop this Card," rev. ad **$3.00**

Crider: "Sunday School Cards"
"Ten Dozen Assorted Cards this size and quality, etc." **$3.00**

D. Heston — humming bird stock card
prices for imprinted cards, quantities from 500 to 10,000 . . . .**$5.00**

Esterbrook's Steel Pens
pen tips, Uncle Sam holds sign imprinted: "Reward of Merit" **$40.00**

Goodall — Advertising Cards, No. 44
Easter style stock card, lith. by: Wemple & Kronheim, N.Y. **$3.00**

Guyott, Card & Job Printer
Harriet Beecher Stowe stock card, rev. ad for printing **$5.00**

Harbach's — floral stock card
"New Year Calling Cards, The Cheapest Place, etc." **$2.00**

Reward of Merit
stock card, beach scene, children make sand castle **$3.00**

Reward of Merit
floral design **$3.00**

Reward of Merit
hand holding flowers **$3.00**

Reward of Merit
lines for student/teacher names, scrap pasted in center box **$5.00**

Roberts — envelope/stamp/clown stock
"Pacific Coast Advertising Card Specialists, S.F.," 1881 . . . .**$5.00**

Seven Wonder of World — stock card
"Printer & Card Dealer, Cards for Collectors at Retail," 1881 . . . . .**$5.00**

Tradesmen Cards. For Sale only by...
stock cut of liquor bottle, spaces for imprinting **$5.00**

Union Card Co. — Greenaway stock card
"Send 25¢" for "100 mixed Chromo Cards" w/name printed **$8.00**

Wm. K. Potter, Jewelry
stock card folder: "In Scrap Books paste this side only..." **$5.00**

Union Card Co., cherub stock card, $5.00.

Ohio Card Company, $25.00.

Stoves, Ovens & Ranges

(See also: Food; Kitchen.)

Stove Images

Trade cards with stove-related advertising offer interesting insights into Victorian culture. The relative quality and abundance of these cards testifies to changes that have occurred over the past century as we have come to take our home heating systems for granted. Many stove cards have color stock images on one side and detailed drawings of stoves on the other. The privately issued stove cards are often beautifully designed and usually printed in lovely colors to showcase nickle trimmings and other decorative features. Within this category one finds ads for parlor heating stoves, basement furnaces, agricultural boilers, kitchen ovens and ranges, and stove polishes. Some collectors also include ads for things like coal, fire screens, and "oil cloths" (fireproof composition rugs upon which stoves could rest) in this grouping.

Historical Notes

Innovations in the steel industry and the emergence of small, highly competitive foundries were critical in the development of the residential stove industry. Starting in the 1840s, numerous designs for cast-iron heating stoves and cooking ranges were experimented with and discarded in frantic succession so that by around the turn of the century, over 7,000 stove designs had been patented. The challenges of heating and cooking were universal, so the stakes were high for the company that could engineer and market the best product. Designs had become efficient and affordable enough by the end of the Civil War that nearly everyone began running stove pipes into their old fireplaces and bricking in their hearths in order to accommodate a new unit.

A family's first purchase was usually a large stove that could burn wood or coal and be used for both heating and cooking. In prosperous times, families added more specialized units designed for specific rooms. At the peak of the stove era during the 1880s to 1900, portable units could be purchased for camping, "art" models with fancy nickle plating and decorative foot rails could be purchased for middle-class parlors, and enormous cooking ranges could be installed for the kitchen servants of the wealthy elite. Coal-burning furnaces were used in some places as early as the 1840s, but they were often seen as unhealthy, and installing them in established homes required massive remodeling on account of the necessary duct work and modifications beneath the house. Homes in many parts of the country were originally built with crawl spaces or cellars, so adding furnaces also entailed digging deeper floors and pouring concrete to seal out water and keep the furnaces dry.

Pricing Tips & Cards to Watch For

Most collectors appreciate nice stove cards, but very few collectors are currently willing to pay more than $25 for even the best of these lovely cards. Stock cards with stove illustrations on the reverse usually sell for $5 to $15. Good privately issued stove cards typically bring $10 to $25. Cards for Round Oak and Acorn stoves are very popular, but so far, few collectors are willing to pay premium prices to get them. Expect these prices to rise as more collectors from outside of the trade card field become aware of these wonderful cards. Keep and eye open for stove cards with images that have special topical appeal, as with cards depicting Uncle Sam, Polar bears, Blacks, etc. because these cards will usually bring the highest prices of any stove cards.

Garland Stoves and Ranges, $20.00.

Acorn Stoves and Ranges, die-cut, $15.00.

Adams & West Lake Oil Stove
"Just the thing for camping," 2 mules camp, hammock, stove **$15.00**

Dixon's Stove Polish
folder, salesboy sings in pipe outside, man hears inside 1884 . . . . . . **$15.00**

Fireside: for Anthracite or Bitum. Coal
early stove in front of fireplace, family reads ad, folder **$40.00**

Florence Oil Stoves & Crown Sewing
man enters, small room stove, wife reads, sewing machine **$20.00**

Florence Oil Stoves & Crown Sewing
2 panels, young people's picnics, with/without stove **$15.00**

Garland Stoves and Ranges
"Bed Time," 3 children gather in night clothes, stove glows **$25.00**

Gold Coin, Chicga Stove Works
3 fairies fly with 1890 coin, banner, stove factory below **$10.00**

Hubbel's Ornamental Metal Corners
stove piped to fireplace, cherubs apply carpet corner, couple **$10.00**

Kelsey Furnace Company
illustration of circulating furnace in basement, burns coal **$15.00**

Peckham Agricultural Furnace
"Soap Day," tiny boy chops wood to stoke boiler for soap **$35.00**

Red Cross Stoves & Ranges
knight in mail, shield, sword, red crosses, "We Challenge..." **$10.00**

Richmond Round Parlor Stove
boy at table, poster ad for stove on wall **$15.00**

Rising Sun Stove Polish
folder "Look yere, old man!/Come in, Ephraim!," Black couple . . **$20.00**

Round Oak Stove
stove, girl plays with baby, clock on mantel **$15.00**

Welcome Base Burner
large fancy stove, winter design, lady in fur, tiny dog barks **$25.00**

Richardson's Perfect Range, $35.00.

Champion Monitor, $25.00.

Lustro Nickel-Plate Polish, $12.00.

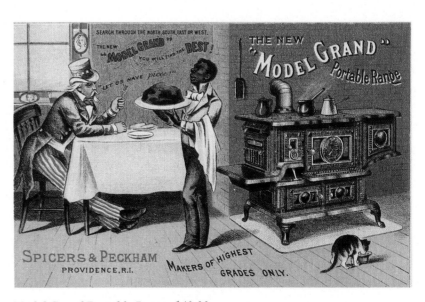

Model Grand Portable Range, $40.00.

Theater & Celebrities

(See also: Entertainment; Fairy Tales & Literary.)

Theater & Celebrity Images

There are two basic types of theater and celebrity trade cards. One type includes cards that were used to advertise upcoming theatrical performances or to promote the careers of specific celebrities. The second, and far more common type, uses allusions to well-know plays or images of celebrities to capture the public's attention in advertisements that have no real connection to the play or celebrity whatsoever. In most cases, cards of this second type were printed without the actual endorsement (or even consent) of the theatrical production or celebrity exploited by the advertisers using the cards.

Black and white stock cards with portraits of celebrities are so common and look so much alike that most collectors pay little attention to them. These cards can be found with imprints for everything from patent medicines to shoe stores, and they come with portraits of stars of every stature. Of more interest to collectors are color cards with references to specific plays (particularly Gilbert and Sullivan productions) or figures (like Sarah Bernhardt or Lillie Langtry) that played significant roles in the history of the stage. The Singer Sewing Machine Company issued some interesting cards around the theme of "Celebrated Singers" that featured celebrities from the concert and opera house circuit. Libby, McNeill & Libby released over two dozen cards with scenes from Shakespearean plays that were popular at the time, but the generic actors depicted in these images lack the historical importance of other cards that can be linked to specific Victorian celebrities. Because of their transitory nature, theater cards tend to be of low quality and were often printed on cheap paper stock.

Historical Notes

The Victorian stage offered a potpourri of entertainment that was as diverse as the mix of films shown in movie theaters today. The line between the "legitimate" and the "not-so-legitimate" stage was not always clear, especially in smaller towns where every traveling act was forced to use the same facility and customers were never quite sure what the next performance in might bring. The advertising trade cards with playbills that were distributed on the day of a troupe's arrival helped clarify expectations, but many of these cards were intentionally printed in vague enough language to allow for the constant adjustments most troupes were forced to make.

On the "low" end of respectability were the acts that came into towns with street entertainment in the form of organ grinders with monkeys, trained bear routines, snake handling, cockfighting, and bare-knuckle fighting. Traveling freak shows, high-wire acts, and sleight of hand performances also fell into this category. Dance halls and saloons sometimes accommodated some of these acts to draw crowds, but they generally preferred the choreographed routines provided by traveling variety troupes using catchy show tunes, blackface skits, female soloists, and cancan dances from Europe. The best of these troupes made their way up from dance halls to opera and theater houses where they participated in the Victorian vaudeville phenomenon.

Vaudeville shows were advertised on the backs of a surprising number of patent medicine trade cards. A typical bill for a good show included a half dozen or more acts ranging from an "Ethiopian sketch" to a twenty minute melodrama, plus a couple of songs by some legitimate star. Variety shows could also include abridged scenes from Shakespeare, animal acts, or even an itinerant lecturer.

The "legitimate" stage featured acts promoting middle-class values in an uplifting spirit of pseudo-refinement. A talented troupe could bring a sophisticated production from New York into a cattle or mining town and hush an audience with a single line. Their plays were often filled with predictable plots, one-dimensional villains, and sappy moralizing, but these actors had genuine talent that mesmerized communities that were unjaded by the level of exposure to talent that we experience today through television and movie theaters.

Pricing Tips & Cards to Watch For

Many great values can be found in trade cards featuring theater and celebrity themes. Black and white stock cards with celebrity portraits usually bring around $5, even for historically significant stars. Most other theater and celebrity cards still sell in the $10 to $15 range. Watch for cards of exceptional beauty and quality, as these are rare in the genre. Also keep an eye open for the many Gilbert and Sullivan cards from their satirical operettas (The *Mikado*, *H.M.S. Pinafore*, *Trial by Jury*, *Patience*, and *Ruddigore* are the most common), as these cards are drawing interest from theater collectors who are just becoming aware of their existence.

Lizzie Evans, "Little Electric Ballery," $15.00.

Alvin Joslin — Chas. L. Davis
"Uncle Alvin Abroad," frumpy actor, umbrella, portrait $15.00

Corinne in Arcadia
Corinne in hat leans on chairback, rev: "greatest Burlesque" $8.00

Corinne — Merrie-Makers
Corrine's fancy coach, street crowd, 2 black horses 1882 . . . .$15.00

Dalys: "Vacation" or Harvard vs. Yale
"Me Too," Thos. Daly as Harry Hall of Harvard, man in suit $15.00

Deakins Liliputian Opera Co.
Scene from Jack the Giant Killer — giant hangs lady by hair $20.00

HMS Pinafore — satirical stock card
"See that Pin-a-fore?," school room — Gilbert & Sullivan $8.00

Libby, McNeill & Libby Meats
Romeo & Juliet, Act II,. Scene VI, Juliet greets the Friar... . . . .$8.00

Mikado — stock card
Sallie Williams as "Peep-Bo," lady in Japanese outfit, fan $15.00

Muldoon's Picnic — Hyde & Behman's
"Great Comedy," families brawl at picnic, bottle as club $20.00

Only a Farmer's Daughter
La Petite Beauty the Greatest Living Child Actress, portrait $15.00

Park Garden Theater (Prov. R.I.)
"Scene from the new opera — The Ambassador's Daughter" $20.00

Peck's Bad Boy — Atkinson Comedy Co.
"Urchin Chastiser," machine spanks boy, mom, girl can't look $15.00

Sallie Wilson in "Morning Dew"
maid in red knocks at door, tray holds card (Rose Tobacco) $15.00

Salsbury's Troubadours in 3 of a Kind
man holds 3 cards with men's faces, lady heart card in back $25.00

Sarah Bernhardt stock card
portrait, issued by "People's Dye" Neb. Druggist imprint $10.00

Singer Sewing Machine: "Nilsson"
portrait card from "Celebrated Singers" set, celebrities $10.00

Uncle Tom's Cabin — Anthony & Ellis'
"Memphis University Students," several scenes, portraits $25.00

Wm. H. Crane in Sharps and Flats
man, big head, hat, suit, rev: "Globe Theatre" engagement $12.00

Ullie Akerstrom, young actress, $12.00.

The Planter's Wife, $12.00.

Brown's Iron Bitters, $12.00.

Tobacco

(See also: Beer, Whiskey & Wine.)

Tobacco Images

Tobacco-related trade cards are among the most hotly collected cards in the hobby. The images of these cards tend to have masculine appeal and are typically printed in strong colors. The illustrations found on tobacco cards range from serious domestic scenes to historical satire. Tobacco cards have an usually high percentage of "humorous," risque, and racially inflammatory illustrations. Stock cards of nearly every quality and type can be found with imprints for tobacco dealers and specific brands, but the cards commissioned by tobacco manufacturers are by far the most interesting to most collectors. Privately issued tobacco cards tend to be unusually high in quality, and they rank well above average in collector appeal.

Tobacco "trading cards" are also popular with many collectors. Trading cards are smaller than most trade cards (typically the size of a modern business card or smaller), and unlike trade cards, they were inserted in cigarette packages to keep the product from bending. Trading cards were issued in large series in order to encourage repeat sales as smokers attempted to complete sets of actresses, athletes, animals, etc. The most valuable nineteenth century tobacco trading cards are the early baseball sets issued for Old Judge, Gypsy Queen, Allen & Ginter, and others. Actually, hundreds of trade cards with baseball images pre-date these mid-1880s trading cards, and some of the early baseball trade cards even carry tobacco advertising.

Historical Notes

One of the first notes Columbus made in 1492 concerning the New World was about the smoke that natives sucked from sticks called "tobaccos." Colonists began planting tobacco in Virginia as early as 1612, and by 1615 a 20,000 pound harvest of the cash crop was hailed as the saviour of Jamestown. The alleged medicinal qualities of tobacco were used to justify its use all the way into the trade card era, at which time some companies promoted their brands as able to improve dispositions, cure nervousness, and soothe upset stomachs.

Concurrent with tobacco's rise in popularity was concern about the dangers and addictive properties of the product. In 1604, King James I of England used such adjectives as "stinking" and "dangerous" to describe the use of tobacco, and in 1624, Pope Urban VIII vowed to excommunicate Catholics who used snuff. Cures for the "Tobacco Habit" were popular during the patent medicine era. A company called "No-To-Bac" issued a hold-to-light trade card that featured two fascinating panels. One panel featured the gladiator "King No-To-Bac" with his foot on the chest of his vanquished foe, "Nicotine." The other panel depicted a man standing beside a couch upon which his distressed wife reclined, with the text including such lines as "He lacked the nerve to make her happy," and "Makes Weak-Nerved Men Strong." When held to the light, the man was shown spitting chew into a cuspidor above the caption, "Don't tobacco spit and smoke your life away!"

Cigarettes came onto the American tobacco scene rather late, but once there, they were quickly recognized as a convenient, clean, and potent alternative to chew, cigars, pipes, and snuff. Early trade cards promote some brands of cigars that were still being hand rolled by tenement dwelling families working out of tiny apartments. By the end of the trade card era around WWI, most tobacco companies had become almost completely mechanized in order to keep up with America's 124 billion cigarettes-a-year habit.

Pricing Tips & Cards to Watch For

Stock cards with tobacco advertising generally sell for $8 to $15, and sometimes more if the image or text is particularly compelling. Privately issued tobacco cards draw some of the most interest of any product in trade cards, with values running $20 to $50 for most cards in very fine condition. Rare and unusual tobacco cards sell for much more. Watch for "Nigger Hair" and "Nigger Head" tobacco cards with archery scenes, as these can bring $200 and up. Prices for the many thousands of tobacco "trading cards" issued with every type of image imaginable vary greatly, depending mostly upon collector interest for each type of image. Sports images definitely command the highest prices, with baseball examples in particular sometimes bringing thousands of dollars each. However, most tobacco trading cards are currently selling in the range of $2 to $10 each.

Miner's Tobacco, $250.00.

Target Plug, $30.00.

Buchanan & Lyall Tobacco
Sultan harem scene, water pipe, dancers, plug border **$25.00**

Capadura Cigar
political: Hendricks & Cleveland puff, cigar box, Capitol Bldg **$40.00**

Capadura Cigar
baseball "Judgment!," man slid under baseman, holds ball up **$35.00**

Enterprise Tobacco Cutters
Sir Raleigh offers "Queen Bess" tobacco cutter, WCE 1893 . . . .**$15.00**

Five Brothers Plug Tobacco
a white & Black kid, bare buns, reading "Tale of Two Cities" **$30.00**

Horse-Head Tobacco
horse with tobacco in mouth sticks head through sign **$20.00**

Jackson's Best Chew
hidden picture "crotchety old man," young couple in chin, nose **$30.00**

Mail Pouch Anti-Dispeptic Tobacco
"Just Found His Mail Pouch," baby grins, hand in diaper **$25.00**

Meerschaum Smoking Tobacco
cat stands on case lid, 4 kittens try to squeeze out **$15.00**

Moorhouse's No. 6 Cigars
man window shops, shoeshine boy sneaks bite, wooden Indian **$25.00**

No-To-Bac Tobacco Habit Cure
H-T-L: "Makes Weak-Nerved Men Strong" in light, man spits **$50.00**

Piper-Heidsieck Plug Tobacco
"Champagne Flavored" river, bottles in basket, grapes, lady **$25.00**

Star Plug
double-sided card, huge plug against fence, crowd gathers **$40.00**

Tansill's Punch 5¢ Cigar — stock card
boys light firecrackers on back of policeman's coat 1883 . . . .**$10.00**

Veteran Cigarettes & Tobacco
"Never Beaten" old soldier, gun up, city in flames behind **$20.00**

Wm. S. Kimball & Co's Cigarettes
sexy lady reclines smoking cigarette, big cat by her head **$40.00**

Bull's Eye Tobacco, $150.00.

Weyman's Copenhagen Snuff, $35.00.

Horse Shoe Cross Bar Tobacco, $20.00.

Toys, Dolls & Games

(See also: Children; Holiday & Santa Claus; Mechanical & Toy Banks; Metamorphic & Novelty.)

Toys, Dolls, & Games Images

Trade cards with images or advertising relating to childhood play are very common and are enjoyed by many collectors. Most of the thousands of cards that show children playing actually advertise things other than toys and games. For example, many patent medicine companies commissioned cards depicting children playing simply to suggest the ability of their products to restore or maintain a child's health. In some cases, the playthings shown in these cards are depicted in wonderful detail. The cards that were designed specifically to advertise Victorian toys, dolls, and games make up a minority of the cards in this category. Stock cards with imprints for toy stores listing examples of the items they sell are not particularly rare, but privately issued cards for brand name items are quite scarce. Some collectors of toy and doll cards limit themselves to these scarce types, while others collect cards with advertisements for anything so long as the images used give an accurate representation of real Victorian toys, dolls, and games.

Some of the play items found in trade card images includes: dolls, doll coaches, and doll houses, Punch and Judy toys, paper toys, balls and sports equipment, rolling toy animals, hoop and ring games, skates, stilts, rocking horses, toy boats, sleds, wagons, balloons, kites, jump ropes, swings, seesaws, bubble blowers, baby rattles, toy guns and swords, puppets, trains, jack-in-the-boxes, banks, toy drums and horns, building blocks, children's bicycles, toy household items (sewing machines, stoves, washboards, etc.), playing cards, toy soldiers, board games, marbles, spinning tops and Diabolo, and yard games like croquet and badminton.

Historical Notes

Among the many changes in American society fueled and documented by trade cards is a shifting view of children. As economic prosperity and education spread through an expanding middle-class, advertising trade cards and department stores helped train consumers to view their children as unique people in need of special products and services. Long-held values and practices were subverted by the new possibilities of an affluent, consumption-based culture. Just as middle-class parents were suddenly finding more opportunities for recreation and materialistic indulgence, so were they providing their children with more time for games and more toys with which to play.

Victorian parents began dressing their children better, at times even to the point of absurdity. Parents began exploring special diets and purchasing cleverly targeted products like Mellin's Food and Imperial Granum. Communities hired experts to implement educational and recreational programs that were sensitive to the "developmental" issues of children. Families began subscribing to magazines like *Youth's Companion* and *St. Nicholas*, and they began filling nursery shelves with books designed with young readers in mind. Special furniture like baby cribs and high chairs were brought into Victorian homes, and child-size cups, plates, and utensils were purchased for table use. Toy departments, and even toy stores, began to flourish. Trade cards promoting and capturing the emergence of new attitudes toward children and a new perspective of the ideal childhood are among the most fascinating of any nineteenth century artifacts, and the legacy of this transition has become our inheritance today.

Pricing Tips & Cards to Watch For

Because trade cards with images of children playing are so common, a wonderful collection of these cards can be assembled for very little money. Most of these cards will be priced according to the type of product advertised and the quality of the image. Check for these cards especially in dealer albums under the product headings of milks, foods, coffees, patent medicines, soaps, and threads. Also check under the topical headings of children, sports, and Santa Claus. The best buys in this category will be found in delightful stock cards that will generally cost $5 or less each. Cards that advertise toy stores and toy manufactures will be much more expensive, with most of these cards falling in the $15 to $75 range. Watch for a John Hancock Insurance novelty card that has a child pointing to a slot in the card. This card is itself a toy bank of sorts, and the card is scarce enough to bring $100 or more. Also watch for cards advertising board games like Parcheesi, Anabasis, and Baaslinda, as the best examples of these cards can bring $100 and up.

None Such Mince Meat, $15.00.

Arbuckle Coffee (#47 of 50)
Ancient Judea, History of Sports & Pastimes, kids spin top **$8.00**

Backgammon stock card
2 children, backgammon board, rev: Gleason's Pictorial ad **$5.00**

Biliousine Cure
"Dolly's Got 'Spepsia," boy & girl playing doctor, bottles **$15.00**

Clark's Thread
2 boys in hats shoot canon at doll, toy balloon with ad on side **$5.00**

Clark's Thread
boys flying 2 kites, thread spools, Prang, 1879 calendar **$12.00**

Clark's Thread Circus Spool Toy
"Chariot," punch-out toy, clown, uses spools for wheels **$10.00**

Halma & Basilinda Games
3 happy children "We are so happy because we play..." **$20.00**

Henderson & Co. Boots & Shoes
2 boys play marbles, red school house, leap frog, hoop, etc. **$10.00**

Highland Evaporated Cream
"Little Doctor," doll in toy bed, boy & girl play doctor, 1890 . . . .**$25.00**

Spurlock's No. 5 Bluing
little girl takes her doll apart, empties out filling **$15.00**

Stock Card — "Dr. Stow's Cure"
3 kids play, toy building blocks, letter blocks, drum **$8.00**

Stock Card — "Red Seal Lye" imprint
seashore, boy in straw hat shows girl toy sailboat **$5.00**

Stock Card — "Schwarz Toy Bazaar"
3 kids play: rocking horse, swing set, bicycle **$15.00**

Stock Card — boy on rocking horse
misc. toys; imprint: "Dolls, Drums, Toys, Doll Coaches, etc" **$15.00**

Stock Card — rev. imprint
girl in lace, toy monkey on a stick **$5.00**

Stock Card: "Merry Christmas, etc."
"New Toy, Fancy Goods & Doll Headquarters," Heyer, Phila. **$5.00**

Union Pacific Tea Company
5 children play "birdie in the cup" game, 3 cats watch **$10.00**

Solar Tip Shoes, $15.00.

J & P Coats Thread, $8.00.

Singer for the Girls, $15.00.

Parker Brothers Toys, Jewelry, etc. $50.00.

Transportation, Ships & Railroad
(See also: Exploration & Travel; Horses.)

Transportation Images

Victorian cards advertising stage lines, ships, and railroads are among the most historically important and highly valued cards in the hobby. Some collectors include general cards with incidental references and images relating to transportation in this category, but there are enough good cards directly promoting transportation companies and vehicle manufacturers to fill a collection if a person can afford the stiff prices that these outstanding cards command. Most of the cards issued by the companies that built horse carriages and coaches were printed in black and white, but Studebaker and a few others did issue a handful of cards in color.

Ship cards come in two basic types. The first type includes the rare clipper ship cards that advertised specific sailing ships by name, typically announcing upcoming voyages and departure dates falling between the California gold rush and the Civil War. These cards are so early and rare that they almost never appear for sale except through special auctions. The second type of ship card advertised specific steamers, steamship lines, or voyages. Most of these cards date from the Centennial Exposition to WWI, with many of the earlier cards featuring illustrations of steamers with masts and sails that sometimes trick inexperienced collectors into mistaking them for clipper ships. Some of these cards promoted recreational excursions or international cruises, but most of these cards were designed to fill ships shuttling back and forth from Europe.

Railroad trade cards also come in several basic styles. There are a few cards that promote specific cars, most notably the Pullman Palace Cars that were leased to all of the major railroad lines from the Civil War on. Far more common are the trade cards promoting passage on specific cross-country routes like the Michigan Central and Great Western Railways or the Chicago and North Western Railway. Less common are cards that advertised local lines like the Columbian Intramural Railroad (Chicago, 1893) or the Mount Washington Railway incline.

Historical Notes

Travelers had very few attractive options prior to the Civil War. Traveling was often such a protracted and brutal ordeal that it was avoided by women and children unless absolutely necessary. Cross-country trips by stage coach or ocean voyages by clipper ship often took weeks, or even months, with unsanitary conditions for eating and sleeping and cramped quarters that left many travelers physically ill or worse. But by the summer of 1869, the transcontinental railroad was complete and deluxe dining and sleeping cars were hustling travelers across the country in first class comfort. By about this same time, steamers had taken command of most ocean routes and travelers could begin looking forward to steadier decks, larger quarters, and quicker arrivals.

Transportation trade cards from the 1870s on played an important role in redefining travel in the minds of American consumers. Speed, safety, comfort, and convenience were emphasized, and in the case of railroad cards, the scenery of the route was often highlighted as well. Spur lines quickly snaked their ways off major railroads into communities not directly on lines, while new paralleled routes were established wherever there were customers enough to justify them. Trade cards advertising western routes encouraged consumers to relocate in order to take advantage of golden opportunities, especially in farmlands in Kansas and Dakota. Steamship cards emphasized the romance of overseas travel, "spacious and cheery" saloons and staterooms, and dining that compared favorably with "that of the best hotels in Eng-

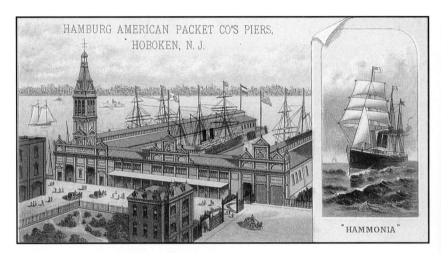

Hamburg American Packer Piers, $60.00.

land." American goods made their way to Europe in the bellies of these ships, and thousands of poor immigrants made their way out of Europe in the "Steerage" compartments during the trip back.

Pricing Tips & Cards to Watch For

Trade cards with images of stage coaches, ships, and trains seldom bring any special price unless the advertising on the card is directly related to the transportation industry. Stock cards with imprints for ticket agents generally run $5 to $15, depending upon the card's image and text. Genuine transportation cards with privately commissioned images and advertising for vehicles and transportation routes usually sell for $25 and up. Cards in very fine condition advertising clipper ships bound for San Francisco during the gold rush basically start at $200 and go up in price from there. Steamship cards mostly sell in the $40 to $125 range. Railroad cards generally bring $30 to $100. Watch for any cards with especially compelling graphics or special historical significance, as these cards will usually bring $75 or more.

Atchison, Topeka & Santa Fe R.R.
engraved card, "Out of Woods/In Woods," farmland promotion **$200.00**

B.T. Babbitt's Whitesboro Machine
"Steam Engines and Boilers," sectional view of locomotive **$75.00**

Belding Bros. Thread
"Sectional view of Cable Street Cars," thread as cable **$250.00**

Colorado Barn Livery, Feed, Stable
early carriage illus., "Stylish Turn-outs...Drivers Furnished" **$75.00**

Erie & Chicago Line Double Track HW
"Pullman Service," man reads paper in fancy train seat **$40.00**

Guion Line U.S. Mail Steamers
"Alaska — fastest Steamer Afloat," shows 4-mast steamer **$125.00**

Inman Steamship Company
harbor, big 3-mast steamship, tug boats, rev. travel info **$60.00**

Lake Shore & Mich. Southern Ry.
Centennial card "Mail Carrier of 100 yrs ago," 1876 train **$75.00**

Michigan Central & Great Western
Buffalo Suspension Bridge, Niagara Falls **$35.00**

Rapid Transit Soap — Colgate & Co.
busy NY street, elevated tracks, trains, horse cars below **$125.00**

Rice Carriage Spring Co.
horse trots log road, "They ride easy...over roughest roads" **$35.00**

Ship in Harbor — stock card
"For Trip across Ocean, Buy Tickets at... Steam Ship Lines" **$8.00**

Starin's Fleet off the Battery
N.Y. Harbor scene, many excursion boats, rates, 1880 . . . .**$40.00**

Storm King! (clipper ship)
"Empire Line for San Fancisco," ship illus. Coleman, 1856 . . . .**$500.00**

Subway stock card — clother imprint
girl sits on baggage, train leaves through tunnel, others wait **$8.00**

Tourists — Theatrical Production
man flirts with lady on RR car, "Do you think... my love." **$20.00**

White Star Line: "Titanic (Building)"
"Largest Steamers in the World," shows Titanic style **$150.00**

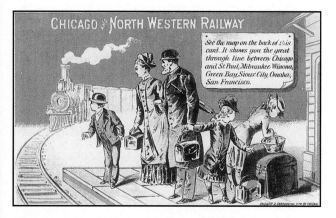

Chicago & North Western Railway, $30.00.

Stage coach stock card, $8.00.

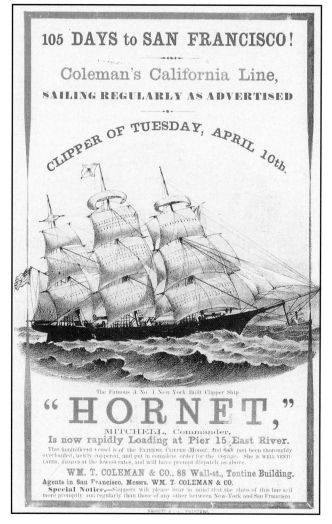

Hornet (clipper ship), $1,500.00.

Uncle Sam

(See also: Columbia; Exposition; Patriotic.)

Cards with Uncle Sam Images

Cards picturing a variety of a lanky red, white, and blue Uncle Sams are among the most widely enjoyed of all the trade cards that people collect. Over 200 different depictions of this famous icon of American capitalism were created for trade cards, thus qualifying Uncle Sam as one of the most commonly used symbols in nineteenth century advertising. Because of the near universal appeal of these images, prices for cards featuring Uncle Sam usually run much higher than similar cards with other images. A good share of these cards date from the proud and patriotic time of the Columbian Exposition (1893), so the quality of these cards is typically very high. Prices for more crudely done Uncle Sams also tend to be strong, as these less sophisticated cards were often produced in more limited quantities and at an early date.

Historical Notes

Uncle Sam is based upon a real "Uncle" Samuel Wilson, who supplied provisions for American troops during the War of 1812. Mr. Wilson had been blessed with dozens of nieces and nephews and was well-respected throughout upstate New York. Those who knew him best often referred to him affectionately as "Uncle Sam." Legend has it that one day a naive soldier (who wasn't used to seeing his young country abbreviated) asked what the letters "U.S." stood for on the barrels. Knowing that it was "Uncle" Sam Wilson's beef in the barrel, someone jokingly replied that U.S. stood for Uncle Sam. The joke caught on and spread until eventually U.S. supplies everywhere were accredited to the benevolence of kindly old Uncle Sam.

As the Uncle Sam joke spread throughout the early 1800s, the original man behind the name became less and less important to the story. Mr. Wilson did, however, leave his mark upon the symbol in several important ways. For one, the tall felt hat came from the real Uncle Sam, as did the swallow-tailed coat, high collar, waistcoat, and bow tie. Samuel Wilson's personality also left an imprint upon the symbol. As with the symbol, the real Uncle Sam was a feisty Yankee capitalist noted for his sense of humor and industry.

Trade cards graphically illustrate the fascinating evolution of Uncle Sam between the time of the nation's Centennial and the release of the famous Uncle Sam "I Want You for U.S. Army" WWI poster. In 1876, Uncle Sam was still competing for his place in American iconography with an eighteenth century character known as "Brother Jonathan." Several fascinating cards from the 1870s show the blurring of these two figures as they merged into the character we know today as Uncle Sam. Trade cards also trace the emerging consensus around the colors of Uncle Sam's wardrobe, hair, and beard.

Pricing Tips & Cards to Watch For

Virtually every full-color Uncle Sam card in good condition will sell for $10 or more. Stock cards with line-drawn illustrations are the possible exception, but here again, many of these can still

bring over $10 because they are both early and scarce. In general, the Uncle Sam cards that bring the most money are the ones that are scarce, attractively designed, and linked to a product that is popular with collectors. The best example of such a card is the highly-prized Uncle Sam mechanical bank card, which can bring upwards to $1,000 when found in excellent condition. The majority of the Uncle Sam cards, however, are not particularly rare, and they can typically be found in the $15 to $40 range.

Uncle Sam cards were produced for nearly every product, so it is best to ask dealers when there isn't time to look through every album. (Dealers generally lump most of their Uncle Sam cards together in one place, regardless of the products advertised.) It is also worth checking a dealer's Brownie cards, as Palmer Cox usually put an Uncle Sam in charge of those little guys when they were at work or play. Also be sure to inspect exposition albums, as Uncle Sam turns up at every expo from 1876 on.

I. W. Harper Whiskey, $100.00.

Berry Brothers Varnish
 Uncle Sam passing out cases to men of world **$30.00**

Clark's ONT Spool Cotton
 Uncle Sam, eagle, cupid, lion, Prang, rev. 1878 calendar **$15.00**

Crown Jewel Stoves
 Uncle Sam dancing with world leaders around stove **$75.00**

Frank Millers Blacking
 Uncle Sam sitting, shaving with eagle **$40.00**

Hub Gore Elastic for Shoes
 Uncle Sam "Talking Automaton" at Columbian Expo **$25.00**

Hygienic Kalsomine
 Uncle Sam on steps at Columbian Expo **$35.00**

Magnolia Ham
 Uncle Sam pointing at big ham, flag **$35.00**

National Cycle Mfg. Co.
 Uncle Sam with bicycle at Pan Am Expo **$150.00**

Pike Whet Stones
 Brother Jonathan with scythe and foot on cases **$75.00**

Preston & Merrill's Yeast Powder
 Uncle Sam on black pot, "Bound to Rise" **$50.00**

Sweet Golden Seal Cigarette
 Uncle Sam talking to large hand, "handy fellow" **$100.00**

Libby, McNeill & Libby Meat, $40.00.

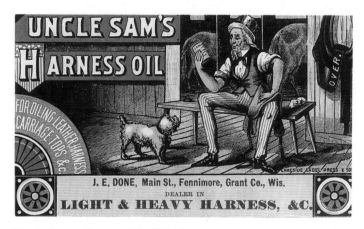

Uncle Sam's Harness Oil, $50.00.

Courtenay Worcestershire Sauce, $50.00.

Boston Baked Beans, $50.00.

Empire Wringer, $15.00.

Vegetable People & Whimsy

(See also: Brownies, Elves & "Little Folks"; Cupids & Cherubs; Humor.)

Vegetable People & Whimsical Images

Whimsical images are popular with collectors and can be found in advertisements from virtually every product category. Whimsical cards can be broken down into numerous sub-groups, each with its own enthusiastic fans. The four most clearly defined and competitively pursued groups in whimsical cards are: 1. Brownies, Elves & "Little People"; 2. Cupids & Cherubs; 3. Vegetable People; and 4. Satirical Substitutions. (The first two groups are treated separately.) Other popular groups include those with anthropomorphic themes, cards with fanciful butterfly or insect scenes, cards with playful distortions of reality or amusing exaggerations, and cards with fantasy or allegorical themes.

Vegetable People trade cards offer some of the most clever images found anywhere in advertising. These cards feature unforgettable "Mr. Potato Head" type characters that are a comical cross between eccentric humans and healthy produce. A typical Vegetable People card captures the essence of a real personality type by merging the appendages of that character with the substance of an aesthetically appropriate fruit or vegetable. The "appendages" of these characters go beyond just arms and feet projecting out from produce, and can include such supporting props as feathered hats, ruffled hair, shoe-less feet, fancy walking sticks, garden tools, musical instruments, or smoldering stogies. As with all good caricatures, most Vegetable People cards do an amazing job of cinching the illustration's theme with eyes and facial expressions that leave the viewer smiling with the thought, "Yes, I've met this person before."

Other versions of these cards feature people with oysters for heads or bodies, and girls with flower bodies or petal clothing. Most collectors also include "Vegetable Bird" cards, "Egg Head" cards, and several of the meat cards that were designed with the same humorous principles in mind. As diverse as these types of cards can be, when placed together in a collection, their kinship in style and whimsical spirit is readily apparent. There are over 125 Vegetable People style cards known, with most of them dating from 1885 to 1888. Nearly all of the Vegetable People cards were produced by New York lithographers, including the earliest known example, a rare Briggs & Bros. color "Flower Girl" card that carries an 1870 copyright date. Vegetable People cards were usually issued as stock cards that could be imprinted for anything, but most of them were used for fertilizer, seed, and county fair advertising.

The most common plants used in Vegetable People images are corn, wheat, potatoes, onions, lettuce, beats, peas, tomatoes, tobacco, cotton, watermelon, grapes, peaches, and oranges. There are also a dozen or so of the "Oyster People" cards, plus at least five of the "Egg Head" cards.

The "Flower Girl" cards are hard to count because many of them were not necessarily designed with the Vegetable People "caricature principle" in mind. For example, J. & P. Coats Thread issued a number of cards in 1887 during the peak of the Vegetable People craze that featured the faces of beautiful girls poking out of flower blossoms. In some cards from the set, the blossoms appear merely to frame the girl's face, whereas in other examples the girl and the flower form an organic unit in the same spirit as the vegetable people cards. Even more questionable are the many whimsical stock cards where girls and women wear large flower blossoms as hats or dresses. The debates about whether such cards are Vegetable People cards or something else will boil down to person preferences.

Pricing Tips & Cards to Watch For

Whimsical trade cards are pervasive enough in trade cards that few of them draw special premiums as topical cards. Stock cards with whimsical illustrations generally sell in the $2 to $8 range, and they will bring more only if they are of exceptional quality with significant imprints. Privately issued whimsical cards draw prices based upon the product advertised, the quality of the card, and its rarity. Black and white whimsical cards are actually quite rare, especially with Vegetable People illustrations, so whimsical cards suffer no special pricing disadvantage when found without full color. Most Vegetable People cards bring $15 to $25. Watch for cards with negative racial themes, or cards from before 1885, as these experience the highest demand. Also keep an eye open for the cards with oyster images, as these can sometimes bring twice the average price or more.

Apple Head, "Forbidden Fruit," $15.00.

Corn Head, $20.00.

Apple Body: "Apple Sauce"
  1887, woman shakes fist in orchard — baking powder imprint **$15.00**

Ayer's Medicines
  "Weather & Med. Signals," bottles dance around globe, 1886 . . . . . **$20.00**

Beetle Whimsy stock card
  2 beatles pull fancy carriage full of roses — fertilizer imprint **$5.00**

Beef Iron Wine "Green Label"
  "Pansies' Playtime," flowers see-saw on fence, Tobin card **$15.00**

Brainerd & Armstrong Threads
  "Seaside Frolic," spools of threads as swimmers, factory **$25.00**

Brown's Household Panacea
  bum carries flaming stove & pipe with bare hands **$20.00**

Butterflies & Shoe Whimsy stock card
  shoe full of kids floats on wings of butterflies — shoe imprint **$8.00**

Clark's Thread
  fancy man with spool head walks dog in park, obelisk **$15.00**

Counselman Hams
  "Nothing hits spot like...," man in top hat walks dog, ham belly . . . **$30.00**

Peach Body: "A Swell Peach"
  1887, man in top hat, cane — clothing imprint **$15.00**

Pear Body: "How do I a'Pear?"
  1887, lady in hat, closed parasol down — A & P Tea imprint **$15.00**

Plum Head: "My Sugar Plum"
  1888, banjo picker on stool, log cabin — rev. medicine imprint . . . **$20.00**

Willimantic Thread
  "People's Favorite Hobby" horse races on spools at track **$15.00**

Roller Skate whimsy stock card, $5.00.

Grasshopper whimsy stock card, $5.00.

Potato body & head, $20.00.

Lettuce dress & hat: "Oh Let-us," $20.00.

Miles' Premium Baking Powder, $15.00.

Women

(See also: Corsets; Cosmetics; Risque.)

Women Images

Women were presented in a fascinating variety of trade card images advertising nearly every type of product. On one end were the predictable images that reinforced and exploited the "traditional" stereotypes of subordinate or helpless Victorian women. These cards featured gentle women who lived to please men, nurture children, and to complete their chores, doing so while encumbered by corsets, bustles, and floor-length skirts. In many of these images, women were presented as the tragic victims of inferior household products. Such women suffered quietly, dreaming of a salvation that could be delivered only through the purchase of a superior brand of soap, a new patent medicine formula, or an improved domestic machine. Advertisements targeted at male consumers typically portrayed women in traditional gender roles that stroked male egos, presenting women who were attractive, eager to please, helpless, or silly.

On the other end are the remarkably abundant images of aggressive women who controlled men, beat up son-in-laws, carried guns, held outside jobs, and capered about away from home. Such images brashly presented a side of the Victorian woman that many "traditionalists" are amazed to discover. Trade cards that advertised items like threads, soaps, and corsets were often the boldest in challenging gender stereotypes, undoubtedly because there was little risk in alienating male consumers from such "feminine" products. The quality of cards with historically significant images of women range from very low to high. The most outrageous of these images are often found on stock cards, because the firms that invested in expensive private designs were rarely interested in risking consumer backlash.

Historical Notes

Victorian trade cards with images of women offer intriguing glimpses into one of the most significant periods of social transition in human history. During the period between the Civil War and WWI, women in America established new definitions of womanhood that the rest of the world has been forced to respond to and live with ever since.

Seeds of political reform and social upheaval were sewn prior to the Civil War by America's prohibitionist and abolitionist movements. Women played leading roles in these movements, and through the church-based chapters that they established across the country, thousands of women honed the skills of effective organizing, attentive listening, and powerful debating. In the aftermath of the Civil War and in the midst of the prosperity of the new age, the energies of these women and their offspring found new forms of expression and new crusades to wage. These women set an agenda that called for nothing less than equal access to education, equal voice in politics, and new relationships with men. And unlike any such dreams from earlier times or other cultures, these women were in a position to get substantial results.

Trade cards provide provocative (and largely unexplored) bits of information about the emergence of the "modern" woman.

First, advertising cards played an important role in fueling consumer demand for manufactured goods, which in turn led to life-changing employment opportunities for women. Trade cards with images of women working outside of the home provide insights on this phenomenon. Second, trade cards disseminated propaganda about time-saving pre-cooked foods and household appliances. In-so-far-as these ads were successful in converting women to radically new homemaking practices, the products that these cards promoted freed time up for women to pursue their own interests and personal growth. And finally, trade cards indirectly document the economic empowerment of women, including the new responsibilities and rewards that such financial decision-making power entailed.

Pricing Tips & Cards to Watch For

Most collectors and social historians have failed to note the significance of trade cards with images of women. As a "topical" group, these cards have few enthusiasts, and they experience very little special demand. Expect to pay the same prices as you would for cards picturing children, pets, or most other common topics. Stock cards will generally bring $3 to $10, and only more if a dealer happens to believe the card is of exceptional beauty or importance. Privately issued cards with images of women will bring the prices commanded by the merchandise advertised, so check the appropriate product headings elsewhere in this reference. Watch for unusual images of women working, acting "liberated," or shown partially naked, as these cards will be the first to rise in value as collectors begin to look at "women" cards in new ways.

White Sewing Machine, $10.00.

Celluloid Collars & Cuffs
father squirts daughter's suitor with hose, she cries **$15.00**

Clark's Thread
"How to keep husbands at home nights," man tied to chair **$8.00**

Fairbank's Soap
lady with club drives man down through chair, "nothing else" **$12.00**

Gold Coin Stoves
"Have dinner ready when I get back, George," lady leaves **$15.00**

Half & Half stock card — clothing
person walking dog: left side is man/right side is woman **$6.00**

Hunting Lady stock card
lady with gun & dog in snow walks past 3 rabbits, 1881 .... **$8.00**

Imperial Diamond Needles
lady runs needle through men and strings them like beans **$10.00**

J. & P. Coats' Thread
courting man swears love through window to lady sewing **$15.00**

Ladies Friend, Goshen Sweeper Co.
woman sweeps carpet in tight neck-to-toe dress **$15.00**

Mm. Fontaine's Bosom Beautifier
breast enlarging & firming cream, Oscar Wilde stock card **$20.00**

Mother-In-Law stock card
ugly lady holds man by neck and punches his head **$6.00**

Nellie Bly on the Fly — med. imprint
she stands on fly's back, "Men don't monopolize success" **$15.00**

Playful Wife stock card — blueing
"on his knee, sits and talks, waiting tea," pinches his cheeks **$5.00**

Quaker Oats Cereal (from set)
"Packing Room," many women at tables making boxes, 1893 .... **$15.00**

Singer Sewing Machine
"Romeo & Juliet," girl leans over wall to kiss boy on machine **$15.00**

Spurlock's No. 5 Bluing — stock card
"Night of Labor," dad walks infant, baby bottle, mom sleeps **$15.00**

Stock Card — hotel imprint
"Speaker of the House," woman with broom yelling at man **$6.00**

Tenexine Egyptian Glue
couple fights, son glues dress to floor, "Divorce Impossible" **$15.00**

Williams' Blood Purifier
Before Taking: sick lady/After Taking: happy to sweep floor **$20.00**

Woman's Suffrage Stove Polish
12 reasons "every Woman wants it" on back of stock card **$10.00**

Hartshorn Shade Rollers, $25.00.

Swanine Laundry Soap, $15.00.

Eureka Thread, $8.00.

Le Page's Glue, $20.00.

Wringers & Washing

(See also: Chinese; Enterprise & Mrs. Potts'; Soap & Soapine.)

Wringer & Washing Images

Trade card images of eccentric Victorian washing machines and early laundry products are popular with many collectors. Such cards from before 1880 are very rare, but dozens of delightful examples can be found dating from 1880 to 1895 when manufactures shifted into high gear and revolutionized "washing day" in America. To discourage families from postponing purchases, Keystone (and others) advertised installment plans when they first introduced their lines around 1880. Prices ranged from $6 to $9 depending upon the model. Because most washing products were "low ticket" items, the quality of trade cards in this group tends to remain below average, with few exceptions.

The most frequently encountered washing cards are the many two and three color stock cards that were issued for the Universal, the Conqueror, and the Eclipse wringers. Most of these cards have simple illustrations of children on the front and detailed line drawings of wringer models and advertising text on the back. All three of these companies issued similar metamorphic cards in the early 1880s. Interestingly enough, the metamorphics used by Eclipse and Universal are virtually identical cards. The only difference between the wringers illustrated in these two cards is the name stamped above the rollers.

Historical Notes

America's first washing machine was introduced in Chicago in 1848. The machine was little more than a crude hand-cranked wringer mounted on the bottom half of an oak barrel with a washboard tucked inside. Prior to mass-produced washboards and wringers, families washed their clothes in tubs and buckets using primitive wooden stompers, or even their own bare feet. Clothes were also rubbed with soap and water against stones or homemade wooden grates, then wrung by hand and hung on ropes to dry. Washing day fell on Monday in almost every home in the country, followed by ironing day on Tuesday. Products like Higgins German Laundry Soap, Oswego Starch, Parsons' Ammonia, and Bengal Bluing were popular laundry aids by the 1880s. Such products reduced the amount of effort required to remove odors and stains, and bluing in particular counteracted the natural yellowing of laundered whites.

Wringers with rubber rollers, gears, and adjustable springs evolved throughout the 1870s. By 1880, several wringers had become practical enough to generate widespread consumer interest. Trade cards advertising wringers played an important role during the 1880s in alerting housewives to the labor-saving possibilities of improved models and thereby reducing some of the frustrations of one of the most despised of all domestic chores. Among the designs that never caught on were several that were powered by foot pedals, and one that was run by a dog-driven treadmill (dog not included).

Early washers with hand-cranked agitators or spinning drums required as much effort as stomping, but shortly after the turn-of-the-century, the Hurley Machine Company introduced a washer that used an electric motor to spin the drum. Maytag (originally a Newton, Iowa, farm equipment manufacturer called the Parsons Band Cutter and Self Feeder Company) soon countered with a machine driven by a small gasoline engine mounted beneath its wooden tub. The motor's exhaust fumes were pumped out a kitchen window through a long flexible exhaust hose. The Maytag model proved to be extremely practical and popular through the early decades of the century when electricity was not yet universally available.

Pricing Tips & Cards to Watch For

Prices for cards advertising washing equipment and laundry products remain very affordable. Stock cards with imprints for laundry soap, starches, bluing, etc. usually sell for $3 to $10, while privately issued cards for these same products usually bring twice those amounts or slightly more. Stock cards with reverse illustrations of wringers generally sell for $5 to $12. Privately commissioned cards for washboards, wringers, and machines usually sell in the $10 to $25 range.

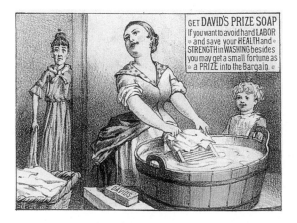

David's Prize Soap, $8.00.

Colby Wringer, $15.00.

American Machine Co. Wringer
   3 children run sheet through wringer, washtub, cat plays $10.00

Bengal Blueing
   "Little Boy Blue," face, "Standard Laundry Blue of America" $20.00

Bixby's French Laundry Blue
   2 women at washtub, clothes basket on floor $12.00

Conqueror Clothes Wringer
   metamorphic — sad family/"Made Jones a Happy Man" $25.00

Empire Wringer
   3 boys, 1 cranks, 1 sticks fingers between rollers $8.00

Eureka Wringer
   1 monkey turns crank, another shoves cat's tail into rollers $20.00

Keystone Wringer
   girl in big red hat turns wringer crank, hold doll $15.00

National Laundry Journal Press
   scene of women working hard, commercial laundry shop $30.00

Parsons' Ammonia, Columbia Chem.
   girl washing dolls clothes in tub outside, clothes line $15.00

Reckitt's Paris Blue
   lady at washtub looks out window, bluing delivery wagon $12.00

Spanish Bluing
   "Will not injure finest fabric," boys leap-frog big bottle, girl $15.00

Star Washer
   illustration of "Washing Machine" tub unit with wringer, etc. $20.00

Universal Clothes Wringer
   folder, Ancient: lady wrings by hand/Modern: lady, wringer $25.00

Welcome Wringer
   engraved card, detailed cut of wringer, dealer imprint below $15.00

Empire Wringer, $12.00.

Empire Wringer, $20.00.

Atlantic Wringer, $25.00.

Ivorine Soap, $10.00.

Victorian Card Glossary:

- **Advertising Post Card:** Evolved from trade cards. Uncommon prior to 1900. Early examples appear similar to trade cards, but marked on back for mailing. Usually approximately 3½" x 5½".
- **Advertising Trade Card:** Usually slightly smaller than a post card, but can range from 1½" x 2½" to 6" x 10" or larger. Designed to merge advertising messages with interesting images to be saved as reminders of goods or services. Most printed between 1876 and 1900.
- **Business & Business Service Cards:** Popular from 1850s to present. Usually printed in one color on one side only, with minimal advertising claims. Includes cards for services like insurance, art and portrait work, plumbing, printing, etc. Service cards offer a unique window into the everyday lives and needs of Victorians.
- **Calling Cards:** These "name cards" were an important part of Victorian etiquette, especially for unmarried men and women. They were also used as sentimental tokens of affection, so were usually small, dainty cards with frilly designs and fancy lettering. They frequently surface in scrapbooks with trade cards. These cards were sometimes collected in large numbers as evidence of popularity or social sophistication.
- **Cameo Cards:** Usually one color with white lettering and design, creating a reversed silhouette or cameo effect. Often printed with embossing and an ornamental border.
- **Chromolithography:** A special printing process employing grease or oil and water, originally using specially prepared limestone plates. Each of the basic colors of a lithograph were applied using a separate stone. A few of Prang's prints used as many as 25 different stones. Most lithographers created some of their hues by simply having colors overlap.
- **Clipper Ship Cards:** Most clipper cards date from the California gold rush and promote voyages from Boston or New York to San Francisco, between 1850 and 1870. Few examples exist outside of museums, thus making them among the most difficult and expensive trade cards to collect.
- **Currier & Ives:** Besides their major business (1857 – 1907) of producing affordable prints for home decoration, Currier & Ives did some additional work for commercial accounts. Most of the 200 or so trade cards they produced carry their name and copyright dates from around 1880. Not to be confused with Courier Lith. of Buffalo.
- **Die-Cut:** Cards that were cut mechanically during production, often into the shapes of animals, palettes, fans, etc. Some cards can appear to be die-cut, but prove upon closer inspection to be regular trade cards that were clipped by hand for scrapbooks.
- **Embossed:** Cards with relief features, where elements of the cards were raised during printing by means pressure stamping.
- **Ephemera:** Term applied to printed items that were created primarily to serve a singular, short-lived purpose. Includes most "paper collectibles."
- **Folder:** Cards designed to be folded, generally of a light stock with two or more panels (four or more pages of illustrations and text). Often show wear along folds, and sometimes found as separated pieces.

- **Hold-To-Light:** (Occasionally called "magic card" or "see-through") Designed so that printing on the back shows through when held to a strong light. HTLs are often very clever. Most common effect is for closed eyelids to "open" with light. Printed on light paper, so frequently found with small flaws.
- **Insert Cards:** Advertising cards that were packaged with a product. Often came in sets to insure customer loyalty. Tobacco, baking soda, and coffee inserts were extremely popular, but many other types were made.
- **Mechanical Cards:** Cards with one or more moving parts. Typically, a mechanical trade card has a window cut out and a cardboard wheel that rotates behind to bring different images into view. Other mechanicals have "pop out" effects, tabs that pull, or arms and legs that move when the card is opened.
- **Mechanical Bank Cards:** Trade cards promoting toy banks that had moving parts. Among the most expensive trade cards.
- **Metamorphic Cards:** Trade cards with a flap that typically folds to form a before and after scene. Can be found for any product.
- **Privately Issued Cards:** (Also called "national issues," or "private designs") Cards that were commissioned by a specific company for their use only. Sometimes found with the name and address of a local retailer stamped on front or back.
- **Prang:** Considered by some the "Father of Chromolithography," Louis Prang of Boston set the early standard for quality in color printing. In addition to his pioneering work in greeting cards, Prang produced many fine trade cards and popularized stock cards with blank boxes for imprinting.
- **Rewards of Merit:** Often found in albums with trade cards. Used originally as student prizes or certificates to honor good behavior.
- **Scrapbooks:** Parlor albums were very popular with many Victorians, who took pride in gathering colorful cards and scraps and gluing them into albums. These old scrapbooks are a prime source for locating trade cards, but sometimes cards were ruined from glue stains or from being cut to fit on an album page.
- **Stock Cards:** These cards were usually printed in large quantities with somewhat generic illustrations. They were generally intended for small, local firms that could imprint their own name, addresses, and messages.
- **Tobacco Cards:** Distinct from the usually smaller tobacco insert cards. Includes stock cards that were imprinted for local retailers, plus many intriguing private designs.
- **Trading Cards:** Generally refers to insert cards post-dating the trade card era. These cards were intended specifically for collecting, with advertising playing little or no role in the design of the card's image.
- **Victorian:** The Victorian period technically covers the years of Queen Victoria's reign in England, 1837 – 1901. In American usage, Victorian most often refers to the fashions, fads, values, architectural styles, etc. popular between our Civil War and WWI (1865 – 1915).

Resources:

Many "primitive" cultures believe that power is obtained through the mastery of names. According to such a view, to share one's name is to relinquish a portion of one's power, and to learn the name of a person or object is to acquire power. I'm not sure about "power," but I can vouch for the extra enjoyment that comes on an afternoon hike when a person knows the names of the streams, trees, and wild flowers discovered along a mountain trail. I can also vouch for the added pleasures found in collecting trade cards when a person knows a bit about the images and history that one holds in his hands.

The information shared in this reference was gathered from a variety of resources ranging from notes taken in graduate level history courses at Western Michigan University to telephone conversations I've had with members of the Trade Card Collector's Association. For those who would like more power/enjoyment with respect to trade cards, I offer the following list of resources as a good place to start.

National Organizations

Trade Card Collector's Association: Membership includes a subscription to an illustrated quarterly magazine covering market and collecting trends, articles on Victorian social history, trade card lithographers, topical collecting, product collecting, and every aspect of buying and selling trade cards. Membership also entitles collectors to special discounts on trade card books, supplies, and annual convention fees. Publishes a show calendar and a membership directory, and accepts display and classified advertising. Write to: TCCA, PO Box 284, Marlton, NJ 08053.

The Ephemera Society of America: Membership includes a subscription to a quarterly newsletter, book discounts, and discounted admissions to all Society-sponsored functions. Avoids price discussions, but takes paper collectibles (including trade cards) very seriously as historical and artistic artifacts. Publishes a show calendar and a membership directory, and accepts display advertising. Write to: Ephemera Society, PO Box 95, Cazenovia, NY 13035.

Books

Ames, Kenneth L. *Death in the Dining Room, & Other Tales of Victorian Culture.* Philadelphia: Temple University Press, 1992.

Bingham, A. Walker. *The Snake Oil Syndrome, Patent Medicine Advertising.* Hanover, MA: Christopher Publishing, 1994.

Burdick, J.R. *The American Card Catalog.* New York: Nostalgia Press (reprint), 1988.

Cheadle, Dave. *Arctic Obsession, The Victorian Race for the North Pole.* Englewood, CO: 1993.

Crane, Ben. *The Before and After Trade Card.* Schoharie, NY: Ephemera Society of America, 1995.

Chronicle of America. New York: Dorling Kindersley, 1995.

Haywood, C. Robert. *Victorian West.* Lawrence: University Press of Kansas, 1991.

Hays, Samuel P. *The Response to Industrialism, 1885-1914.* Chicago: University of Chicago Press, 1957.

Jay, Robert. *The Trade Card in Nineteenth-Century America.* Columbia, MO: University of Missouri Press, 1987.

Schieber, Ron. *Currier & Ives Trade Card Checklist.* Akron, OH: Schieber, 1995.

Schlereth, Thomas J. *Victorian America, Transformations in Everyday Life, 1876-1915.* New York: HarperCollins, 1991.

Smith, Page. *The Rise of Industrial America.* New York: McGraw-Hill, 1984.

Periodicals & Catalogs

Advertising Trade Card Quarterly, PO Box 284, Marlton, NJ 08053.

Aiglatson Catalogs, PO Box 3173 A, Framingham, MA 01701.

American Enterprise Catalogs, Wm. Frost Mobley, PO Box 10, Schoharie, NY 12157.

Cards from Grandma's Trunk, PO Box 404, Northport, MI 49670.

Ephemera News, PO Box 95, Cazenovia, NY 13035.

Paper Collectors' Marketplace, PO Box 128, Scandinavia, WI 54977.

Reflections, Kit Barry Ephemera Auctions, 109 Main St., Brattleboro, VT 05301.

Victorian Images Auctions, Catalogs #1-#27, PO Box 284, Marlton, NJ 08053.

Acknowledgments:

My special thanks goes to the people who have been my greatest resources throughout this project:

My wife, Audrey, who encouraged, supported, and covered for me constantly. My good friend Russ Mascieri, who initiated this project and lent his time and expertise to see it through. And Evie Eysenburg, who has hunted down many of the best cards in my collection and who has caught more of my mistakes than anybody other than my father.